A WRITER'S RECOLLECTIONS

MARY WARD
(MRS HUMPHRY WARD)

Published by Mer Publishing 2007
First published in 1918

A CIP catalogue record for this book
is available on request from the British Library
ISBN 978-0-9555849-4-7

Printed in Poland

Mer Publishing Ltd
8 Drake Close, London SE16 6RS
www.merpublishing.com

CONTENTS

Chapter		Page
I.	**Early Days.**	6
	Tasmania. Arnold of Rugby and his Children.	
	My Father and New Zealand.	
II.	**Fox How**	21
	My Grandmother.	
	Charlotte Brontë and Matthew Arnold.	
III.	**The Family of Fox How**	28
	Mrs Forster. Matthew Arnold. A Letter from Lansdowne	
	House. An Oxford Election.	
IV.	**Other Children of Fox How**	45
	William Delafield Arnold. 'Oakfield.' 'A Summer Night.'	
	'Aunt Mary.'	
V.	**The Friends of Fox How**	58
	Wordsworth. An Unpublished Letter. A Vision of the Poet.	
	Arthur Hugh Clough. Dean Stanley.	
VI.	**Young Days at Oxford**	73
	Balliol and the Master. The Pattisons. George Eliot.	
	M. Taine. Swinburne. The Paters.	
VII.	**Balliol and Lincoln**	94
	The Master Again. Thomas Hill Green. Cardinal Newman.	
	Dr Pusey. Canon Liddon.	
VIII.	**Early Married Life**	105
	First Attempts at Writing. Mandell Creighton.	
	John Richard Green. Mr Freeman. Bishop Stubbs.	
	A First Talk with M. Renan. Sarah Bernhardt.	
	Mme Mohl. Dr Lushington.	

IX.	**The History of 'Robert Elsmere'**	120
	Spanish History. Work on the West Goths. Meaning and Weight of Testimony. The Bampton Lectures, 1881. 'Unbelief and Sin.' A First Sketch of 'Robert Elsmere'. M. Renan at Oxford. Work on The *Times*. London. Dublin, 1880. Mr Forster's Chief Secretaryship. The Education Bill of 1870.	
X.	**London in the Eighties**	135
	John Morley. His Editorship of *Macmillan*. My Work for Him. His 'Life of Gladstone.' Russell Square and Borough Farm. 'Miss Bretherton.' Henry James. Laura Lyttelton.	
XI.	**London and Other Friends**	152
	Edmond Scherer. Amiel's *Journal*. Mr Balfour at Whittinghame. Mr Goschen. Lord Acton. Mr Clemenceau. Mr Chamberlain. Robert Browning. James Russell Lowell.	
XII.	**Publication of 'Robert Elsmere'**	168
	How the Book was Written. My Mothers Death. Conversations with Mr Gladstone. Death of Matthew Arnold. The Rush for 'Robert Elsmere'. Mr Pater's Review. Henry James's Letters and many others. Appearance of the Book in America. Oliver Wendell Holmes. Goldwin Smith. M. Brunetière and 'Robert Elsmere'.	
XIII.	**First Visits to Italy**	188
	The Story of a First Folio. Mr Gladstone at Hawarden. 'The New Reformation.' First Sketch of 'David Grieve'. Emily Lawless. Contessa Pasolini. A summer at Hampden. Visitors to Hampden. The Huxleys. Sir Alfred Lyall. M. Jusserand. M. André Chevrillon.	
XIV.	**Amalfi and Rome**	203
	Lord Dufferin. Publication of 'David Grieve'. Lord Derby. We Settle at Stocks. Beginnings of 'Marcella'. Foundation of the Passmore Edwards Settlement. The Jowett Lectureship. Lord Carlisle. Stopford Brooke. James Martineau. The Death of the Master.	

XV.	**Helbeck of Bannisdale**	**221**
	Publication of 'Marcella'. Letters from Mr Gladstone.	
	His Death and Funeral. Huxley on the 'Sentimental	
	Deists'. Lady Wemyss. The Origins of 'Helbeck'.	
	Spring at Levens. Publication of 'Helbeck'.	
	An Hour with the Empress Frederick.	
XVI.	**The Villa Barberini. Henry James**	**236**
	A Spring at Castel Gandolfo. Henry James at Nemi.	
	Henry James's Art.	
XVII.	**Roman Friends. 'Eleanor'**	**243**
	Sir William Harcourt at Rome. Commendatore Boni.	
	Monseigneur Duchesne. Cardinal Vaughan.	
	Appearance of 'Eleanor'. Modern Italy.	
Epilogue		**257**
	Some Thoughts on Literature and Religion.	
	Tennyson and Meredith. Stevenson. Thomas Hardy.	
	Rudyard Kipling. Mr Wells. Mr Arnold Bennett.	
	Mr Conrad. Mr Galsworthy. Father Tyrell.	
	The Effects of the War on the Country Districts.	
	A Visit to the United States. A Journey through Canada.	

CHAPTER I
Early Days

Do we all become garrulous and confidential as we approach the gates of old age? Is it that we instinctively feel, and cannot help asserting our one advantage over the younger generation, which has so many over us? — the one advantage of *time*!

After all, it is not disputable that we have lived longer than they. When they talk of past poets, or politicians, or novelists, whom the young still deign to remember, of whom for once their estimate agrees with ours, we can sometimes put in a quiet — 'I saw him' — or 'I talked with him' — which for the moment wins the conversational race. And as we elders fall back before the brilliance and glitter of the New Age, advancing 'like an army with banners', this mere prerogative of years becomes in itself a precious possession. After all, we cannot divest ourselves of it, if we would. It is better to make friends with it, to turn it into a kind of *panache* — to wear it with an air, since wear it we must.

So as the years draw on towards the Biblical limit, the inclination to look back, and to tell some sort of story of what one has seen, grows upon most of us. I cannot hope that what I have to say will be very interesting to many. A life spent largely among books, and in the exercise of a literary profession, has very obvious drawbacks, as a subject matter, when one comes to write about it. I can only attempt it with any success, if my readers will allow me a large psychological element. The thoughts and opinions of one human being, if they are sincere, must always have an interest for some other human beings. The world is there to think about; and if we have lived, or are living, with any sort of energy, we *must* have thought about it, and about ourselves in relation to it — thought 'furiously' often. And it is out of the many 'thinkings' of many folk, strong or weak, dull or far-ranging, that thought itself grows. For progress surely, whether in men or nations, means only a richer knowledge; the more impressions therefore on the human intelligence that we can seize and record, the more sensitive becomes that intelligence itself.

But of course the difficulty lies in the seizing and recording — in the choice, that is, of what to say, and how to say it. In this choice, as I look back over more than half a century, I can only follow — and trust — the same sort of instinct that one follows in the art of fiction. I shall be telling what is primarily true, or as true as I can make it; as distinguished from what is primarily imagination, built on truth. But the truth one uses in fiction must be interesting! Milton expresses that in the words 'sensuous' and 'passionate', which he applies to poetry in the *Areopagitica.* And the same thing applies to autobiography, where selection is even more necessary than fiction. Nothing ought to be told, I think, that does not interest or kindle one's own mind in looking back; it is the only condition on which one can hope to interest or kindle other minds. And this means that one ought to handle things broadly, taking only the salient points in the landscape of the past, and of course with as much detachment as possible. Though probably in the end one will have to admit — egotists that we all are! — that not much detachment *is* possible.

For me, the first point that stands out is the arrival of a little girl of five, in the year 1856, at grey stone house in a Westmorland valley, where fourteen years earlier, the children of Arnold of Rugby, the 'Doctor' of 'Tom Brown's Schooldays', had waited on a June day, to greet their father expected from the South, only to hear, as the summer day died away, that two hours' sharp illness, that very morning, had taken him from them. Of what preceded my arrival as a black-haired, dark-eyed child, with my father, mother, and two brothers, at Fox How, the holiday house among the mountains which the famous headmaster had built for himself in 1834, I have but little recollection. I see dimly another house in wide fields, where dwarf lilies grew, and I know that it was a house in Tasmania, where at the time of my birth my father, Thomas Arnold, the Doctor's second son, was organising education in the young colony. I can just recall too, the deck of a ship which to my childish feet seemed vast — but the *William Brown* was a sailing ship of only 400 tons! — in which we made the voyage home in 1856. Three months and a half we took about it, going round the Horn in bitter weather, much run over by rats at night, and expected to take our baths by day in two huge barrels full of sea water on the deck, into which we children were plunged shivering by our nurse, two or three times a week. My father and mother, their three children, and some small cousins, who were going to England under my mother's care, were the only passengers.

I can remember too being lifted — weak and miserable with toothache — in my father's arms to catch the first sight of English shores as we neared the mouth of the Thames; and then the dismal inn by the docks where we first took shelter. The dreary room where we children slept the first night, its dingy ugliness and its barred windows, still come back to me as a vision of horror. Next day, like angels of rescue, came an aunt and uncle, who took us away to other and cheerful quarters, and presently saw us off to Westmorland. The aunt was my godmother, Dr Arnold's eldest daughter — then the young wife of William Edward Forster, a Quaker manufacturer, who afterwards became the well-known Education Minister of 1870, and was Chief Secretary for Ireland in the terrible years 1880-82.

To my mother and her children, Fox How and its inmates represented much that was new and strange. My mother was the grand-daughter of one of the first Governors of Tasmania, Governor Sorell, and had been brought up in the colony, except for a brief schooling at Brussels. Of her personal beauty in youth we children heard much, as we grew up, from her old Tasmanian friends and kinsfolk who would occasionally drift across us; and I see as though I had been there, a scene often described to me — my mother playing Hermione in the 'Winter's Tale', at Government House when Sir William Denison was Governor — a vision, lovely and motionless, on her pedestal, till at the words 'Music! Awake her! Strike!' she kindled into life. Her family were probably French in origin. Governor Sorell had been a man of promise in his youth. His father, General William Alexander Sorell, of the Coldstream Guards, was a soldier of some eminence, whose two sons William and Thomas both served under Sir John Moore, and at the Cape. But my great-grandfather ruined his military career, while he was Deputy Adjutant General at the Cape, by a love-affair with a brother officer's wife, and was banished or promoted — whichever one pleases to call it — to the new colony of Tasmania, of which he became Governor in 1816. His eldest son, by the wife he had left behind him in England, went out as a youth of twenty-one or so, to join his father the Governor, in Tasmania, and I possess a little calf-bound diary of my grandfather written in a very delicate and refined hand, about the year 1823. The faint entries in it show him to have been a devoted son. But when in 1830 or so, the Governor left the colony, and retired to Brussels, my grandfather remained in Van Diemen's Land, as it was then generally called, became very much attached to the colony, and filled the post of Registrar of Deeds for many years under its successive Governors. I just remember him, as a gentle, affectionate, upright being, a gentleman of an old punctilious school, strictly honourable and exact, content with a small sphere, and much loved within it. He would sometimes talk to his children of early days in Bath, of his father's young successes and promotions, and of his grandfather, General Sorell, who as Adjutant of the Coldstream Guards, from 1744 to 1758, and associated with all the home and foreign service of that famous regiment during those years, through the Seven Years' War, and up to the opening of the American War of Independence, played a vaguely brilliant part in his grandson's recollections. But he himself was quite content with the modest affairs of an infant colony, which even in its earliest days achieved, whether in its landscape or its life, a curiously English effect; as though an English midland county had somehow got loose, and drifting to the Southern seas, had there set up — barring a few black aborigines, few convicts, its mimosas, and its treeferns — another quiet version of the quiet English life it had left behind.

But the Sorells all the same had some foreign and excitable blood in them. Their story of themselves was that they were French Huguenots, expelled in 1685, who had settled in England, and coming of a military stock, had naturally sought careers in the English army. There are points in this story which are puzzling; but the foreign touch in my mother, and in the Governor — to judge from the only picture of him which remains — was unmistakable. Delicate features, small, beautifully shaped hands and feet, were accompanied in my mother by a French vivacity and quickness, an overflowing energy, which never forsook her through all her trials and misfortunes. In the Governor, the same physical characteristics make a rather decadent and foppish impression — as of an old stock run to seed. The stock had been re-invigorated in my mother, and one of its original elements which certainly survived in her temperament and tradition was of great importance both for her own life and for her children's. This was the Protestant — the *French* Protestant element; which no doubt represented in the family from which she came, a history of long suffering at the hands of Catholicism. Looking back upon her Protestantism, I see that it was not the least like English Evangelicalism, whether of the Anglican or dissenting type. There was nothing emotional or 'enthusiastic' in it — no breath of Wesley or Wilberforce; but rather something drawn from deep wells of history, instinctive and invincible. Had some direct Calvinist ancestor of hers, with a soul on fire, fought the tyranny of Bossuet and Madame de Maintenon, before — eternally hating and resenting 'Papistry' — he abandoned his country and kinsfolk, in the search for religious liberty? That is the impression which — looking back upon her life — it often makes upon me. All the more strange that to her it fell, unwittingly, imagining, indeed, that by her marriage with a son of Arnold of Rugby, she was taking a step precisely in the opposite direction, to be, by a kind of tragic surprise, which yet was no one's fault, the wife of a Catholic.

And that brings me to my father, whose character and story were so important to all his children that I must try and draw them, though I cannot pretend to any impartiality in doing so — only to the insight that affection gives; its one abiding advantage over the critic and the stranger.

He was the second son of Dr Arnold of Rugby, and the younger brother — by only eleven months — of Matthew Arnold. On that morning of June 12, 1842, when the Headmaster who in fourteen years' rule at Rugby had made himself so conspicuous a place, not merely in the public school world, but in English life generally[1], arose, in the words of his poet son — to tread —

---

[1] At the moment of correcting these proofs, my attention has been called to a foolish essay on my grandfather by Mr Lytton Strachey, none the less foolish because it is the work of an extremely clever man. If Mr Strachey imagines that the effect of my grandfather's life and character upon men like Stanley and Clough, or a score of others who could be named, can be accounted for by the eidôlon he presents to his readers in place of the real human being, one can only regard it as one proof the more of the ease with which a certain kind of ability outwits itself.

> In the summer morning, the road —
> Of death, at a call unforeseen —
> Sudden —

— my father, a boy of eighteen, was in the house, and witnessed the fatal attack of *angina pectoris* which, in two hours, cut short a memorable career, and left those who till then, under a great man's shelter and keeping, had —

> Rested as under the boughs
> Of a mighty oak. . .
> Bare, unshaded, alone.

He had been father's special favourite among the elder children, as shown by some verses in my keeping addressed to him as a small boy, at different times, by 'the Doctor'. Those who know their 'Tom Brown's Schooldays' will perhaps remember the various passages in the book where the softer qualities of the man whom 'three hundred reckless childish boys' feared with all their hearts, 'and very little besides in heaven or earth' are made plain in the language of that date. Arthur's illness, for instance, when the little fellow, who has been at death's door, tells Tom Brown, who is at last allowed to see him — 'You can't think what the Doctor's like when one's ill. He said such brave and tender and gentle things to me — I felt quite light and strong after it, and never had any more fear'. Or East's talk with the Doctor, when the lively boy of many scrapes has a moral return upon himself — and says to his best friend — 'You can't think how kind and gentle he was, the great grim man, whom I've feared more than anybody on earth. When I stuck, he lifted me, just as if I'd been a little child. And he seemed to know all I'd felt, and to have gone through it all'. This tenderness and charm of a strong man, which in Stanley's biography is specially mentioned as growing more and more visible in the last months of his life, was always there for his children. In a letter written in 1828 to his sister, when my father as a small child not yet five was supposed to be dying, Arnold says, trying to steel himself against the bitterness of coming loss — 'I might have loved him, had he lived, too dearly — you know how deeply I do love him now'. And three years later, when 'little Tom', on his eighth birthday, had just said wistfully — with a curious foreboding instinct — 'I think

11

that the eight years I have now lived will be the happiest of my life' — Arnold, painfully struck by the words, wrote some verses upon them which I still possess. 'The Doctor' was no poet, though the best of his historical prose — the well-known passage in the Roman History, for instance, on the death of Marcellus — has some of the essential notes of poetry — passion, strength, music. But the gentle Wordsworthian quality of his few essays in verse will be perhaps interesting to those who are aware of him chiefly as the great Liberal fighter of eighty years ago. He replies to his little son: —

> Is it that aught prophetic stirred
> Thy spirit to that ominous word,
> Foredating in thy childish mind
> The fortune of thy Life's career —
> That nought of brighter bliss shall cheer
> What still remains behind?
>
> Or is thy Life so full of bliss
> That come what may, more blessed than this
> Thou canst not be again?
> And fear'st thou, standing on the shore,
> What storms disturb with wild uproar
> The years of older men?
>
> . . . .
>
> At once to enjoy, at once to hope —
> That fills indeed the largest scope
> Of good our thoughts can reach.
> Where can we learn so blest a rule,
> What wisest sage, what happiest school,
> Art so divine can teach?

The answer, of course, in the mouth of a Christian teacher is that in Christianity alone is there both present joy and future hope. The passages in Arnold's most intimate diary, discovered after his death, and published by Dean Stanley, show what the Christian faith was to my grandfather, how closely bound up with every action and feeling of his life.

The impression made by his conception of that faith, as interpreted by his own daily life, upon a great school, and, through the many strong and able men who went out from it, upon English thought and feeling, is part of English religious history.

But curiously enough the impression upon his own sons *appeared*, at any rate, to be less strong and lasting than in the case of others. I mean, of course, in the matter of opinion. The famous father died, and his children had to face the world without his guiding hand. Matthew and Tom, William and Edward, the four eldest sons, went in due time to Oxford, and the youngest boy into the Navy. My grandmother made her home at Fox How under the shelter of the fells, with her four daughters, the youngest of whom was only eight when their father died. The devotion of all the nine children to their mother, to each other, and to the common home was never weakened for a moment by the varieties of opinion that life was sure to bring out in the strong brood of strong parents. But the development of the two elder sons at the University was probably very different from what it would have been had their father lived. Neither of them, indeed, ever showed, while there, the smallest tendency to the 'Newmanism' which Arnold of Rugby had fought with all his powers; which he had denounced with such vehemence in the Edinburgh article on 'The Oxford Malignants'. My father was at Oxford all through the agitated years which preceded Newman's secession from the Anglican communion. He had rooms in University College in the High Street, nearly opposite St Mary's, in which John Henry Newman, then its Vicar, delivered Sunday after Sunday those sermons which will never be forgotten by the Anglican church. But my father only once crossed the street to hear him, and was then repelled by the mannerism of the preacher. Matthew Arnold occasionally went, out of admiration, my father used to say, for that strange Newmanic power of words, which in itself fascinated the young Balliol poet, who was to produce his first volume of poems two years after Newman's secession to the Church of Rome. But he was never touched in the smallest degree by Newman's opinions. He and my father and Arthur Clough, and a few other kindred spirits lived indeed in quite another world of thought. They discovered George Sand, Emerson and Carlyle, and orthodox Christianity no longer seemed to them the sure refuge that it had always been to the strong teacher who trained them as boys. There are many allusions of many dates in the letters of my father and uncle to each other, as to their common Oxford passion for George Sand. *Consuelo*, in particular, was a revelation to the two young men brought up under the 'earnest' influence of Rugby. It seemed to open to them a world of artistic beauty and joy of which they had never dreamed; and to loosen the bands of an austere conception of life, which began to appear to them too narrow for the facts of life. *Wilhelm Meister*, read in Carlyle's translation at the same time, exercised a similar liberating and enchanting power upon my father. The social enthusiasms of George Sand also affected him greatly, strengthening whatever he had inherited of his father's discontent with an iron world, where the poor suffer too much and work too hard. And this discontent, when the time came for him to leave Oxford, assumed a form which startled his friends.

He had done very well at Oxford, taking his two Firsts with ease, and was offered a post in the Colonial Office immediately on leaving the University. But the time was full of schemes for a new heaven and a new earth, wherein should dwell equality and righteousness. The storm of '48 was preparing in Europe; the Corn Laws had fallen; the Chartists were gathering in England. To settle down to the old humdrum round of Civil Service promotion seemed to my father impossible. This revolt of his, and its effect upon his friends, of whom the most intimate was Arthur Clough, has left its mark on Clough's poem, the 'Vacation Pastoral', which he called 'The Bothie of Tober-na-Vuolich,' or, as it runs in my father's old battered copy which lies before me — 'Tober-na-Fuosich'. The Philip of the poem, the dreamer and democrat, who says to Adam the Tutor

> Alas, the noted phrase of the prayer-book
> Doing our duty in that state of life to which God has called us,
> Seems to me always to mean, when the little rich boys say it,
> Standing in velvet frock by Mama's brocaded flounces,
> Eying her gold-fastened book, and the chain and watch at her bosom,
> Seems to me always to mean, eat, drink, and never mind others,

— was in broad outline drawn from my father, and the impression made by his idealist, enthusiastic youth upon his comrades. And Philip's migration to the Antipodes at the end — when he

> rounded the sphere to New Zealand,
> There he hewed and dug; subdued the earth and his spirit —

— was certainly suggested by my father's similar step in 1847, the year before the poem appeared. Only in my father's life there had been as yet no parallel to the charming love-story of 'The Bothie'. His love-story awaited him on the other side of the world.

At that moment New Zealand, the land of beautiful mountain and sea, with its even temperate climate, and its natives whom English enthusiasm hoped not only to govern but to civilise and assimilate, was in the minds of all to whom the colonies seemed to offer chances of social reconstruction beyond any that were possible in a crowded and decadent Europe. 'Land of Hope', I find it often called in these old letters. 'The gleam' was on it, and my father, like Browning's Waring, heard the call.

> After it; follow it. Follow the gleam!

He writes to his mother in August 1847 from the Colonial Office:

> Everyone whom I meet pities me for having to return to London at this dull season, but to my own feelings, it is not worse than at other times. The things which would make me loathe the thought of passing my life or even several years in London, do not depend on summer or winter. It is the chronic, not the acute ills of London life which are real ills to me. I meant to have talked to you again before I left home about New Zealand, but I could not find a good opportunity. I do not think you will be surprised to hear that I cannot give up my intention — though you may think me wrong, you will believe that no cold-heartedness towards home has assisted me in framing my resolution. Where or how we shall meet on this side the grave will be arranged for us by a wiser will than our own. To me, however strange and paradoxical it may sound, this going to New Zealand is become a work of faith, and I cannot but go through with it.

And later on when his plans are settled, he writes in exultation to his eldest sister:

> The weather is gusty and rainy, but no cheerlessness without can repress a sort of exuberant buoyancy of spirit which is supplied to me from within. There is such an indescribable blessedness in looking forward to a manner of life which the heart and conscience approve, and which at the same time satisfies the instinct for the heroic and beautiful. Yet there seems little enough in a homely life in New Zealand forest; and indeed there is nothing in the thing itself, except in so far as it flows from a principle, a faith.

And he goes on to speak in vague exalted words of the 'equality' and 'brotherhood' to which he looks forward in the new land; winding up with an account of his life on London, its daily work at the Colonial Office, his walks, the occasional evenings at the Opera where he worships Jenny Lind, his readings and practisings in his lodgings. My poor father! He little knew what he was up, or the real conditions of the life to which he was going.

For though the Philip of 'The Bothie' may have 'hewed and dug' to good purpose in New Zealand, success in colonial farming was a wild and fleeting dream in my father's case. He was born for academic life and a scholar's pursuits. He had no practical gifts, and knew nothing whatever of land or farming. He had only courage, youth, sincerity, and a charming presence which made him friends at sight. His mother, indeed, with her gentle wisdom, put no obstacles in his way. On the contrary, she remembered that her husband had felt a keen imaginative interest in the colonies, and had bought small sections of land near Wellington, which his second son now proposed to take up and farm. But some of the old friends of the family felt and expressed consternation. In particular Baron Bunsen, then Prussian Ambassador to England, Arnold of Rugby's dear and faithful friend, wrote a letter of earnest and affectionate remonstrance to the would-be colonist. Let me quote it, if only that it may remind me of days long ago, when it was still possible for a strong and tender friendship to exist between a Prussian and an Englishman!

Bunsen points out to 'young Tom' that he has only been eight or nine months in the Colonial Office, not long enough to give it a fair trial, that the drudgery of his clerkship will soon lead to more interesting things, that his superiors speak well of him; above all that he has no money, and no practical experience of farming, and that if he is going to New Zealand in the hope of building up a purer society, he will soon find himself bitterly disillusioned.

> Pray, my dear young friend, do not reject the voice of a man nearly sixty years, who has made his way through life under much greater difficulties perhaps than you imagine — who was your father's dear friend — who feels deeply attached to all that bears the honoured and blessed name of Arnold — who in particular had *your father's promise* that he would allow me to offer to *you*, after I had seen you in 1839, something of that care and friendship he had bestowed upon Henry — (Brunsen's own son) — do not

reject the warning voice of that man, if he entreats you solemnly not to take a *precipitate* step. Give yourself time. Try a change of scene. Go for a month or two to France or Germany. I am sure you wish to satisfy your friends that you are acting wisely, considerately, in giving up what you have.

Spartam quam nactus es, orna — was Niebuhr's word to me when once, about 1825, wearied with diplomatic life, I resolved to throw up my place, and go — not to New Zealand, but to German University. Let me say that concluding word to you and believe me, my dear young friend

Your sincere and affectionate friend
Bunsen.

P.S. If you feel disposed to have half an hour's quiet conversation with me alone, pray come to-day at six o'clock, and then dine with us quietly at half-past six. I go tomorrow to Windsor Castle for four days.

Nothing could have been kinder, nothing more truly felt and meant. But the young make their own experience, and my father, with the smiling open look which disarmed opposition, and disguised all the time a certain stubborn independence of will, characteristic of him through life, took his own way. He went to New Zealand, and now that it was done, the interest and sympathy of all his family and friends followed him. Let me give the touching letter, which Arthur Stanley, his father's biographer, wrote to him the night before he left England.

Univ. Coll. Oxford, Nov. 4, 1847.

Farwell! — (if you will let me once again recur to a relation so long since past away) farewell — my dearest, earliest, best of pupils. I cannot let you go without asking you to forgive those many annoyances which I fear I must have unconsciously inflicted upon you in the last year of your Oxford life — nor without expressing the interest which I feel and shall I trust ever feel, beyond all that I can say, in your future course. You know — or perhaps you hardly can know — how when I came back to Oxford after the summer of 1842, your presence here was to me the stay and charm of my life — how the walks — the lectures — the Sunday evenings with you, filled up the void which had been left in my interests,[1] and endeared to me all the beginnings of my College labours. That particular feeling, as is natural, has passed away — but it may still be a pleasure to you to feel in your distant home that whatever may be my occupations, nothing will more cheer and support me through them than the belief that in that new world your dear father's name is in you still loved and honoured, and bringing forth the fruits which he would have delighted to see.

---

[1] By the sudden death of Dr Arnold.

Farewell, my friend. May God in whom you trust be with you.

Do not trouble yourself to answer this — only take it as the true expression of one who often thinks how little he has done for you in comparison with what he would.

Ever yours,
A.P.Stanley

But, of course, the inevitable happened. After a few valiant but quite futile attempts to clear his land with his own hands, or with the random labour he could find to help him, the young colonist fell back on the education he had held so cheap in England, and bravely took schoolwork wherever in the rising townships of the infant colony he could find it. Meanwhile his youth, his pluck, and his Oxford distinctions had attracted the kindly notice of the Governor, Sir George Gray, who offered him his private secretaryship — one can imagine the twinkle in the Governor's eye, when he first came across my father building his own hut on his section outside Wellington! The offer was gratefully refused. But another year of New Zealand life brought reconsideration. The exile begins to speak of 'loneliness' in his letters home, to realise that it is 'collision' with other kindred minds that 'kindles the spark of thought', and presently, after a striking account of a solitary walk across unexplored country in New Zealand, he confesses that he is not sufficient for himself, and that the growth and vigour of the intellect were, for him at least, 'not compatible with loneliness'.

A few months later, Sir William Denison, the newly appointed Governor of Van Diemen's Land, hearing that a son of Arnold of Rugby, an Oxford First Class man, was in New Zealand, wrote to offer my father the task of organising primary education in Van Diemen's Land.

He accepted — yet not I think without a sharp sense of defeat at the hands of Mother Earth! — set sail for Hobart, and took possession of a post that might easily have led to great things. His father's fame preceded him, and he was warmly welcomed. The salary was good and the field free. Within a few months of his landing he was engaged to my mother. They were married in 1850, and I, their eldest child, was born in June 1851.

And then the unexpected, the amazing thing happened. At the time of their marriage, and for some time after, my mother, who had been brought up in a Protestant 'scriptural' atmosphere, and had been originally drawn to the younger 'Tom Arnold', partly because he was the son of his father, as Stanley's 'Life' had now made the headmaster known to the world, was a good deal troubled by the heretical views of her young husband. She had some difficulty in getting him to consent to the baptism of his elder children. He was still in may respects the 'Philip' of the 'Bothie', influenced by Goethe, and the French romantics, by Emerson, Kingsley and Carlyle, and in touch still with all that Liberalism of the later forties in Oxford, of which his most intimate friend, Arthur Clough, and his elder brother, Matthew Arnold, were to become the foremost representatives. But all the while, under the surface, an extraordinary transformation was going on. He was never able to explain it afterwards, even to me, who knew him best of all his children. I doubt whether he ever understood it himself. But he who had only once crossed the High Street to hear Newman preach, and felt no interest in the sermon, now, on the other side of the world, surrendered to Newman's influence. It is uncertain if they had ever spoken to each other at Oxford; yet that subtle pervasive intellect which captured for years the critical and sceptical mind of Mark Pattison, and indirectly transformed the Church of England after Newman himself had left it, now, reaching across the world, laid hold on Arnold's son, when Arnold himself was no longer there to fight it. A general reaction against the negations and philosophies of his youth set in for 'Philip', as inevitable in his case as the revolt against St Sulpice was for Ernest Renan. For my father was in truth born for religion, as his whole later life showed. In that he was the true son of Arnold of Rugby. But his speculative Liberalism had carried him so much further than his father's had ever gone, that the recoil was correspondingly great. The steps of it are dim. He was 'struck' one Sunday with the 'authoritative' tone of the First Epistle of Peter. Who and what was Peter? What justified such a tone? At another time he found a Life of St Brigit of Sweden at a country inn, when he was on one of his school-inspecting journeys across the island. And he records a mysterious influence or 'voice' from it, as he rode in meditative solitude through the sunny spaces of the Tasmanian bush. Last of all, he 'obtained' — from England no doubt — the 'Tracts for the Times'. And as he went through them, the same documents, and the same arguments, which had taken Newman to Rome, nine years before, worked upon his late and distant disciple. But who can explain 'conversion'? Is it not enough to say, as was said of old — 'The Holy Ghost fell on them that believed'? The great 'Malignant' had indeed triumphed. In October, 1854, my father was received at Hobart, Tasmania, into the Church of Rome; and two years later, after he had reached England, and written to Newman asking the new Father of the Oratory to receive him, Newman replied —

> How strange it seems! What a world this is! I knew your father a little, and I really think I never had any unkind feeling towards him. I saw at Oriel on the Purification before (I think) his death (January 1842). I was glad to meet him. If I said ever a harsh thing against him I am very sorry for it. In seeing you, I should have a sort of pledge that he at the moment of his death made it all up with me. Excuse this. I came here last night, and it is so marvellous to have your letter this morning.

So, for the moment, ended one incident in the long bout between two noble fighters, Arnold and Newman, each worthy of the other's steel. For my father, indeed, this act of surrender was but the beginning of a long and troubled history. My poor mother felt as though the earth had crumbled under her. Her passionate affection for my father endured till her latest hour, but she never reconciled herself to what he done. There was in her an instinctive dread of Catholicism, of which I have suggested some of the origins — ancestral and historical. It never abated. Many years afterwards, writing 'Helbeck of Bannisdale', I drew upon what I remembered of it in describing some traits in Laura Fountain's inbred, and finally indomitable resistance, to the Catholic claim upon the will and intellect of men.

And to this trial in the realm of religious feeling there were added all the practical difficulties into which my father's action plunged her, and his children. The Tasmanian appointment had to be given up, for the feeling in the colony was strongly anti-Catholic; and we came home, as I have described, to a life of struggle, privation, and constant anxiety, in which my mother suffered not only for herself, but for her children.

But after all there were bright spots. My father and mother were young; my mother's eager sympathetic temper brought her many friends; and for us children, Fox How and its dear inmates opened a second home, and new joys, which upon myself in particular left impressions never to be effaced or undone. Let me try in it, as they were in 1856.

Chapter II
Fox How

The grey stone house stands now, as it stood then, on a 'how' or rising ground in the beautiful Westmorland valley leading from Ambleside to Rydal. The 'Doctor' built it as a holiday paradise for himself and his children, in the year 1833. It is a modest building, with ten bedrooms and three sitting-rooms. Its windows look straight into the heart of Fairfield, the beautiful semi-circular mountain which rears its hollowed front and buttressing scaurs against the north, far above the green floor of the valley. That the house looked north never troubled my grandfather or his children. What they cared for was the perfect outline of the mountain wall, the 'pensive glooms', hovering in that deep breast of Fairfield, the magic never-ending chase of sunlight and cloud across it on fine days, and the beauty of the soft woodland clothing its base. The garden was his children's joy as it became mine. Its little beck with its mimic bridges, its encircling river, its rocky knolls, its wild strawberries and wild raspberries, its queen of birch trees rearing a stately head against the distant mountain, its rhododendrons growing like weeds on its mossy banks, its velvet turf, and long silky grass in the parts left wild — all these things have made the joy of three generations.

Inside, Fox How was comfortably spacious, and I remember what a place it appeared to my childish eyes, fresh from the tiny cabin of a 400-ton sailing-ship, and the rough life of a colony. My grandmother, its mistress, was then sixty-one. Her beautiful hair was scarcely touched with grey, her complexion was still delicately clear, and her soft brown eyes had the eager sympathetic look of her Cornish race. Charlotte Brontë, who saw her a few years earlier, while on a visit to Miss Martineau, speaks of her as having been a 'very pretty woman', and credits her and her daughters with 'the possession of qualities the most estimable and endearing'. In another letter, however, written to a less familiar correspondent, to whom Miss Bronte, as the literary lady, with a critical reputation to keep up, expresses herself in a different and more artificial tone, she again describes my grandmother as good and charming, but doubts her claim to 'power and completeness of character'. The phrase occurs in a letter describing a call at Fox How, and its slight pomposity makes the contrast with the passage in which Matthew Arnold describes the same visit the more amusing.

> At seven came Miss Martineau, and Miss Brontë (Jane Eyre); talked to Miss Martineau (who blasphemes frightfully) about the prospects of the Church of England, and, wretched man that I am, promised to go and see her cow-keeping miracles tomorrow, I who hardly know a cow from a sheep. I talked to Miss Brontë (past thirty and plain, with expressive grey eyes through) of her curates, of French novels, and her education in a school at Brussels, and sent the lions roaring to their dens at half-past nine.

No one indeed would have applied the word 'power' to my grandmother, unless they had known her very well. The general impression was always one of gentle sweetness and soft dignity. But the phrase 'completeness of character', happens to sum up very well the impression left by her life both on kindred and friends. What Miss Bronte exactly meant by it, it is difficult to say. But the widowed mother of nine children, five of them sons, and all of them possessed of strong will and quick intelligence, who was able so to guide their young lives, that to her last hour, thirty years after her husband's death had left her alone with her task, she possessed their passionate reverence and affection, and that each and all of them would have acknowledged her as among the dearest and noblest influences in their lives, can hardly be denied 'completeness of character'. Many of her letters lie before me. Each son and daughter, as he or she went out into the world, received them with the utmost regularity. They knew that every incident in their lives interested their mother; and they in their turn were eager to report to her everything that came to them, happy or unhappy, serious or amusing. And this relation of the family to their mother only grew and strengthened with the years. As the daughters married, their husbands became so many new and devoted sons to this gentle, sympathetic, and yet firm-natured woman. Nor were the daughters-in-law less attached to her, and the grandchildren who in due time began to haunt Fox How. In my own life I trace her letters from my earliest childhood, through my life at school, to my engagement and marriage; and I have never ceased to feel a pang of disappointment that she died before my children were born. Matthew Arnold adored her, and wrote her every week of his life. So did her other children. William Forster, throughout his busy life in Parliament, vied with her sons in tender consideration and unfailing loyalty. And every grandchild thought of a visit to Fox How as not only a joy but an honour. Indeed nothing could have been more 'complete', more rounded, than my grandmother's character and life as they developed through her eighty-three years. She made no conspicuous intellectual claim, though her quick intelligence, her wide sympathies and clear judgement, combined with something ardent and responsive in her temperament, attracted and held able men; but her personality was none the less strong because it was so gently, delicately served by looks and manner.

Perhaps the 'completeness' of my grandmother's character will be best illustrated by one of her family letters, a letter which may recall to some readers Stevenson's delightful poem on the mother who sits at home watching the fledglings depart from the nest.

> So from the hearth the children flee,
>   By that almighty hand
> Austerely led; so one by sea
>   Goes forth, and one by land;
>   Nor aught of all man's sons escapes from that command.
>
> . . . .
>
> And as the fervent smith of yore
>   Beat out the glowing blade,
> Nor wielded in the front of war
>   The weapons that he made,
>   But in the tower at home still plied his ringing trade;
> So like a sword the son shall roam
>   On nobler missions sent;
> And as the smith remained at home
>   In peaceful turret pent,
>   So sits the wild at home the mother well content.

The letter was written to my father in New Zealand in the year 1848, as a family chronicle. The brothers and sisters named in it are Walter, the youngest of the family, a middy of fourteen, on board hip, and not very happy in the Navy, which he was ultimately to leave for Durham University and business; Willy, in the Indian Army, afterwards the author of 'Oakfield', a novel attacking the abuses of Anglo-Indian life, and the first Director of Public Instruction in the Punjab — commemorated by his poet brother in 'A Southern Night'; Edward, at Oxford; Mary, the second daughter, who at the age of twenty-two had been left a widow after a year of married life; and Fan, the youngest daughter of the flock, who now, in 1917, alone represents them in the grey house under the fells, the little Westmorland farm described is still exactly as it was; and has still a Richardson for master, though of a younger generation. And Rydal Chapel, freed now from the pink cement which clothed it in those days, and from the high pews familiar to the children of Fox How, still sends the cheerful voice of its bells through the valley on Sunday mornings.

The reader will remember, as he reads it, that he is in the troubled year of '48, with Chartism at home and revolution abroad. The 'painful interest' with which the writer has read Clough's 'Bothie', refers I think, to the fact that she has recognised her second son, my father, as to some extent the hero of the poem.

Fox How, Nov. 19, 1848.

My Dearest Tom, — . . . I am always intending to send you something like a regular journal, but twenty days of the month have now passed away, and it not done. Dear Matt, who was with us at the beginning, and who I think bore a part in our last letters to you, has returned to his post in London, and I am not without hope of hearing by tomorrow's post that he has run down to Portsmouth to see Walter before he sails on a cruise with the Squadron which I believe he was to do today. But I should think they would hardly leave Port in such dirty weather, when the wind howls and the rain pours, and the whole atmosphere is thick and lowering as I suppose you rarely or never see it in New Zealand. I wish the more that Matt may get down to Spithead, because the poor little man has been in a great ferment about leaving his ship and going into a smaller one. By the same post I had a letter from him, and Capitan Daws, who had been astonished and grieved by Walter's coming to him and telling him he wished to leave the ship. It was evident that Capitan D. was quite distressed about it.

She then discusses, very shrewdly and quietly, the reasons for her boy's restlessness, and how best to meet it. The letter goes on: —

Certainly there is great comfort in having him with so true and good a friend as Capitan D. and I could not feel justified in acting against his counsel. But as he gets to know Walter better, I think it very likely that he will himself think it better for him to be in some ship not so likely to stay about in harbour as the St. Vincent; and will judge that with a character like his it might be better for him to be on some more distant stations.

I write about all this as coolly as if he were not my own dear youngest born, the little dear son whom I have so cherished, and who was almost a nursling still, when the bond which kept us all together was broken. But I believe I do truly feel that if my beloved sons are good and worthy of the name they bear, are in fact true, earnest, Christian men, I have no wish left for them — no selfish longings after their companionship, which can for a moment be put in comparison with such joy. This almost seemed strange to me when in a letter the other day from Willy to Edward, in reference to his — E's — future destination — Willy rather urged upon him a home, domestic life, on *my* account, as my sons were already so scattered. As I say, those loving words seemed strange to me; because I have such an overpowering feeling that the all-in-all to me is that my sons should be in just that vocation in life most suited to them, and most bringing out what is highest and best in them; whether it might be in England, or at the furthest extremity of the world.

. . . .

November 24, 1848. — I have been unwell for some days, dearest Tom, and this makes me less active in all my usual employments, but it shall not if I can help it, prevent my making some progress in this letter, which in less than a week may perhaps be on its way to New Zealand. I have just sent Fan downstairs, for she nurses her Mother till I begin to think some change good for her. She has been reading aloud to me, and now, as the evening advances I have asked some of them to read to me a long poem by Clough — (the 'Bothie') which I have no doubt will reach you. It does not *look* attractive to me, for it is in English Hexameters, which are to me very cumbrous and uninviting; but probably that may be for some want of knowledge in my own ear and taste. The poem is addressed to his pupils of last summer, and in scenery etc. will have, I suppose, many touches from his highland residence; but, in a brief Preface, he says that the tale itself is altogether fiction.

. . . .

To turn from things domestic to at large, what a state of things is this at Berlin! A state of siege declared, and the King at open issue with his representatives! — from the country districts, people flocking to give him aid, while the great towns are almost in revolt. 'Always too late' might, I suppose, have been his motto; and when things have been given with one hand, he has seemed too ready to withdraw them with other. But, after all, I must and do believe that he has noble qualities, so to have won Bunsen's love and respect.

November 25. — Mary is preparing a long letter, and it will therefore matter the less if mine is not so long as I intended. I have not yet quite made up the way I have lost in my late indisposition, and we have such volumes of letters from dear Willy to answer, that I believe this folio will be all I can send to you, my own darling; but you do not dwell in my heart or my thoughts less fondly. I long inexpressibly to have some definite ideas of what you are now — after some eight months of residence — doing, thinking, feeling; what are your occupations in the present, what your aims and designs for the future. The assurance that it is your first and heartfelt desire to please God my dear son; that you have struggled to do this and not allowed yourself to shrink from whatever you felt to be involved in it, this is, and will be my deepest and dearest comfort, and I pray to Him to guide you into all truth. But though supported by this assurance, I do not pretend to say that often and often I do not yearn over you in my thoughts, and long to bestow upon you in act and word as well as in thought, some of that overflowing love which is cherished for you in your home.

And here follows a tender mother-word in reference to an early and unrequited attachment of my father's, the fate of which may possibly have contributed to the restlessness which sent beyond the seas.

But, dear Tom, I believe that though the hoped for flower and fruit have faded, yet that the plant has been strengthened and purified . . . . It would be a grief to me not to believe that you will yet be most happy in married life and when you can make to yourself a home I shall perhaps lose some of my restless longing to be near you and ministering to your comfort, and sharing in your life — if I can think of you as cheered and helped by one who loved you as I did your own beloved father.

Sunday, November 26. — Just a year, my son, since you left England! But I really must not allow myself to dwell on this, and all the thoughts it brings with it; for I found last night that the contrast between the fullness of thought and feeling, and my own powerlessness to express it weighed on me heavily; and not having yet quite recovered my usual tone I could not well bear it. So I will just try to collect for you a few more home Memoranda, and then have done. . . . Our new tenant, James Richardson, is now fairly established at his farm, and when I went up there and saw the cradle and the happy childish faces around the table, and the rows of oatmeal cake hanging up, and the cheerful, active Mother going hither and thither — now to her Diary — now guiding the steps of the little one that followed her about — and all the time preparing things for her husband's return from his work at night, I could not but feel that it was a very happy picture of English life. Alas! That there are not larger districts where it exists! But I hope there is still much of it; and I feel that while there is an awful under-current of misery and sin — the latter both caused by the first and causing it — and while, on the surface, there is carelessness, and often recklessness and hardness and trifling, yet that still, in our English society, there is, between these two extremes, a strength of good mixed with baser elements, which must and will, I fully believe, support us nationally in the troublous times which are at hand — on which we are actually entered.

But again I am wandering, and now the others have gone off to Rydal Chapel without me this lovely Sunday morning. There are bells sounding invitingly across the valley, and the evergreens are white and sparkling in the sun.

I have a note from Clough. . . . His poem is as remarkable, I think, as you would expect, coming from him. Its *power* quite overcame my dislike to the measure — so far at least as to make me read it with great interest — often, though, a painful one. And now I must end.

As to Miss Brontë's impressions of Matthew Arnold in that same afternoon call of 1850, they were by no means flattering. She understands that he was already the author of 'a volume of poems' (The Poems by A, 1849), and remarks that his manner 'displeases from its seeming foppery', but she recognises, nevertheless, in conversation with him, 'some genuine intellectual aspirations!' It was but a few years later that my uncle paid his poet's homage to the genius of the two sisters — to Charlotte of the 'expressive grey eyes' — to Emily of the 'chainless soul'. I often try to picture their meeting in the Fox How drawing-room: Matthew Arnold, tall, handsome, in the rich opening of his life, his first poetic honours thick upon him, looking with a half-critical, half-humorous eye at the famous little lady whom Miss Martineau had brought to call upon his mother; and beside him that small intrepid figure, on which the worst storms of life had already beaten, which was but five short years from its own last rest. I doubt whether, face to face, they would ever have made much of each other. But the sister who could write of a sister's death as Charlotte wrote, in the letter that every lover of great prose ought to have by heart: —

Emily suffers no more from pain or weakness now, she never will suffer more in this world. She is gone, after a hard, short conflict. . . . We are very calm at present, why should we be otherwise? The anguish of seeing her suffer is over; the funeral day is past. We feel she is at peace. No need now to tremble for the hard frost and the keen wind. *Emily does not feel them.* —

— must have stretched out spiritual hands to Matthew Arnold, had she lived to read 'A Southern Night' — that loveliest, surely, of all laments of brother for brother.

CHAPTER III

The Family of Fox How

Dr Arnold's eldest daughter, Jane Arnold, afterwards Mrs W. E. Forster, my godmother, stands out for me on the tapestry of the past, as one of the noblest personalities I have ever known. She was twenty-one when her father died, and she had been his chief companion among his children for years before death took him from her. He taught her Latin and Greek, he imbued her with his own political and historical interests, and her ardent Christian faith answered to his own. After his death she was her mother's right hand at Fox How; and her letters to her brothers — to my father especially, since he was longest and farthest away — show her quick and cultivated mind, and all the sweetness of her nature. We hear of her teaching a young brother Latin and Greek; she goes over to Miss Martineau on the other side of the valley to translate some German for that busy woman; she reads Dante beside her mother, when the rest of the family have gone to bed; she sympathises passionately with Mazzini and Garibaldi; and every week, she walks over Loughrigg through fair weather and foul, summer and winter, to teach in a night school at Skelwith. Then the young Quaker manufacturer William Forster appears on the scene, and she falls happily and completely in love. Her letters to the brother in New Zealand become, in a moment, all joy and ardour, and nothing could be prettier than the account, given by one of the sisters, of the quiet wedding in Rydal Chapel, the family breakfast, the bride's simple dress and radiant look, Matthew Arnold giving his sister away — with the great fells standing sentinel. And there exists a delightful unpublished letter by Harriet Martineau which gives some idea of the excitement roused in the quiet Ambleside valley by Jane Arnold's engagement to the tall Yorkshireman who came from surroundings so different from the academic and scholarly world in which the Arnolds had been brought up.

Then followed married life at Rawdon near Bradford, with supreme happiness at home, and many and growing interests in the manufacturing, religious and social around the young wife. In 1861 William Forster became member for Bradford, and in 1869 Gladstone included him in that Ministry of all the talents, which foundered under the onslaught of Disraeli in 1874. Forster became Vice-President of the Council, which meant Minister for Education, with a few other trifles like the cattle-plague thrown in. The Education Bill, which William Forster brought in, in 1870 — (as a girl of eighteen, I was in the Ladies' Gallery in the House of Commons on the great day to hear his speech) — has been the foundation stone ever since of English popular education. It has always been clear to me that the scheme of the Bill was largely influenced by William Forster's wife, and through her, by the convictions and beliefs of her father. The compromise by which the Church schools, with the creeds and the Church catechism, were preserved, under a conscience clause, while the dissenters got their way as to the banishment of creeds and catechisms, and the substitution for them of 'simple Bible teaching', in the schools founded under the new School Boards, which the Bill set up all over England, has practically — with of course modifications — held its ground for nearly half a century. It was illogical; and the dissenters have never ceased to resent the perpetuation of the Church school which it achieved. But English life is illogical. It met the real situation; and it would never have taken the shape it did — in my opinion — but for the ardent beliefs of the young and remarkable woman, at once a strong Liberal, and devoted daughter of the English Church, as Arnold, Kingsley and Maurice understood it, who had married her Quaker husband in 1850, and had thereby been the innocent cause of his automatic severance from the Quaker body. His respect for her judgement and intellectual power was only equalled by his devotion to her. And when the last great test of his own life came, how she stood by him! — through those terrible days of the Land League struggle, when, as Chief Secretary for Ireland, Forster carried his life in his hand month after month, to be worn out finally by the double toil of Parliament and Ireland, and to die just before Mr Gladstone split the Liberal party in 1886, by the introduction of the Home Rule Bill, in which Forster would not have followed him.

I shall, however, have something to say later on in these Reminiscences about those tragic days. To those who watched Mrs Forster through them, and who knew her intimately, she was one of the most interesting figures of that crowded time. Few people, however, outside the circle of her kindred, knew her intimately. She was of course in the ordinary social and political world, both before and after her husband's entrance upon office, and admission to the Cabinet; dining out and receiving at home; attending Drawing-rooms and public functions; staying at country houses, and invited to Windsor, like other Ministers' wives, and keenly interested in all the varying fortunes of Forster's party. But though she was in that world, she was never truly of it. She moved through it, yet veiled from it, by that pure, unconscious selflessness, which is the saint's gift. Those who ask nothing for themselves, whose whole strength is spent on affections that are their life, and on ideals at one with their affections, are not easily popular, like the self-seeking, particoloured folk who make up the rest of us; who flatter, caress, and court, that we in our turn may be flattered and courted. Their gentleness masks the indomitable soul within; and so their fellows are often unaware of their true spiritual rank.

It is interesting to recall the instinctive sympathy with which a nature so different from Charlotte Brontë's as that of Arnold's eldest daughter, met the challenge of the Brontë genius. It would not have been wonderful — in those days — if the quiet Fox How household, with its strong religious atmosphere, its daily psalms and lessons, its love for 'The Christian Year', its belief in 'discipline' (how that comes out in all the letters!) had been repelled by the blunt strength of 'Jane Eyre'; just as it would not have been wonderful if they had held aloof from Miss Martineau, in the days when it pleased that remarkable woman to preach mesmeric atheism, or atheistic mesmerism, as we choose to put it. But there was a lifelong friendship between them and Harriet Martineau; and they recognised at once the sincerity and truth — the literary rank in fact — of 'Jane Eyre'. Not long after her marriage, Jane Forster with her husband went over to Haworth to see Charlotte Brontë. My aunt's letter, describing the visit to the dismal parsonage and church, is given without her name in Mrs Gaskell's 'Life', and Mr Shorter in reprinting it in the second of his large volumes, does not seem to be aware of the identity of the writer.

> Miss Brontë put me so in mind of her own 'Jane Eyre' (wrote my godmother). She looked smaller than ever, and moved about so quietly and noiselessly, just like a little bird, as Rochester called her; except that all birds are joyous, and that joy can never have entered that house since it was built. And yet, perhaps when that old man (Mr Brontë) married and took home his bride, and children's voices and feet were heard about the house, even that desolate graveyard and biting blast could not quench cheerfulness and hope. Now (i.e. since the deaths of Emily and Anne) there is something touching in the sight of that little creature entombed in such a place, and moving about herself there like a spirit; especially when you think that the slight still frame encloses a force of strong, fiery life, which nothing has been able to freeze or extinguish.

This letter was written before my birth, and about six years before the writer of it appeared, as an angel of help, in the dingy dockside inn, where we tired travellers had taken shelter on our arrival from the other side of the world, and where I was first kissed by my godmother. As I grew up into girlhood, 'Aunt K.' (K. was the pet name by which Matthew Arnold always wrote to her) became for me part of the magic of Fox How, through? I saw her a passionate and troubled affection. She was to me 'a thing enskied' and heavenly — for all her quick human interests, and her sweet ways with those she loved. How could anyone be so good! — was often the despairing reflection of the child who adored her, caught herself in the toils of a hot temper and a stubborn will; but all the same to see her enter a room was joy, and to sit by her the highest privilege. I don't know whether she could be strictly called beautiful. But to me everything about her was beautiful — her broad brow, her clear brown eyes, and wavy brown hair, the touch of stately grace with which she moved, the mouth so responsive and soft, yet, at need, so determined, the hand so delicate, yet so characteristic.

She was the eldest of the nine. Of her relation to the next of them — her brother Matthew — there are many indications in the collection of my uncle's letters, edited by Mr George Russell. It was to her that 'Resignation' was addressed, in recollection of their mountain walks and talks together; and in a letter to her, the sonnet to Shakespeare — 'Others abide our question — thou art free' — was first written out. Their affection for each other, in spite of profound differences of opinion, only quickened and deepened with time.

Between my father and his elder brother Matthew Arnold there was barely a year's difference of age. The elder was born in December 1822, and the younger in November 1823. They were always warmly attached to each other, and in spite of much that was outwardly divergent — sharply divergent — they were more alike fundamentally than was often suspected. Both had derived from some remoter ancestry — possibly through their Cornish mother, herself the daughter of a Penrose and a Trevenen — elements and qualities which were lacking in the strong personality of their father. Imagination, 'rebellion against fact', spirituality, a tendency to dream, unworldliness, the passionate love of beauty and charm, 'ineffectualness' in the practical competitive life — these, according to Matthew Arnold, when he came to lecture at Oxford on 'The Study of Celtic Literature', were and are the characteristic marks of the Celt. They were unequally distributed between the two brothers. 'Unworldliness', 'rebellion against fact', 'ineffectualness' in common life, fell rather to my father's share than my uncle's; though my uncle's 'worldliness', of which he was sometimes accused, if it was ever existed, was never more than skin-deep. Imagination in my father led to a life-long and mystical preoccupation with religion; it made Matthew Arnold one of the great poets of the nineteenth century.

There is a sketch of my father made in 1847, which preserves the dreamy, sensitive look of early youth, when he was the centre of a band of remarkable friends — Clough, Stanley, F. T. Palgrave, Alfred Domett (Browning's Waring) and others. It is the face — nobly and delicately cut — of one whom the successes of the practical, competitive life could never be of the same importance as those events which take place in thought, and for certain minds are the only real events. 'For ages and ages the world has been constantly slipping ever more and more out of the Celt's grasp', wrote Matthew Arnold. But all the while the Celt has great compensations. To him belongs another world than the visible; the world of phantasmagoria, of emotion, the world of passionate beginnings, rather than of things achieved. After the romantic and defiant days of his youth, my father, still pursuing the same natural tendency, found all that he needed in Catholicism, and specially, I think, in that endless poetry and mystery of the Mass, which keeps Catholicism alive.

Matthew Arnold was very different in outward aspect. The face, strong and rugged, the large mouth, the broad lined brow, and vigorous coal-black hair, bore no resemblance, except for that fugitive yet vigorous something which we call 'family likeness', to either his father or mother — still less to the brother so near to him in age. But the Celtic trace is there, though derived, I have sometimes thought, rather from an Irish than a Cornish source. Dr Arnold's mother, Martha Delafield, according to a genealogy I see no reason to doubt, was partly of Irish blood; one finds, at any rate, Fitzgeralds and Dillons among the names of her forebears. And I have seen in Ireland faces belonging to the 'black Celt' type — faces full of power, and humour, and softness, visibly moulded out of the good common earth by the nimble spirit within, which have reminded me of my uncle. Nothing indeed at first sight could have been less romantic or dreamy than his outer aspect. 'Ineffectualness' was not to be thought of in connection with him. He stood four-square — a courteous, competent man of affairs, an admirable inspector of schools, a delightful companion, a guest whom everybody wanted, and no one could bind for long; one of the sanest, most independent, most cheerful and loveable of mortals. Yet his poems show what was the real inner life and genius of the man; how rich in that very 'emotion', 'love of beauty and charm', 'rebellion against fact', 'spirituality', 'melancholy' which he himself catalogued as the cradle gifts of the Celt. Crossed indeed, always, with the Rugby 'earnestness', with that in him which came to him from his father.

It is curious to watch the growing perception of 'Matt's' powers among the circle of his nearest kin, as it is reflected in these family letters to the emigrant brother, which reached him across the seas from 1847 to 1856, and now lie under my hand. The 'Poems by A.' came out, as all lovers of English poetry know, in 1849. My grandmother writes to my father in March of that year, after protesting that she has not much news to give him: —

But the little volume of Poems! — that is indeed a subject of new and very great interest. By degrees we hear more of public opinion concerning them, and I am very much mistaken if their power both in thought and execution is not more and more felt and acknowledged. I had a letter from dear Miss Fenwick today, whose first impressions were that they were by *you*, for it seems she had heard of the volume as much admired, and as by one of the family, and she had hardly thought it could be by one so moving in the busy haunts of men as dear Matt. . . . Matt himself says 'I have learned a good deal as to what is *practicable* from the objections of people, even when I thought them not reasonable, and in some degree they may determine my course as to publishing; e.g. I had thoughts of publishing another volume of short poems next spring, and a tragedy I have long had in my head, the spring after: at present I shall leave the short poems to take their chance, only writing them when I cannot help it, and try to get on with my Tragedy (Merope), which however will not be a very quick affair. But as that must be in regular and usual from, it may perhaps, if it succeeds, enable me to use metres in short poems which seem proper to myself; whether they suit the habits of readers at first sight or not. But all this is rather vague at present.... I think I am getting quite indifferent about the book. I have given away the only copy I had, and now never look at them. The most enthusiastic people about them are young men of course; but I have heard of one or two people who found pleasure in "Resignation" and poems of that stamp, which is what I like.'

'The most enthusiastic people about them are young men, of course'. The sentence might stand as the motto of all poetic beginnings. The young poet writes first of all for the young of his own day. They make his bodyguard. They open to him the gates of the House of Fame. But if the divine power is really his, it soon frees itself from the shackles of Time and Circumstance. The true poet becomes, in the language of the Greek epigram on Homer, 'the ageless mouth of all the world'. And if 'The Strayed Reveller', and the Sonnet 'To Shakespeare', and 'Resignation', delighted those who were young in 1849, that same generation, as the years passed over it, instead of outgrowing their poet, took him all the more closely to their hearts. Only so can we explain the steady spread and deepening of his poetic reputation which befell my uncle up to the very end of his life, and had assured him by then — leaving out of count the later development of his influence both in the field of poetry and elsewhere — his place in the history of English literature.

But his entry as a poet was gradual, and but little heralded, compared to the *débuts* of our own time. Here is an interesting appreciation from his sister Mary, about whom I shall have more to say presently. At the time this letter was written, in 1849, she was twenty-three, and already a widow, after a tragic year of married life during which her young husband had developed paralysis of the brain. She was living in London, attending Bedford College, and F.D. Maurice's sermons, much influenced, like her brothers, by Emerson and Carlyle, and at this moment, a fine, restless, immature creature, much younger than her years in some respects, and much older in others, with eyes fast opening on worlds hitherto unsuspected in the quiet home life. She writes: —

> I have been in London for several months this year, and I have seen a good deal of Matt, considering the very different lives we lead. I used to breakfast with him sometimes, and then his Poems seemed to make me know Matt so much better than I had ever done before. Indeed it was almost like a new Introduction to him. I do not think those Poems could be read, quite independently of their poetical power — without leading one to expect a great deal from Matt; without raising I mean the kind of expectation one has from and for those who have, in some way or other, come face to face with life and asked it, in real earnest, what it means. I felt there was so much more of this practical questioning in Matt's book than I was at all prepared for; in fact that it showed a knowledge of life and conflict which was *strangely like experience* if it was not have looked for. I do not yet know the book well, but I think that 'Mycerinus' struck me most perhaps, as illustrating what I have been speaking of.

And again, to another member of the family: —

> It is the moral strength, or, at any rate, the *moral consciousness* which struck and surprised me so much in the poems. I could have been prepared for any degree of poetical power, for there being a great deal more than I could at all appreciate; but there is something altogether different from this, something which such a man as Clough has, for instance, which I did not expect to find in Matt; but it is there. Of course when I speak of his Poems I only speak of the impression received from those I understand. Some are perfect riddles to me, such as that to the Child at Douglas, which is surely more poetical than true.

Strangely like experience! The words are an interesting proof of the difficulty we all have in seeing with accuracy the persons and things which are nearest to us. The astonishment of the sisters — for the same feeling is expressed by Mrs Forster — was very natural. In these early days, 'Matt' often figures in the family letters as the worldling of the group — the dear one who is making way in surroundings quite unknown to the Fox How circle, where under the shadow of the mountains, the sisters, idealists all of them, looking out a little austerely, for all their tenderness, on the human scene, are watching with a certain anxiety lest Matt should be 'spoiled'. As Lord Lansdowne's private secretary, very much liked by his chief, he goes among rich and important people, and finds himself as a rule much cleverer than they; above all, able to amuse them, so often the surest road to social and other success. Already at Oxford 'Matt' had been something of an exquisite — or as Miss Bronte puts it, a trifle 'foppish'; and in the (manuscript) 'Fox How Magazine,' to which all the nine contributed, and in which Matthew Arnold's boyish poems may still be read, there are many family jests levelled at Matt's high standard in dress and deportment.

But how soon the nascent dread lest their poet should be somehow separated from them by the 'great world' passes away from mother and sisters — for ever! With every year of his life Matthew Arnold, beside making the sunshine of his own married home, became a more attached, a more devoted son and brother. The two volumes of his published letters are there to show it. I will only quote here a sentence from a letter of Mrs Arnold's written in 1850, a year after the publication of the 'Poems by A.'. She and her eldest daughter, then shortly to become William Forster's wife, were at the time in London. 'K.' had been seriously ill, and the marriage had been postponed for a short time.

> Matt (says Mrs Arnold) has been with us almost every day since we came up — now so long ago! — and it is pleasant indeed to see his dear face, and to find him always so affectionate, and so unspoiled by his being so much sought after in a kind of society entirely different from anything we can enter into.

But, indeed, the time saved, day after day, for an invalid sister, by a run-after young man of twenty-seven, who might so easily have made one or other of the trifling or selfish excuses we are all so ready to make, was only a prophecy of those many 'nameless unremembered acts' of simple kindness, which filled the background of Matthew Arnold's middle and later life, and were not revealed, many of them, even to his own people, till after his death — kindness to a pupil-teacher, an unsuccessful writer, a hard-worked schoolmaster or schoolmistress, a budding poet, a schoolboy. It was not possible to 'spoil' Matthew Arnold. Meredith's 'Comic Spirit' in him, his irrepressible humour, would alone have saved him from it. And as to his relation to 'society', and the great ones in it, no one more frankly amused himself — within certain very definite limits — with the 'cakes and ale' of life, and no one held more lightly to them. He never denied — none but the foolish ever do deny — the immense personal opportunities and advantages of an aristocratic class, wherever it exists. He was quite conscious — none but those without imagination can fail to be conscious — of the glamour of long descent and great affairs. But he laughed at the 'Barbarians', the materialised or stupid holders of power and place, and their 'fortified posts', i.e. the country houses, just as he laughed at the Philistines and Mr Bottles; when he preached a sermon in later life, it was on Menander's motto — 'Choose Equality'; and he and Clough — the Republican — were not really far apart. He mocked even at Clough indeed, addressing his letters to him — 'Citizen Clough, Oriel Lyceum Oxford'; but in the midst of the revolutionary hubbub of '48 he pours himself out to Clough only — he and 'Thyrsis', to use his own expression in a letter, 'agreeing like two lambs in a world of wolves', and in his early sonnet (1848) 'To a Republican Friend' (who was certainly Clough), he says: —

> If sadness at the long heart-wasting show
> Wherein earth's great ones are disquieted;
> If thoughts, not idle, while before me flow
> The armies of the homeless and unfed —
> If these are yours, if this is what you are,
> Then I am yours, and what you feel, I share.

Yet, as he adds, in the succeeding sonnet, he has no belief in sudden radical change, nor in any earthly millennium —

> Seeing this vale, this earth, whereon we dream,
> Is on all sides o'ershadowed by the high
> Uno'erleaped mountains of necessity,
> Sparing us narrower margin than we dream.

On the eagerness with which Matthew Arnold followed the revolutionary spectacle of '48, an unpublished letter written — piquantly enough! From Lansdowne House itself, on February 28, in that famous year, to my father in New Zealand, throws a vivid light. One feels the artist in the writer. First, the quiet of the great house and courtyard, the flower-pricked grass, the 'still-faced babies': then the sudden clash of the street-cries! 'Your uncle's description of this house', writes the present Lord Lansdowne, in 1910, 'might almost have been written yesterday, instead of in 1848. Little is changed, Romulus and Remus and the she-wolf are still on the top of the bookcase, and the clock is still hard by; but the picture of the Jewish Exiles... has been given to a local School of Art in Wiltshire! The green lawn remains, but I am afraid the crocuses, which I can remember as a child, no longer come up through the turf. And lastly one of the "still-faced babies" (i.e. Lord Lansdowne himself) is still often to be seen in the gravel court! He was three years old when the letter was written'.

Here then is the letter: —

Lansdowne House, Feb 8, 1848.

My Dearest Tom, — ... Here I sit, opposite a marble group of Romulus and Remus and the wolf; the two children fighting like mad, and the limp-uddered she-wolf affectionately snarling at the little demons struggling on her back. Above it is a great picture, Rembrandt's Jewish Exiles, which would do for Consuelo and Albert resting in one of their wanderings, worn out upon a wild stony heath sloping to the Baltic — she leaning over her two children who sleep in their torn rags at her feet. Behind me a most musical clock, marking now 24 Minutes past 1 p.m. On my left two great windows looking out on the court in front of the house, through one of which, slightly opened, comes in gushes the soft damp breath, with a tone of spring-life in it, which the close of an English February sometimes brings — so different from a November mildness. The green lawn which occupies nearly half the court is studded over with crocuses of all colours — growing out of the grass, for there are no flower beds; delightful for the large still-faced white-robed babies whom their nurses carry up and down on the gravel court where it skirts the green. And from the square and the neighbouring streets, through the open door whereat the civil porter moves to and fro, come the sounds of vehicles and men, in all gradations, some from near and some from far, but mellowed by the time they reach this backstanding lordly mansion.

But above all cries comes one whereat every stone in this and other lordly mansions may totter and quake for fear:

'Se...c...ond Edition of the Morning Herald — L...a...test news from Paris: — arrival of the King of the French.'

I have gone out and bought the said portentous Herald, and send it herewith, that you may read and know. As the human race for ever stumbles up its great steps, so it is now. You remember the Reform Banquets (in Paris) last summer? — well! — the diners omitted the King's health, and abused Guizot's majority as corrupt and servile: the Majority and the King grew excited; the Government forbade the Banquets to continue. The King met the Chamber with the words 'passions aveugles' to characterise the dispositions of the Banqueters: and Guizot grandly declared against the spirit of Revolution all over the world. His practice suited his words, or seemed to suit it, for both in Switzerland and Italy, the French Government incurred the charge of siding against the Liberals. Added to this the corruption cases you remember, the Praslin murder, and later events, which powerfully stimulated the disgust (moral indignation that People does not feel!) entertained by the lower against the governing class.

Then Thiers, seeing the breeze rising, and hoping to use it, made most telling speeches in the debate on the Address, clearly defining the crisis as a question between revolution and counter-revolution, and declaring enthusiastically for the former. Lamartine and others, the sentimental and the plain honest, were very damaging on the same side. The Government were harsh — abrupt — almost scornful. They would not yield — would not permit banquets: would give no Reform till they chose. Guizot spoke (alone in the Chamber I think) to this effect. With decreasing Majorities the Government carried the different clauses of the address, amidst furious scenes; opposition members crying that they were worse than Polignac. It was resolved to hold an Opposition banquet in Paris in spite of the Government, last Tuesday, the 22nd. In the week between the close of the debate and this day there was a profound uneasy excitement, but nothing I think to appall the rulers. They had the fortifications: all kinds of stores; and 100,000 troops of the line. To be quite secure however, they take a formal legal objection to the banquet at the doors; but not to prevent the procession thereto. On that the Opposition published a proclamation inviting the National Guard, who sympathised, to form part of the procession in uniform. Then the Government forbade the meeting altogether — absolutely — and the Opposition resigned themselves to try the case in a Court of Law.

So did not the people!

They gathered all over Paris: the National Guard, whom Ministers did not trust, were not called out: the Line checked and dispersed the mob on all points. But next day the mob were there again: the Ministers in a constitutional fright called out the National Guard: a body of these hard by the Opera refused to clear the street: they joined the people. Troops were brought up: the Mob and the National Guard refused to give them passage down the Rue Le Pelletier which they occupied: after a moment's hesitation, they were marched on along the Boulevard.

This settled the matter! Everywhere the National Guard fraternised with the People: the troops stood indifferent. The King dismissed the Ministers: he sent for Molé; a shade better: not enough: he sent for Thiers — a pause; this was several shades better — still not enough: meanwhile the crowd continued, and attacks on different posts, with slight bloodshed, increased the excitement: finally *The King abdicated* in favour of the Count of Paris and fled. The Count of Paris was taken by his mother to the Chamber — the People broke in; too late — not enough: — a Republic — an appeal to the people. The royal family escaped to all parts, Belgium, Eu, England: *a Provisional Government named.*

You will see how they stand: they have adopted the last measures of Revolution. — News has just come that the National Guard have declared against a Republic, and that a collision is inevitable.

If possible I will write by the next mail, and send you a later paper than the Herald by this mail.

Your truly affectionate, dearest Tom
M. Arnold

To this, let me add here two or three other letters or fragments, all unpublished, which I find among the papers from which I have been drawing, ending, for the present, with the jubilant letter describing his election to the Poetry Professorship at Oxford, in 1857. Here, first of all, is an amusing reference, dated 1849, to Keble, then the idol of every well-disposed Anglican household: —

I dined last night with a Mr Grove[1], a celebrated man of science: his wife is pretty and agreeable, but not on a first interview. The husband and I agree wonderfully in some points. He is a bad sleeper, and hardly ever free from headache; he equally dislikes and disapproves of modern existence and the state of excitement in which everybody lives: and he sighs after a paternal despotism and the calm existence of a Russian or Asia-

---

[1] Afterwards Sir William Grove, F.R.S., author of the famous essay on 'The Correlation of Physical Force'.

tic. He showed me a picture of Faraday, which is wonderfully fine: I am almost inclined to get it: it has a curious likeness to Keble, only with a calm, earnest look unlike the latter's Flibbertigibbet, fanatical, twinkling expression.

Did ever anybody apply such adjectives to John Keble before! Yet if anyone will look carefully at the engraving of Keble so often seen in quiet parsonages, they will understand, I think, exactly, what Matthew Arnold meant.

In 1850 great changes came upon the Arnold family. The 'Doctor's' three elder children — Jane, Matthew, and my father — married in the year, and a host of new interests sprang up for every member of the Fox How circle. I find in a letter to my father from Arthur Stanley, his father's biographer, and his own Oxford Tutor, the following reference to 'Matt's' marriage, and to the second series of Poems — containing 'Sohrab and Rustum' — which were published in 1854. 'You will have heard' — writes Stanley — 'of the great success of Matt's poems. He is in good heart about them. He is also — I must say so — though perhaps I have no right to say so, greatly improved by his marriage — retaining all the genius and nobleness of mind which you remember, with all the lesser faults pruned and softened down'. Matt himself wrote to give news of his wedding, to describe the bride — Judge Wightman's daughter, the dear and gracious little lady whom we grandchildren knew and loved as 'Aunt Fanny Lucy' — and to wish my father joy of his own. And then there is nothing among the waifs and strays that have come to me worth printing, till 1855, when my uncle writes to New Zealand: —

> I hope you have got my book by this time. What you will like best, I think, will be the 'Scholar Gipsy'. I am sure that old Cumner and Oxford country will stir a chord in you. For the preface I doubt if you will care, not having much before your eyes the sins and offences at which it is directed: the first being that we have numbers of young gentlemen with really wonderful powers of perception and expression, but to whom there is wholly wanting a 'bedeutendes Individuum' — so that their productions are most unedifying and unsatisfactory. But this is a long story.
>
> As to Church matters. I think people in general concern themselves less with them than they did when you left England. Certainly religion is not, to all appearance at least, losing ground here: but since great people of Newman's party went over, the disputes among the comparatively unimportant remains of them do not excite much interest. I am

going to hear Manning at the Spanish Chapel next Sunday. Newman gives himself up almost entirely to organising and educating the Roman Catholics, and is gone off greatly, they say, as a preacher.

God bless you, my dearest Tom: I cannot tell you the almost painful longing I sometimes have to see you once more.

The following year the brothers met again; and there followed, almost immediately, my uncle's election to the Poetry Professorship at Oxford. He writes, in answer to my father's congratulations: —

Hampton, May 15, 1857.

My Dear Tom, — My thoughts have often turned to you during my canvass for the Professorship — and they have turned to you more than ever during the last few days which I have been spending at Oxford. You alone of my brothers are associated with that life at Oxford, the *freest* and most delightful part, perhaps, of my life, when with you and Clough and Walrond I shook off all the bonds and formalities of the place, and enjoyed the spring of life and that unforgotten Oxfordshire and Berkshire country. Do you remember a poem of mine called 'The Scholar Gipsy'? It was meant to fix the remembrance of those delightful wanderings of ours in the Cumner hills before they were quite effaced — and as such, Clough and Walrond accepted it, and it has had much success at Oxford, I am told, as was perhaps likely from its *couleur locale.* I am hardly ever at Oxford now, but the sentiment of the place is overpowering to me when I have leisure to feel it, and can shake off the interruptions which it is not so easy to shake off now as it was when we were young. But on Tuesday afternoon I smuggled myself away, and got up into one of our old coombs among the Cumner hills, and into a field waving deep with cowslips and grasses, and gathered such a bunch as you and I used to gather in the cowslip field on Lutterworth road long years ago.

You dear old boy, I love your congratulations although I see and hear so little of you, and alas! *can* see and hear but so little of you. I was supported by people of all opinions, the great bond of union being, I believe, the affectionate interest felt in papa's memory. I think it probable that I shall lecture in English: there is no direction whatever in the Statute as to the language in which the lectures shall be: and the Latin has so died out, even among scholars, that it seems idle to entomb a lecture which, in English, might be stimulating and interesting.

On the same occasion, writing to his mother, the new Professor gives an amusing account of the election day, when my uncle and aunt came up to town from Hampton, where they were living, in order to get telegraphic news of the polling from friends at Oxford. 'Christ Church' — i.e. the High Church party in Oxford — had put up an opposition candidate, and the excitement was great. My uncle was by this time the father of three small boys, Tom, Trevenen — *alias* Budge — and Richard 'Diddy'.

> We went first to the telegraph station at Charing Cross. Then, about 4, we got a message from Walrond — 'nothing certain is known, but it is rumoured that you are ahead'. Then we went to get some toys for the children in the Lowther Arcade, and could scarcely have found a more genuine distraction than in selecting wagons for Tom and Trev, with horses of precisely the same colour, not one of which should have a hair more in his tail than the other — and a musical cart for Diddy. A little after five we went back to the telegraph office, and got the following message — 'Nothing declared, but you are said to be quite safe. Go to Eaton Place'. ('Eaton Place' was then the house of Judge Wightman, Mrs Matthew Arnold's father.) 'To Eaton Place we went, and then a little after 6 o'clock we were joined by the Judge in the highest state of joyful excitement with the news of my majority of 85, which had been telegraphed to him from Oxford after he had started and had been given to him at Paddington Station.... The income is £130 a year or thereabouts: the duties consist as far as I can learn in assisting to look over the prize compositions, in delivering a Latin oration in praise of founders at every alternate commemoration, and in preparing and giving three Latin lectures on ancient poetry in the course of the year. *These lectures I hope to give in English.*

The italics are mine. The intention expressed here and in the letter to my father was, as is well known, carried out, and Matthew Arnold's Lectures at Oxford, together with the other poetic and critical work produced by him during the years of his professorship, became so great a force in the development of English criticism and English taste, that the life-like detail of this letter acquires a kind of historical value. As a child of fourteen I first made acquaintance with Oxford, while my uncle was still Professor. I remember well some of his lectures, the crowded lecture-hall, the manner and personality of the speaker, and my own shy pride in him — from a great distance. For I was a self-conscious, bookish child, and my days of real friendship with him were still far ahead. But during the years that followed, the ten years that he held his professorship, what a spell he wielded over Oxford, and literary England in general! Looking back one sees how the first series of 'Essays in Criticism', the 'Lectures on Celtic Literature', or 'On translating Homer', 'Culture and Anarchy' and the rest, were all the time working on English taste and feeling, whether through sympathy or antagonism; so that after those ten years, 1857-1867, the intellectual life of the country had absorbed, for good and all, an influence, and a stimulus, which had set it moving on new paths to new ends. With these thoughts in mind, supplying a comment on the letter which few people could have foreseen in 1857, let me quote a few more sentences: —

> Keble voted for me after all. He told the Coleridges he was so much pleased with my letter (to the electors) that he could not refrain..... I had support from all sides. Archdeacon Denison voted for me, also Sir John Yarde Buller, and Henley, of the Tory party. It was an immense victory — some 200 more voted than have ever, it was said, voted in a Professorship election before. It is a great lesson to Christchurch, which was rather disposed to imagine it could carry everything by its great numbers.
>
> Goodbye my dearest mother.... I have just been up to see the three dear little brown heads on their pillows, all asleep.... My affectionate thanks to Mrs Wordsworth and Mrs Fletcher for their kind interest in my success.

It is pleasant to think of Wordsworth's widow, in her 'old age serene and bright', and of the poet's old friend, Mrs Fletcher, watching and rejoicing in the first triumphs of the younger singer.

So the ten years of approach and attack — in the intellectual sense — came to an end, and the ten central years of mastery and success began. Towards the end of that time, as a girl of sixteen I became a resident in Oxford. Up to then Ruskin — the 'Stones of Venice', and certain chapters in 'Modern Painters' — had been my chief intellectual passion in a childhood and first youth that cut but a very poor figure, as I look back upon them, beside the 'wonderful children' of this generation! But it must have been about 1868 that I first read 'Essays in Criticism'. It is not too much to say that the book set for me the currents of life; its effect heightened, no doubt, by the sense of kinship. Above all it determined in me as in many others, an enduring love of France and of French literature, which played the part of schoolmaster to a crude youth. I owe this to my uncle, and it was a priceless boon. If he had only lived a little longer — if he had not died so soon after I had really begun to know him — how many debts to him would have been confessed, how many things said, which, after all, were never said!

CHAPTER IV

Other Children of Fox How

I have now to sketch some other figures in the Fox How circle, together with a few of the intimate friends who mingled with it frequently, and very soon became names of power to the Tasmanian child also.

Let me take first Dr Arnold's third son, 'Uncle Willy' — my father's junior by some four years. William Delafield Arnold is secure of long remembrance, one would fair think, if only as the subject of Matthew Arnold's two memorial poems — 'A Southern Night' and 'Stanzas from Carnac'. But in truth he had many and strong claims of his own. His youth was marked by that 'restlessness', which is so often spoken of in the family letters as a family quality and failing. My father's restlessness' made him throw up a secure niche in English life, for New Zealand adventure. The same temperament in Mary Twining, the young widow of twenty-two, took her to London, away from the quiet of the Ambleside valley, and made her an ardent follower of Maurice, Kingsley and Carlyle. And in Willy, the third son, it showed itself first in revolt against Oxford, while he was still at Christchurch, leading to his going out to India, and joining the Indian Army, at the age of twenty, only to find the life of an Indian subaltern all but intolerable, and to plunge for a time at least into fresh schemes of change.

Among the early photographs at Fox How, there is a particularly fine daguerreotype of a young officer in uniform, almost a boy, slim and well proportioned, with piled curly hair, and blue eyes, which in the late fifties I knew as 'Uncle Willy'; and there were other photographs on glass of the same young man, where this handsome face appeared again, grown older — much older — the boyish look replaced by an aspect of rather grave dignity. In the later pictures he was grouped with children, whom I knew as my Indian cousins. But him, in the flesh, I had never seen. He was dead. His wife was dead. On the landing bookcase of Fox

How, there was however a book in two blue volumes, which I soon realised as a 'novel', called 'Oakfield', which had been written by the handsome young soldier in the daguerreotype. I tried to read it, but found it was about things and persons in which I could then take no interest. But its author remained to me a mysteriously attractive figure: and when the time came for me to read my Uncle Matthew's poems, 'A Southern Night', describing the death at Gibraltar of this soldier uncle, became a great favourite with me. I could see it all as Matthew Arnold described it — the steamer approaching Gibraltar, the landing, and the pale invalid with the signs on him of that, strange thing called 'death', which to a child that 'feels its life in every limb', has no real meaning, though the talk of it may lead vaguely to tears, as that poem often did with me.

Later on, of course, I read 'Oakfield', and learnt to take a more informed pride in the writer of it. But it was not until a number of letters written from India by William Arnold to my father in New Zealand between 1848 and 1855, with a few later ones, came into my possession, at my father's death, that I really seemed to know this dear vanished kinsman, though his orphaned children had always been my friends.

The letters of 1848 and '49 read like notes for 'Oakfield'. They were written in bitterness of soul by a very young man, with high hopes and ideals, fresh from the surroundings of Oxford and Rugby, from the training of the Schoolhouse and Fox How, and plunged suddenly into a society of boys — the subalterns of the Bengal Native Infantry — living for the most part in idleness, often a vicious idleness, without any restraining public opinion, and practically unshepherded, amid the temptations of the Indian climate and life. They show that the novel is indeed, as was always supposed, largely autobiographical, and the references in them to the struggle with the Indian climate point sadly forward to the writer's own fate, ten years later, when like the hero of his novel, Edward Oakfield, he fell a victim to Indian heat and Indian work. The novel was published in 1853, while its author was at home on a long sick leave, and is still remembered for the anger and scandal it provoked in India, and the reforms to which, no doubt, after the Mutiny, it was one of the contributing impulses. It is indeed full of interest for any student of the development of Anglo-Indian life and society; even when one remembers how, soon after it was published, the great storm of the Mutiny came rushing over the society it describes, changing and uprooting everywhere. As fiction, it suffers from the Rugby 'earnestness' which overmasters in it any purely artistic impulse, while infusing a certain fire and unity of its own. But various incidents in the story — the quarrel at the mess-table, the horse-whipping, the court-martial, the death of Vernon, and the meeting between Oakfield and Stafford, the villain of the piece, after Chilianwallah — are told with force, and might have led on, had the writer lived, to something more detached and mature in the way of novel-writing.

But there were few years left to him, 'poor gallant boy!' — to quote the phrase of his poet-brother; and within them he was to find his happiness and his opportunity in love and in public service, not in literature.

Nothing could be more pathetic than the isolation and revolt of the early letters. The boy Ensign is desperately homesick, pining for Fox How, for his mother and sisters, for the Oxford he had so easily renounced, for the brothers parted from him by such leagues of land and sea.

> The fact that one learns first in India (he says bitterly) is the profound ignorance which exists in England about it. You know how one hears it spoken of always as a magnificent field for exertion, and is true enough in one way, for if a man does emerge at all, he emerges the more by contrast — he is a triton among minnows. But I think the responsibility of those who keep sending out here young fellows of sixteen and seventeen fresh from a private school or Addiscombe is quite awful. The stream is so strong, the society is so utterly worldly and mercenary in its best phase, so utterly and inconceivably low and profligate in its worst, that it is not strange that at so early an age, eight out of ten sink beneath it.... One soon observes here how seldom one meets a happy man.
>
> I came out here with three great advantages (he adds). First, being twenty instead of seventeen; secondly, not having been at Addiscombe; third, having been at Rugby and Christchurch. This gives me a sort of position — but still I know the danger is awful — for constitutionally I believe I am as little able to stand the peculiar trials of Indian life as anybody.

And he goes on to say, that if ever he feels himself in peril of sinking to the level of what he loathes — 'I will go at once'. By coming out to India he had bound himself to one thing only — 'to earn my own bread'. But he is not bound to earn it 'as a gentleman'. The day may come

> When I shall ask for a place on your farm, and if you ask how I am to get there, you, Tom, are not the person to deny that a man who is in earnest and capable of forming a resolution can do more difficult things than getting from India to New Zealand!

And he winds up with yearning affection towards the elder brother so far away.

> I think of you very often — our excursion to Keswick and Greta Hall, our walk over Hardknot and Wrynose, our bathes in the old Allen Bank bathing-place (Grasmere), our parting in the cab at the corner of Mount St. One of my pleasantest but most difficult problems is when and where we shall meet again.

In another letter written a year later, the tone is still despondent. 'It is no affection to say that I feel my life, in one way, cannot now be a happy one'. He feels it his duty for the present to 'lie still', as Keble says to think, it may be to suffer. 'But in my castle-buildings I often dream of coming to you'. He appreciates, more fully than ever before, Tom's motives in going to New Zealand — the desire that may move a man to live his own life in a new and freer world. 'But when I am asked, as I often am, why you went, I always grin and let people answer themselves; for I could not hope to explain without preaching a sermon an act of faith and conviction cannot be understood by the light of worldly motives and interests; and to blow out this light, and bring the true one, is not the work of a young man with his own darkness to struggle through; so I grin as aforesaid'. 'God is teaching us', — he adds, i.e. the different members of the family 'by separation, absence, and suffering'. And he winds up — 'Goodbye. I never like finishing a letter to you — it seems like letting you fall back again to such infinite distance. And you are often very near me, and the thought of you is often cheery and helpful to me in my own conflict'. Even up to January, 1850, he is still thinking of New Zealand, and signing himself, 'ever, dear Tom, whether I am destined to see you soon, or never again in this world — Your most truly affectionate brother'.

Alack, the brothers never did meet again, in this world which both took so hardly. But for Willy a transformation scene was near. After two years in India, his gift and his character had made their mark. He had not only been dreaming of New Zealand; besides his daily routine, he had been working hard at Indian languages and history. The Lawrences, both John and Henry, had found him out, and realised his quality. It was at Sir Henry Lawrence's house in the spring of 1850, that he met Miss Fanny Hodgson, daughter of the distinguished soldier and explorer, General Hodgson, discoverer of the sources of the Ganges, and at that time the Indian Surveyor-General. The soldier of twenty-three fell instantly in love, and tumult and despondency melted away. The next letter to New Zealand is pitched in quite another key. He still judges Indian life and Indian government with a very critical eye. 'The Alpha and Omega of the whole evil in Indian Society' is 'the regarding India as a rupee-mine, instead of a Colony, and ourselves as Fortune-hunters and Pension-earners rather than as emigrants and missionaries'. And outside his domestic life his prospects are still uncertain. But with every mail one can see the strained spirit relaxing, yielding to the spell of love and to the honourable interests of an opening life.

'Today, my Thomas (October 2, 1850) I sit, a married man in the Bengal army writing to a brother, it may be a married man, in Van Diemen's Land'. (Rumours of Tom's courtship of Julia Sorell had evidently just reached him.) He goes on to describe his married home at Hoshyarpore, and his work at Indian languages. He has been reading Carlyle's 'Cromwell', and marvelling at the 'rapid rush of thought which seems more and more to be engrossing people in England!' 'In India you will easily believe that the torpor is still unbroken'. (The Mutiny was only seven short years ahead!) And he is still conscious of the 'many weights which do beset and embitter a man's life in India'. But a new stay within, the reconciliation that love brings about between a man and the world, upholds him.

'" To draw homewards to the general life," which you, and dear Matt himself, and I, and all of us, are, or at least may be — living, independent of all the accidents of time and circumstance — this is a great alleviation'. The *'fundamentals'* are safe. He dwells happily on the word — 'a good word, in which you and I, so separated, as far as accidents go, it may be for all time, can find great comfort, speaking as it does of Eternity'. One sees what is in his mind — the brother's little book of poems' published a year before: —

> Yet they, believe me, who await
> No gifts from chance, have conquered fate,
> They, winning room to see and hear,
> And to men's business not too near
> Though clouds of individual strife
> Draw homeward to the general life.
>
> . . . .
>
> To the wise, foolish; to the world
> Weak; — yet not weak, I might reply,
> Not foolish, Fausta, in His eye,
> To whom each moment in its race,
> Crowd as we will its neutral space,
> Is but a quiet watershed
> Whence, equally, the seas of life and death are fed.

Six months later the younger brother has heard 'as a positive fact' of Tom's marriage, and writes, with affectionate 'chaff': —

> I wonder whether it has changed you much? — not made a Tory of you, I'll undertake to say! But it is wonderfully sobering. After all, Master Tom, it is not the very exact *finale* which we should have expected to your Republicanism of the last three or four years, to find you a respectable married man, holding a permanent appointment!

Matt's marriage, too, stands pre-eminent among the items of family news. What blind judges sometimes, the most attached brothers are of each other!

> I hear too by this mail of Matt's engagement, which suggests many thoughts. I own that Matt is one of the very last men in the world whom I can fancy happily married — or rather happy in matrimony. But I daresay I reckon without my host, for there was such a 'longum intervallum' between dear old Matt and me, that even that last month in town, when I saw so much of him, through there was the most entire absence of elderbrotherism on his part, and only the most kind and thoughtful affection, for which I shall always feel grateful, yet our intercourse was that of man and boy; and though the difference of years was not so formidable as between 'Matthew' and Wordsworth, yet we were less than they a 'pair of Friends,' though a pair of very loving brothers.

But even in this gay charming letter, one begins to see the shadows cast by the doom to come. The young wife has gone to Simla, having been 'delicate' for some time. The young husband stays behind, fighting the heat.

> The hot weather, old boy, is coming on like a tiger. It is getting on for ten at night; but we sit with windows all wide open, the Punkah going, the thinnest conceivable garments, and yet we sweat, my brother, very profusely . . . Tomorrow I shall be up at gunfire, about half-past four a.m. and drive down to the civil station, about three miles off, to see a friend, an officer of our own corps . . . who is sick, return, take my Bearer's daily account, write a letter or so, and lie down with Don Quixote under a punkah, go to sleep the first Chapter that Sancho lets me, and sleep till ten, get up, bathe, re-dress and breakfast; do my daily business, such as it is — hard work, believe me, in a hot sleep-inducing, intestine-withering climate, till sunset, when doors and windows are thrown open . . . and mortals go out to 'eat the air' as the natives say.

The climate indeed had already begun its deadly attack upon an organism as fine and sensitive as any of the myriad victims which the secret forces of India's sun and soil have exacted from her European invaders. In 1853, William Delafield Arnold came home invalided, with his wife and his two elder children. The third, Oakeley (the future War Minister in Mr Balfour's Government), was born in England in 1855. There were projects of giving up India and settling at home. The younger soldier whose literary gift, always conspicuous among the nine in the old childish Fox How days, and already shown in 'Oakfield', was becoming more and more marked, was at this time a frequent contributor to *The Times*, *The Economist* and *Fraser*, and was presently offered the Editorship of *The Economist*. But just as he was about to accept it, came a flattering offer from India, no doubt through the influence of Sir John Lawrence, of the Directorship of Public Instruction in the Punjab. He thought himself bound to accept it, and with his wife and two children went out again at the end of 1855. His business was to organise the whole of native education in the Punjab, and he did it so well during the short time that remained to him before the Mutiny broke out, that during all that time of terror, education in the Punjab was never interrupted, the attendances at the schools never dropped, and the young Director went about his work, not knowing often, indeed, whether the whole province might not aflame within twenty-four hours, and its Anglo-

Indian administration wiped out, but none the less undaunted and serene.

To this day, three portrait medals in gold and silver are given every year to the best pupils in the schools of the Punjab, the product of a fund raised immediately after his death by William Arnold's fellow-workers there, in order to commemorate his short heroic course in that far land, and to preserve if they could some record of that 'sweet stateliness' of aspect, to use the expression of one who loved him, which 'had so fascinated his friends'.

The Mutiny passed. Sir John Lawrence paid public and flattering tribute to the young official who had so amply justified a great man's choice. And before the storm had actually died away, within a fortnight of the fall of Delhi, while it was not yet certain that the troops on their way would arrive in time to prevent further mischief, my uncle, writing to my father of the awful days of suspense from the 14th to the 30th of September, says: —

A more afflicted country than this has been since I returned to it in November 1855 — afflicted by Dearth — Deluge — Pestilence — far worse than war, if would be hard to imagine. *In the midst of all, the happiness of our domestic life has been almost perfect.*

With that touching sentence the letters to my father, so far at least as I possess them, come to an end. Alas! In the following year the gentle wife and mother, worn out by India, died at a hill-station in the Himalayas, and a few months later, her husband, ill and heartbroken, sent his motherless children home by long sea, and followed himself by the overland route. Too late! He was taken ill in Egypt, struggled on to Malta, and was put ashore at Gibraltar to die. From Cairo he had written to the beloved mother who was waiting for him in that mountain home he so longed to reach, that he hopes to be able to travel in a fortnight.

But do not trust to this . . . Do not in fact expect me till you hear that I am in London. I much fear that it may be long before I see dear, dear Fox How. In London I must have advice, and I feel sure I shall be ordered to the South of England till the hot weather is well advanced. I must wait too in London for the darling children. But once in London, I cannot but think my dearest mother will manage to see me, and I have even had visions of your making one of your spring tours, and going with me to Torquay or whatever I may go. . . . Plans — plans — plans! They will keep.

And a few days later: —

As I said before, do not expect me in England till you hear I am there. Perhaps I was too eager to get home. Assuredly I have been checked, and I feel as if there were much trouble between me and home yet . . . I see in the papers the death of dear Mrs.Wordsworth . . .

> Ever my beloved mother . . .
> Your very loving son,
> W. D. Arnold.

He started for England, but at Gibraltar, a dying man was carried ashore. His younger brother, sent out from England in post haste, missed him by ill chance at Alexandria and Malta, and arrived too late. He was buried under the shelter of the Rock of Spain and the British flag. His intimate friend, Meredith Townsend, the joint editor and creator of the *Spectator*, wrote to *The Times* shortly after his death: —

William Arnold did not live long enough (he was thirty-one) to gain his true place in the world, but he had time enough given him to make himself of importance to a Government like that of Lord Dalhousie, to mould the education of a great province, and to win the enduring love of all with whom he ever came in contact.

It was left, however, for his poet-brother to build upon his early grave 'the living record of his memory'. A month after 'Willy's' death, 'Matt' was wandering where —

> Beneath me, bright and wide
> Lay the low coast of Brittany —

With the thought of 'Willy' in his mind, as he turns to the sea that will never now bring the wanderer home.

> O, could he once have reached the air
> Freshened by plunging tides, by showers!
> Have felt this breath he loved, of fair
> Cool northern fields, and grain, and flowers.
>
> He longed for it — pressed on! — In vain!
> At the Straits failed that spirit brave,
> The south was parent of his pain,
> The south is mistress of his grave.

Or again, in 'A Southern Night' — where he muses on the 'two jaded English', man and wife, who lie, one under the Himalayas, the other beside 'the soft Mediterranean'. And his first thought is that for the 'spent ones of a workday age', such graves are out of keeping.

> In cities should we English lie
>   Where cries are rising ever new,
> And men's incessant stream goes by! —
>
> . . . .
>
> Not by those hoary Indian hills,
>   Not by this gracious Midland sea
> Whose floor tonight sweet moonshine fills
>   Should our graves be!

Some Eastern sage pursuing 'the pure goal of being' — 'He by those Indian mountains old, might well repose'. Crusader, troubadour, or maiden dying for love:

> Such by these waters of romance
> 'Twas meet to lay!

And then he turns upon himself. For what is beauty, what wisdom, what romance, if not the tender goodness of women, if not the high soul of youth?

> Mild o'er her grave, ye mountains, shine!
>   Gently by his, ye waters, glide!
> To that in you which is divine
>   They were allied.
>
> . . . .

Only a few days after their father's death, the four orphan children of the William Arnolds arrived at Fox How. They were immediately adopted as their own by William and Jane Forster, who had no children; and later they added the name of Forster to that of Arnold. At that moment

I was at school at Ambleside, and I remember well my first meeting with the Indian children and how I wondered at their fair skins and golden hair and frail ethereal looks.

By this time, Fox How was in truth a second home to me. But I have still to complete the tale of those who made it so. Edward Penrose, the Doctor's fourth son, who died in 1878, on the threshold of fifty, was a handsome bearded man of winning presence, and of many friends. He was at Balliol, then a Fellow of All Souls, and in Orders. But he first found his real vocation as an Inspector of Schools in Devon and Cornwall, and for eighteen years, from 1860 to 1878, trough the great changes in elementary education produced by his brother-in-law's Education Act, he was the ever-welcome friend of teachers and children all over the wide and often remote districts of the West Country which his work covered. He had not the gifts of his elder brothers, —neither the genius of Matthew nor the restless energy and initiative of William Delafield, nor the scholarly and researching tastes of my father; and his later life was always a struggle against ill-health. But he had Matthew's kindness, and Matthew's humour — the 'chaff' between the two brothers was endless! — and a large allowance of William's charm. His unconscious talk in his last illness was often of children. He seemed to see them before him in the country schoolrooms, where his coming — the coming of 'the tall gentleman with the kind blue eyes', as an eye-witness describes him — was a festa, excellent official though he was. He carried enthusiasm into the cause of popular education, and that is not a very common enthusiasm in this country of ours. Yet the cause is nothing more nor less than the cause of *the national intelligence*, and its sharpening for the national tasks. But education has always been the Cinderella of politics; this nation apparently does not love to be taught! Those who grapple with its stubbornness in this field can never expect the ready palm that falls to the workers in a dozen other fields. But in the seed sown, and the human duty done, they find their reward.

'Aunt Mary', Arnold's second daughter, I have already spoken of. When my father and mother reached England from Tasmania, she had just married again, a Leicestershire clergyman, with a house and small estate near Loughborough. Her home — Woodhouse — on the borders of

Charnwood Forest, and the beautiful Beaumanoir Park, was another fairy-land to me and to my cousins. Its ponds and woods and reed-beds; its distant summer house between two waters, where one might live and read and dream through long summer hours, undisturbed; its pleasant rooms, above all the 'tapestry room' where I generally slept, and which I always connected with the description of the huntsman on the 'arras', in 'Tristram and Iseult'; the Scott novels I devoured there; and the 'Court' nights at Beaumanoir, where some feudal customs were still kept up, and its beautiful mistress, Mrs Herrick, the young wife of an old man, queened it very graciously over neighbours and tenants: — all these are among the lasting memories of life. Mrs Herrick became identified in my imagination with each successive Scott heroine, — Rowena, Isabella, Rose Bradwardine, the White Lady of Avenel, and the rest. But it was Aunt Mary herself after all, who held the scene. In that Leicestershire world of High Toryism, she raised the Liberal flag — her father's flag — with indomitable courage, but also with a humour, which after the tragic hours of her youth, flowered out in her like something new and unexpectedly delightful. It must have been always there, but not till marriage and motherhood, and F. D. Maurice's influence, had given her peace of soul does it seem to have shown itself as I remember it, — a golden and pervading quality, which made life unfailingly pleasant beside her. Her clear dark eyes, with their sweet sincerity, and the touch in them of a quiet laughter, of which the causes were not always clear to the bystanders, her strong face with its points of likeness to her father's, and all her warm and most human personality — they are still vividly present to me, though it is nearly thirty years, since, after an hour or two's pain, she died suddenly and unexpectedly, of the same malady that killed her father. Consumed in her youth by a passionate idealism, she had accepted at the hands of life, and by the age of four and twenty, a lot by no means ideal: — a home in the depths of the country, among neighbours often uncongenial, and far from the intellectual pleasures she had tasted during her young widowhood in London. But out of this lot she made something beautiful, and all her own — by sheer goodness, conscience, intelligence. She had her angles and inconsistencies; she often puzzled those who loved her; but she had a large brain and a large heart; and for us colonial children, conscious of many disadvantages beside our English-born cousins, she had a peculiar tenderness, a peculiar laughing sympathy, that led us to feel in 'Aunt Mary', one of our best friends.

Susan Arnold, the Doctor's fourth daughter, married Mr John Cropper in 1858, and here too, in her house beside the Mersey, among fields and trees that still maintain a green though be-smutted oasis in the busy heart of Liverpool, that girdles them now on all sides, and will soon engulf them, there was kindness and welcome for the little Tasmanians. She died a few years ago, mourned and missed by her own people — those life-long neighbours who know truly what we are. Of the fifth daughter, Frances, 'Aunt Fan', I may not speak, because she is still with us in the old house — alive to every political and intellectual interest of these darkened days, beloved by innumerable friends in many worlds, and making sunshine still for Arnold's grandchildren, and their children's children. But it was to her that my own stormy childhood was chiefly confided at Fox How; it was she who taught the Tasmanian child to read, and grappled with her tempers; and while she is there, the same magic as of old clings about Fox How for those of us who have loved it and all it stands for, so long.

CHAPTER V

The Friends of Fox How

It remains for me now to say something of those friends of Fox How and my father, whose influence, or whose living presence, made the atmosphere in which the second generation of children who loved Fox How grew up.

Wordsworth died in 1850, the year before I was born. He and my grandfather were much attached to each other — 'old Coleridge', says my grandfather, 'inoculated a little knot of us with the love of Wordsworth' — though their politics were widely different, and the poet sometimes found it hard to put up with the reforming views of the younger man. In a letter printed in Stanley's 'Life' my grandfather mentions 'a good fight' with Wordsworth over the Reform Bill of '32, on a walk to Greenhead Ghyll. And there is a story told of a girlfriend of the family who, once when Wordsworth had been paying a visit at Fox How, accompanied him and the Doctor part of the way home to Rydal Mount. Something was inadvertently said to stir the old man's Toryism, and he broke out in indignant denunciation of some views expressed by Arnold. The storm lasted all the way to Pelter Bridge, and the girl on Arnold's left stole various alarmed glances at him to see how he was taking it. He said little or nothing, and at Pelter Bridge they all parted, Wordsworth going on to Rydal Mount, and the other two turning back towards Fox How. Arnold paced along, his hands behind his back, his eyes on the ground, and his companion watched him, till he suddenly threw back his head with a laugh of enjoyment. — 'What *beautiful* English the old man talks!'

The poet complained sometimes — as I find from an amusing passage in the letter to Mr Howson quoted below, that he could not see enough of his neighbour, the Doctor, on a mountain walk, because Arnold was always so surrounded with children and pupils, 'like little dogs' running round and after him. But no differences, great or small, interfered with his constant friendship to Fox How. The garden there was largely planned by him during the family absences at Rugby: the round chimneys of the house are said to be of his design; and it was for Fox How, which still possesses the MS., that the fine sonnet was written, beginning —

> Wansfell, this household has a favoured lot
> Living with liberty on thee to gaze.

— a sonnet which contains, surely, two or three of the most magical lines that Wordsworth ever wrote.

It is of course no purpose of these notes to give any fresh account of Wordsworth at Rydal, or any exhaustive record of the relations between the Wordsworths and Fox How, especially after the recent publication of Professor Harper's fresh, interesting, though debatable biography. But from the letters in my hands I glean a few things worth recording. Here for instance is a passing picture of Matthew Arnold and Wordsworth in the Fox How drawing-room together, in January 1848, which I find in a letter from my grandmother to my father: —

Matt has been very much pleased I think by what he has seen of dear old Wordsworth since he has been at home, and certainly he manages to draw him out very well. The old man was here yesterday, and as he sat on the stool in the corner beside the fire which you knew so well, he talked of various subjects of interest, of Italian poetry, of Coleridge etc. etc.; and he looked and spoke with more vigour than he has often done lately.

But the poet's health was failing. His daughter Dora's death in 1847 had hit him terribly hard, and his sister's state — the helpless though gentle insanity of the unique, the beloved Dorothy — weighed heavily on his weakening strength. I find a touching picture of him in the unpublished letter referred to on a previous page, written in this very year — 1848 — to Dean Howson, as a young man, by his former pupil the late Duke of Argyll, the distinguished author of 'The Reign of Law' — which Dean Howson's son and the Duke's grandson allow me to print. The Rev J. S. Howson, afterwards Dean of Chester, married a sister of the John Cropper who married Susan Arnold, and was thus a few years later brought into connection with the Arnolds and Fox How. The Duke and Duchess had set out to visit both the Lakes and the Lakes 'celebrities', advised evidently as to their tour by the Duke's old tutor, who was already familiar with the valleys and some of their inmates. Their visit to Fox How is only briefly mentioned, but of Wordsworth and Rydal Mount the Duke gives a long account. The picture, first, of drooping health and spirits, and then of the flaming out of the old poetic fire, will I think interest any true Wordsworthian.

On Saturday (writes the Duke) we reached Ambleside and soon after drove to Rydal Mount. We found the Poet seated at his fireside, and a little languid in manner. He became less so as he talked. . . He talked incessantly, but not generally interestingly . . . I looked at him often and asked myself if that was the man who had stamped the impress of his own mind so decidedly on a great part of the literature of his age! He took us to see a waterfall near his house, and talked and chattered, but said nothing remarkable or even thoughtful . . . Yet I could see that all this was only that we were on the surface, and did not indicate any decay of mental powers. Still — we went away with no other impression than the vaguest of having seen the man, whose writings we knew so well — and with no feeling that we had seen anything of the mind which spoke through them.

On the following day, Sunday, the Duke with a friend walked over to Rydal, but found no one at the Mount, but an invalid lady, very old, and apparently paralysed, 'drawn in a bath chair by a servant'. They did not realise that the poor sufferer, with her wandering speech and looks, was Dorothy Wordsworth, whose share in her great brother's fame will never be forgotten while literature lasts.

In the evening, however —

— after visiting Mrs Arnold we drove together to bid Wordsworth goodbye, as we were to go next morning. We found the old man as before, seated by the fireside and languid and sleepy in manner. Again he awakened as conversation went on, and, a stranger coming in, we rose to go away. He seemed unwilling that we should go so soon, and said he would walk out with us. We went to the mound in front and the Duchess then asked if he would repeat some of his own lines to us. He said he hardly thought he could do that, but that he would have been glad to read some to us. We stood looking at the view for some time, when Mrs Wordsworth came out and asked us back to the house to take some tea. This was just what we wanted. We sat for about half an hour at tea, during which I tried to direct the conservation to interesting subjects — Coleridge, Southey, etc. He gave a very different impression from the preceding evening. His memory seemed clear and unclouded — his remarks forcible and decided — with some tendency to run off to irrelevant anecdote.

When tea was over, we renewed our request that he should read to us. He said — 'Oh dear, that is terrible!' — but consented, asking what we chose. He jumped at 'Tintern Abbey' in preference to any part of the Excursion.

He told us he had written 'Tintern Abbey' in 1798, taking four days to compose it; the last twenty lines or so being composed as he walked down the hill from Clifton to Bristol. It was curious to feel that we were to hear a Poet read his own verses composed fifty years before.

He read the introductory lines descriptive of the scenery in a low clear voice. But when he came to the thoughtful and reflective lines, his tones deepened and he poured them forth with a fervour and almost passion of delivery, which was very striking and beautiful. I observed that Mrs Wordsworth was strongly affected during the reading. The strong emphasis that he put on the words addressed to the person to whom the poem is written struck me as almost unnatural at the time. 'My Dear, Dear friend!' — and on the words, 'In thy wild eyes'. It was not till after the reading was over that we found out that the poor paralytic invalid we had seen in the morning was the *sister* to whom 'Tintern Abbey' was addressed, and her condition, now, accounted for the fervour with which the old Poet read lines which reminded him of their better days. But it was melancholy to think that the vacant gaze we had seen in the morning was from the 'wild eyes' of 1798.

. . . We could not have had a better opportunity of bringing out in his reading the source of the inspiration of his poetry, which it was impossible not to feel was the poetry of the heart. Mrs Wordsworth told me it was the first time he had read since his daughter's death, and that she was thankful to us for having made him do it, as he was apt to fall into a listless, languid state. We asked him to come to Inverary. He said he had not courage; as he had last gone through that country with his daughter, and he feared it would be too much for him.

Less than two years after this visit, on April 23, 1850, the death day of Shakespeare and Cervantes, Arnold's youngest daughter, now Miss Arnold of Fox How, was walking with her sister Susan on the side of Loughrigg which overlooks Rydal Mount. They knew that the last hour of a great poet was near, to my aunts, not only a great poet, but the familiar friend of their dead father and all their kindred. They moved through the April day, along the mountainside, under the shadow of death; and suddenly, as they looked at the old house opposite, unseen hands drew down the blinds; and by the darkened windows, they knew that the life of Wordsworth had gone out.

Henceforward, in the family letters to my father, it is Mrs Wordsworth who comes into the foreground. The old age prophesied for her by her poet bridegroom in the early Grasmere days was about her for the nine years of her widowhood, 'lovely as a Lapland night'; or rather like one of her own Rydal evenings when the sky is clear over the perfect little lake, and the reflections of island and wood and fell, go down and down, unearthly far into the quiet depths, and Wansfell still 'parleys with the setting sun'. My grandmother writes of her — of 'her sweet grace and dignity,' and the little friendly acts she is always doing for this person and that, gentle or simple, in the valley — with a tender enthusiasm. She is 'dear Mrs Wordsworth' always, for them all. And it is my joy that in the year '56 or '57 my grandmother took me to Rydal Mount, and that I can vividly recollect sitting on a footstool at Mrs Wordsworth's feet. I see still the little room, with its plain furniture, the chair beside the fire, and the old lady in it. I can still recall the childish feeling that this was no common visit, and the house no common house — that a presence still haunted it. Instinctively the childish mind said to itself 'Remember!' — and I have always remembered.

A few years later, I was again, as a child of eight, in Rydal Mount. Mrs Wordsworth was dead, and there was a sale in the house. From far and near the neighbours came, very curious, very full of real regret, and a little awe-stricken. They streamed through the rooms where the furniture was arranged in lots. I wandered about by myself, and presently came upon something which absorbed me so that I forgot everything else — a store of Easter eggs, with wonderful drawings and devices, made by 'James', the Rydal Mount factotum, in the poet's day. I recollect sitting down with them in a nearly empty room, dreaming over them in a kind of ecstasy, because of their pretty, strange colours and pictures.

Fifty-two years passed, and I found myself, in September 1911, the tenant of a renovated and rebuilt Rydal Mount, for a few autumn weeks. The house was occupied then, and is still occupied by Wordsworth's great-granddaughter and her husband — Mr and Mrs Fisher Wordsworth. My eldest daughter was with me, and a strange thing happened to us. I arrived at the Mount before my husband and daughter. She joined me there on September 13. I remember how eagerly I showed her the many Wordsworthiana in the house, collected by the piety of its mistress — the Haydon portrait on the stairs, and the books, in the small low-ceiled room to the right of the hall, which is still just as it was in Wordsworth's day; the garden too, and the poet's walk. All my own early recollections were alive; we chattered long and late. And now let the account of what happened afterwards be given in my daughter's words as she wrote it down for me the following morning.

Rydal Mount, September 14, 1911

Last night, my first at Rydal Mount, I slept in the corner room, over the small sitting-room. I had drawn up the blind about halfway up the window before going to bed, and had drawn the curtain aside, over the back of a wooden armchair that stood against the window. The window, a casement, was wide open. I slept soundly, but woke quite suddenly, at what hour I do not know, and found myself sitting bolt upright in bed looking towards the window. Very bright moonlight was shining into the room and I could just see the corner of Loughrigg out in the distance. My first impression was of bright moonlight, but then I became strongly conscious of the moonlight striking something, and I saw perfectly clearly the figure of an old man sitting in the arm-chair by the window. I said to myself — 'That's Wordsworth!' He was sitting with either hand resting on the arms of the chair, leaning back, his head rather bent and he seemed to be looking down, straight in front of him with a rapt expression. He was not looking at me, nor out of the window. The moonlight lit up the top of his head and the silvery hair and I noticed that the hair was very thin. The whole impression was of something solemn and beautiful, and I was not in the very least frightened. As I looked — I cannot say, when I looked again, for I have no recollection of ceasing to look, or looking away — the figure disappeared, and I became aware of the empty chair. — I lay back again, and thought for a moment in a pleased and contented way — 'That was Wordsworth'. And almost immediately I must have fallen asleep again. I had not, to my knowledge, been dreaming about Wordsworth before I woke; but I had been reading Hutton's essay on 'Wordsworth's Two Styles' out of Knight's 'Wordsworthiana', before I fell asleep.

I should add that I had a distinct impression of the high collar and stock, the same as in the picture on the stairs in this house.

Neither the seer of this striking vision — unique in her experience — nor I, to whom she told it within eight hours, make any claim for it to a supernatural origin. It seemed to us an interesting example of the influence of mind and association on the visualising power of the brain. A member of the Psychical Society, to whom I sent the contemporary record, classified it as 'a visual hallucination', and I don't know that there is anything more to be said about it. But the pathetic coincidence remains still to be noted — we did not know it till afterwards — that the seer of the vision was sleeping in Dorothy Wordsworth's room, where Dorothy spent so many sad years of death-in-life; and that in that very corner by the window, Wordsworth must have sat, day after day, when he came to visit what remained to him of that creature of fire and dew, that child of genius, who had been the inspiration and support of his poetic youth.

In these rapid sketches of the surroundings and personal influences amid which my own childhood was passed, I have already said something of my father's intimate friend, Arthur Hugh Clough. Clough was of course a Rugbeian, and one of Arnold's ablest and most devoted pupils. He was about three years older than my father, and was already a Fellow of Oriel when Thomas Arnold, the younger, was reading for his First. But the difference of age made no difference to the friendship which grew up between them in Oxford, a friendship only less enduring and close than that between Clough and Matthew Arnold, which has been 'eternised', to use a word of Fulke Greville's, by the noble dirge of 'Thyrsis'. Not many years before his own death, in 1895 my father wrote of the friend of his youth: —

> I loved him, oh so well: and also respected him more profoundly than any man, anywhere near my own age, whom I ever met. His pure soul was without stain: he seemed incapable of being inflamed by wrath, or tempted to vice, or enslaved by any unworthy passion of any sort. As to 'Philip' something that he saw in me helped to suggest the character — that was all. There is much in Philip that is Clough himself, and there is a dialectic force in him that certainly was never in me. A great yearning for possessing one's soul in freedom — for trampling on ceremony and palaver, for trying experiment in equality, being common to me and Philip, sent me out to New Zealand; and in the two years before I sailed (Dec. 1847) Clough and I were a great deal together.

It was partly also the visit paid by my father and his friend John Campbell Shairp, afterwards Principal Shairp of St. Andrew's, to Clough's reading party at Drumnadrochit in 1845, and their report of incidents which had happened to them on their way along the shores of Loch Ericht, which suggest the scheme of the 'Bothie'. One of the half-dozen short poems of Clough which have entered permanently into literature — *Qui laborat orat* — was found by my father one morning on the table of his bachelor rooms in Mount St., after Clough had spent the night on a shake-up in his sitting-room, and on his early departure had left the poem behind him as payment for his night's lodging. In one of Clough's letters to New Zealand I find — 'Say not the struggle nought availeth' — another of the half-dozen — written out by him; and the original copy — 'tibi primo confisum', of the pretty though unequal verses, 'A London Idyll'. The little volume of miscellaneous poems, called 'Ambarvalia', and the 'Bothie of Toberna-Vuolich' were sent out to New Zealand by Clough, at the same moment that Matt was sending his brother the 'Poems by A.'.

Clough writes from Liverpool in February 1849, — having just received Matt's volume —

At last our own Matt's book! Read mine first, my child if our volumes go forth together. Otherwise you won't read mine — Ambarvalia — at any rate, at all. Froude also has published a new book of religious biography, auto or otherwise (The Nemesis of Faith) and therewithal resigns his fellowship. But the Rector (of Exeter) talks of not accepting the resignation, but having an expulsion — fire and fagot fashion. Quo usque?

But when the books arrive, my father writes to his sister with affectionate welcome indeed of the 'Poems by A.' but with enthusiasm of the 'Bothie'.

It greatly surpasses my expectations! It is on the whole a noble poem, well held together, clear, full of purpose, and full of promise. With joy I see the old fellow bestring himself, 'awakening like a strong man out of sleep and shaking his invincible locks'; and if he remains true and works, I think there is nothing too high or too great to be expected from him.

'True', and a worker, Clough remained to the last hours of his short life. But in spite of a happy marriage, the burden and perplexity of philosophic thought, together with the strain of failing health, checked, before long, the strong poetic impulse shown in the 'Bothie', its buoyant delight in natural beauty, and in the simplicities of human feeling and passion. The 'music of his 'rustic' flute'

> Kept not for long its happy, country tone;
> Lost it too soon, and learnt a stormy note
> Of men contention-tost, of men who groan.

The poet of the 'Bothie' becomes the poet of 'Dipsychus', 'Easter Day', and the 'Amours de Voyage'; and the young republican who writes in triumph — all humorous joy and animation — to my father, from the Paris of '48, which has just seen the overthrow of Louis Philippe, says, a year later — February 24, 1849 —

Today, my dear brother republican, is the glorious anniversary of '48, whereof what shall I now say? Put not your trust in republics, nor in any constitution of man! God be praised for the downfall of Louis Philippe. This with a faint feeble echo of that loud last year's scream of 'A bas Guizot!' seems to be the sum total. Or are we to salute the rising sun, with 'Vive l'Empereur!' and the green liveries? President for life I think they'll make him, and then begin to tire of him. Meanwhile the Great Powers are to restore the Pope, and crush the renascent Roman Republic, of which Joseph Mazzini has just been declared a citizen!

A few months later, the writer — at Rome — 'was in at the death' of this same Roman Republic, listening to the French bombardment in bitterness of soul.

I saw the French enter (he writes to my father). Unto this has come our grand Lib. Eq. and Frat. Revolution! And then I went to Naples — and home. I am full of admiration for Mazzini . . . . But on the whole — 'Farewell Politics!' utterly! - What can I do? Study is much more to the purpose.

So in disillusion and disappointment, 'Citizen Clough' leaving Oxford and politics behind him, settled down to educational work in London, married, and became the happy father of children, wrote much that was remarkable, and will be long read — whether it be poetry or no — by those who find perennial attraction in the lesser-known ways of literature and thought, and at last closed his short life at Florence in 1862, at the age of forty-one, leaving an indelible memory in the hearts of those who had talked and lived with him.

> To a boon southern country he is fled,
>   And now in happier air,
> Wandering with the Great Mother's train divine
>   (And purer of more subtle soul than thee,
>   I trow the mighty Mother doth not see)
> Within a folding of the Apennine,
>
> Thou hearest the immortal chants of old! —

But I remember him, in an English setting, and on the slopes of English hills. In the year 1858, as a child of seven, I was an inmate of a little school kept at Ambleside, by Miss Anne Clough, the poet's sister afterwards the well-known head of Newnham College, Cambridge, and wisest leader in the cause of women. It was a small day-school for Ambleside children of all ranks, and I was one of two boarders, spending my Sundays often at Fox How. I can recall one or two golden days, at long intervals, when my father came for me, with 'Mr Clough', and the two old friends, who after nine years' separation, had recently met again, walked up the Sweden Bridge lane into the heart of Scandale Fell, while I, paying no more attention to them, than they — after a first ten minutes — did to me, went wandering, and skipping, and dreaming by myself. In those days every rock along the mountain lane, every boggy patch, every stretch of silken, flower-sown grass, every bend of the wild stream, and all its sounds, whether it chattered gently over stony shallows, or leapt full-throated into deep pools, swimming with foam — were to me the never-ending joys of a 'land of pure delight'. Should I find a ripe wild strawberry in a patch under a particular rock I knew by heart? — or the first Grass of Parnassus, or the bog auricula, or streaming cotton-plant, amid a stretch of wet moss ahead? I might quite safely explore these enchanted spots under male eyes, since they took no account, mercifully, of a child's boots and stockings — male tongues besides being safely busy with books and politics. Was that a dipper, rising and falling along the stream, or — positively — a fat brown trout in hiding under that shady bank? — or that a buzzard, hovering overhead? Such hopes and doubts kept a child's heart and eyes as quick and busy as the 'beck' itself. It was a point of honour with me to get to Sweden

Bridge — a rough crossing for the shepherds and sheep, near the head of the valley — before my companions; and I would sit dangling my feet over the unprotected edge of its grass-grown arch, blissfully conscious on a summer day of the warm stretches of golden fell folding in the stream, the sheep, the hovering hawks, the stony path that wound up and up to regions beyond the ken of thought; and of myself, queening it there on the weather-worn keystone of the bridge, dissolved in the mere physical joy of each contented sense: — the sun on my cotton dress, the scents from grass and moss, the marvellous rush of cloud-shadow along the hills, the brilliant browns and blues in the water, the little white stones on its tiny beaches, or the purples of the bigger rocks, whether in the stream or on the mountainside. How did they come there — those big rocks? I puzzled my head about them a good deal, especially as my father, in the walks we had to ourselves, would sometimes try and teach me a little geology.

I have used the words 'physical joy', because, although such passionate pleasure in natural things as has been my constant Helper (on the sense of the Greek επικουρος) through life, has connected itself no doubt, in process of time, with various intimate beliefs, philosophic or religious, as to the Beauty which is Truth, and therewith the only conceivable key to man's experience, yet I could not myself endorse the famous contrast in Wordsworth's 'Tintern Abbey', between the 'haunting passion' of youth's delight in Nature, and the more complex feeling of later years, when Nature takes an aspect coloured by our own moods and memories, when our sorrows and reflections enter so much into what we feel about the 'bright and intricate device' of earth and her and her seasons, that 'in our life alone doth Nature live'. No one can answer for the changing moods that the future, long or short, may bring with it. But so far, I am inclined to think of this quick, intense pleasure in natural things, which I notice in myself and others, as something involuntary and inbred; independent — often selfishly independent — of the real human experience. I have been sometimes ashamed — pricked even with self-contempt — to remember how in the course of some tragic or sorrowful hours, concerning myself, or others of great account to me, I could not help observing some change in the clouds, some effect of colour in the garden, some picture on the wall, which pleased me even —

for the moment — intensely. The impression would be gone, perhaps, as soon as felt, rebuked by something like a flash of remorse. But it was not in my power to prevent its recurrence. And the delight in natural things — colours, forms, scents — when there was nothing to restrain or hamper it, has often been a kind of intoxication, in which thought and consciousness seemed suspended — 'as though of hemlock one had drunk'. Wordsworth has of course expressed it constantly, though increasingly, as life went on, in combination with his pantheistic philosophy. But it is my belief that it survived in him in its primitive form, almost to the end.

The best and noblest people I have known have been, on the whole — except in first youth — without this correspondence between some constant pleasure-sense in the mind, and natural beauty. It cannot therefore be anything to be proud of. But it is certainly something to be glad of — 'amid the chances and changes of this mortal life'; it is one of the joys, 'in widest commonalty spread' — and that may last longest. It is therefore surely to be encouraged both in oneself, and in children; and that, although I have often felt that there is something inhuman, or infrahuman in it, as though the earth-gods in us all — Pan, or Demeter — laid ghostly hands again, for a space, upon the soul and sense that nobler or sadder faiths have ravished from them.

In these Westmorland walks, however, my father had sometimes another companion — a frequent visitor at Fox How, where he was almost another son to my grandmother, and an elder brother to her children. How shall one ever make the later generation understand the charm of Arthur Stanley? There are many — very many — still living, in whom the sense of it leaps up, at the very mention of his name. But for those who never saw him, who are still in their twenties and thirties, what shall I say? That he was the son of a Bishop of Norwich, and a member of the old Cheshire family of the Stanleys of Alderley, that he was a Rugby boy and a devoted pupil of Arnold, whose 'Life' he wrote, so that it stands out among the biographies of the century, not only for its literary merit, but for its wide and varied influence on feeling and opinion; that he was an Oxford tutor and Professor all through the great struggle of Liberal thought against the reactionary influences let loose by Newman and the Tractarian movement; that, as Regius Professor at Oxford, and Canon of Canterbury, if he added little to learning, or research, he at least kept alive — by his power of turning all he knew in to image and colour — that great 'art' of history which the Dryasdusts so willingly let die; that as Dean of Westminster, he was still the life and soul of all the Liberalism in the church, still the same generous friend and champion of all the spiritually oppressed that he had ever been? None of the old 'causes' beloved of his youth could ever have said of him as of so many others: —

> Just for a handful of silver he left us
> Just for a ribbon to stick in his coat —

He was no doubt the friend of kings and princes, and keenly conscious, always, of things long-descended, with picturesque or heroic associations. But it was he who invited Colenso to preach in the Abbey, after his ex-communication by the fanatical and now forgotten Bishop of Cape Town; it was he who brought about that famous Communion of the Revisers in the Abbey, where the Unitarian received the Sacrament of Christ's death beside the Wesleyan and the Anglican, and who bore with unflinching courage the idle tumult which followed; it was he too who first took special pains to open the historical Abbey to working-men, and to give them an insight into the meaning of its treasures. He was not a social reformer in the modern sense; that was not his business. But his unfailing power of seeing and pouncing upon the *interesting* — the *dramatic* — in any human lot, soon brought him into relation with men of callings and types the most different from his own; and for the rest he fulfilled to perfection that hard duty — 'the duty of our equals'. on which Mr Jowett once preached a caustic and suggestive sermon. But for him John Richard Green would have abandoned history, and student after student, heretic after heretic, found in him the man who eagerly understood them, and chivalrously fought for them.

And then, what a joy he was to the eye! His small spare figure, miraculously light, his delicate face of tinted ivory — only that ivory is not sensitive and subtle, and incredibly expressive, as were the features of the little Dean; the eager thin-lipped mouth, varying with every shade of feeling in the innocent great soul behind it; the clear eyes of china-blue; the glistening white hair, still with the wave and spring of youth in it; the slender legs, and Dean's dress, which becomes all but the portly, with, on festal occasions, the red ribbon of the Bath crossing the mercurial frame: — there are still a few pictures and photographs by which these characteristics are dimly recalled to those at least who knew the living man. To my father, who called him 'Arthur', and to all the Fox How circle he was the most faithful of friends, though no doubt my father's conversion to Catholicism to some extent, in later years, separated him from Stanley. In the letter I have printed on a former page, written on the night before my father left England for New Zealand in 1847, and cherished by its recipient all his life, there is a yearning, personal note, which was, perhaps, sometimes lacking in the much-surrounded, much-courted Dean of later life. It was not that Arthur Stanley, any more than Matthew Arnold, ever became a worldling in the ordinary sense. But 'the world' asks too much of such men as Stanley. It heaps all its honours and all its tasks upon them, and without some slight stiffening of its substance the exquisite instrument cannot meet the strain.

Mr Hughes always strongly denied that the 'George Arthur' of 'Tom Brown's Schooldays' had anything whatever to do with Arthur Stanley. But I should like to believe that at least some anecdote of Stanley's schooldays had entered into the well-known scene where Arthur, in class, breaks down in construing the last address of Helen to the dead Hector. Stanley's memory, indeed, was alive with the great things or the picturesque detail of literature and history, no less than with the humorous or striking things of contemporary life. I remember an amusing instance of it at my own wedding breakfast. Stanley married us, and a few days before, he had buried Frederick Denison Maurice. His historical sense was pleased by the juxtaposition of the two names Maurice and Arnold, suggested by the funeral of Maurice and the marriage of Arnold's granddaughter. The consequence was that his speech at the wedding breakfast was quite as much concerned with 'graves and worms and epitaphs' as with things hymeneal. But from 'the little Dean' all things were welcome.

My personal memory of him goes back to much earlier days. As a child at Fox How, he roused in me a mingled fascination and terror. To listen to him quoting Shakespeare or Scott or Macaulay was fascination;

to find his eye fixed on one, and his slender finger darting towards one, as he asked a sudden historical question — 'Where did Edward the First die?' — 'Where was the Black Prince buried?' — was terror — lest, at seven years old, one should not be able to play up. I remember a particular visit of his to Fox How, when the dates and places of these royal deaths and burials kept us — myself in particular — in a perpetual ferment. It must, I think, have been when he was still at Canterbury, investigating, almost with the zest and passion of the explorer of Troy or Mycenae, what bones lay hid, and where, under the Cathedral floor, what sands — 'fallen from the ruined sides of Kings' — that this passion of deaths and dates was upon him. I can see myself as a child of seven or eight, standing outside the drawing-room door at Fox How, bracing myself in a mixture of delight and fear, as to what 'Dr Stanley' might ask me when the door was opened; then the opening, and the sudden sharp turn of the slight figure, writing letters at the middle table, at the sight of 'little Mary' — and the expected thunderbolt:

'Where did Henry the Fourth die?'

Confusion — and blank ignorance!

But memory leaps forward to a day four or five years later, when my father and I invaded the dark high room in the old Deanery, and the Dean standing at his reading-desk. He looks round — sees 'Tom', and the child with him. His charming face breaks into a broad smile; he remembers instantly, though it is some years since he and 'little Mary' met. He holds out his hands to me —

'Come and see the place where Henry the Fourth died!'

And off we ran together to the Jerusalem Chamber.

CHAPTER VI

Young Days at Oxford

How little those who are schoolgirls to today can realise what it was to be a schoolgirl in the fifties or the early sixties of the last century! A modern girls' school, equipped as scores are now equipped throughout the country, was of course not to be found in 1858, when I first became a school boarder, or in 1867 when I ceased to be one. The games, the gymnastics, the solid grounding in drawing and music, together with the enormously improved teaching in elementary science, or literature and languages, which are at the service of the schoolgirl to today, had not begun to be when I was at school. As far as intellectual training was concerned, my nine years from seven to sixteen were practically wasted. I learnt nothing thoroughly or accurately, and the German, French, and Latin, which I soon discovered after my marriage to be essential to the kind of literary work I wanted to do, had all to be re-learnt before they could be of any real use to me; nor was it ever possible for me — who married at twenty — to get that firm hold on the structure and literary history of any language, ancient or modern, which my brother William, only fifteen months my junior, got from his six years at Rugby, and his training there in Latin and Greek. What I learnt during those years was learnt from personalities; from contact with a nature so simple, sincere and strong as that of Miss Clough; from the kindly old German governess, whose affection for me helped me through some rather hard and lonely school years spent at a school in Shropshire; and from a gentle and high-minded woman, an ardent Evangelical, with whom a little later, at the age of fourteen or fifteen, I fell headlong in love, as was the manner of schoolgirls then, and is I understand frequently the case with schoolgirls now, in spite of the greatly increased variety of subjects on which they may spend their minds.

English girls' schools today providing the higher education are, so far as my knowledge goes, worthily representative of that astonishing rise in the intellectual standards of women, which has taken place in the last half century. They are almost entirely taught by women, and women with whom, in many cases, education — the shaping of the immature human creature to noble ends — is the sincerest of passions; who find indeed, in the task that same creative joy which belongs to literature or art, or philanthropic experiment. The school-mistress to whom money is the sole or even the chief motive of her work, is, in my experience rare today, though we have all in our time heard tales of modern 'academics' of the Miss Pinkerton type, brought up to date — fashionable, exclusive, and luxurious — where, as in some boys' preparatory schools (before the war!) the more the parents paid, the better they were pleased. But I have not come across them, The leading boarding-schools in England and America, at present, no less than the excellent day-schools for girls of the middle class, with which this country has been covered since 1870, are genuine products of that Women's Movement, as we vaguely call it, in the early educational phases of which I myself was much engaged; whereof the results are now widely apparent, though as yet only half-grown. If one tracks it back to somewhere near its origins, its superficial origins at any rate, one is brought up, I think, as in the case of so much else, against one leading cause — *railways*! With railways and a cheap press, in the second third of the nineteenth century, there came in, as we all know, the break-up of a thousand mental stagnations, answering to the old physical disabilities and inconveniences. And the break-up has nowhere had more startling results than in the world of women, and the training of women for life. We have only to ask ourselves what the women of Benjamin Constant, or of Beyle, or Balzac, would have made of the keen schoolgirl and college girl of the present day, to feel how vast is the change through which some of us have lived. Exceptional women, of course, have led much the same kind of lives in all generations. Mrs Sidney Webb has gone through a very different sort of self-education from that of Harriet Martineau; but she has not thought more widely, and she will hardly influence her world so much as that staunch fighter of the past. It is the rank and file — the average woman — for whom the world has opened up so astonishingly. The revelation of her widespread and various capacity that the present war has brought about, is only the suddenly conspicuous result of the liberating forces set in action by the scientific and mechanical development of the nineteenth century. It rests still with that world 'after the war', to which we are looking forward with mingled hope and fear, to determine the new forms, sociological and political, through which this capacity, this heightened faculty, must some day organically express itself.

In the years when I was at school, however, — 1858 to 1867 — these good days were only beginning to dawn. Poor teaching, poor schoolbooks, and, in many cases, indifferent food and much ignorance as to the physical care of girls — these things were common in my school-time. I loved nearly all my teachers; but it was not till I went home to live at Oxford, in 1867, that I awoke intellectually to a hundred interests and influences that begin much earlier nowadays to affect any clever child. I had few tools and little grounding; and I was much more childish than I need have been. A few vivid impressions stand out from these years: the great and to me mysterious figure of Newman haunting the streets of Edgbaston, where, in 1861, my father became head classical master of the Oratory School; the news of the murder of Lincoln, coming suddenly into a quiet garden in a suburb of Birmingham, and an ineffaceable memory of the pale faces and horror-stricken looks of those discussing it; the haunting beauty of certain passages of Ruskin which I copied out and carried about with me, without in the least caring to read as a whole the books from which they came; my first visit to the House of Commons in 1863; the recurrent visits to Fox How, and the winter and summer beauty of the fells; together with an endless storytelling phase in which I told stories to my school-fellows, on condition they told stories to me; coupled with many attempts on my part at poetry and fiction, which make me laugh and blush when I compare them today with similar efforts of my own grand-children. But on the whole they were starved and rather unhappy years; through no one's fault. My parents were very poor and perpetually in movement. Everybody did the best they could.

With Oxford, however, and my seventeenth year, came a radical change.

It was in July 1865, while I was still a schoolgirl, that in the very middle of the Long Vacation, I first saw Oxford. My father, after some five years as Dr Newman's colleague at the Oratory School, had then become the subject of a strong temporary reaction against Catholicism. He left the Roman church in '65, to return to it again, for good, eleven years later. During the interval he took pupils at Oxford, produced a very successful 'Manual of English Literature', edited the works of Wycliffe for the Clarendon Press, made himself an Anglo-Saxon scholar, and became one of the most learned editors of the great 'Rolls Series'. To look at the endless piles of his notebooks is to realise how hard, how incessantly he worked. Historical scholarship was his destined field; he found his happiness in it through all the troubles of life. And the return to Oxford, to its memories, its libraries, its stately, imperishable beauty, was delightful to him. So also, I think, for some years, was the sense of intellectual freedom. Then began a kind of nostalgia, which grew and grew till it took him back to the Catholic haven in 1876, never to wander more.

But when he first showed me Oxford he was in the ardour of what seemed a permanent severance from an admitted mistake. I see a deserted Oxford street, and a hansom coming up it — myself and my father inside it. I was returning from school, for the holidays. When I had last seen my people, they were living near Birmingham. I now found them at Oxford, and I remember the trill of excitement with which I looked from side to side as we neared the colleges. For I knew well even at fourteen, that this was 'no mean city'. As we drove up Beaumont Street we saw what was the 'new Balliol' in front of us, and a jutting window. 'There lives the arch-heretic!' said my father. It was a window in Mr Jowett's rooms. He was not yet Master of the famous College, but his name was a rallying-cry, and his personal influence almost at its zenith. At the same time, he was then rigorously excluded from the university pulpit; it was not till a year later that even his close friend Dean Stanley ventured to ask him to preach in Westminster Abbey; and his salary as Greek Professor, due to him from the revenues of Christ Church, and withheld from him on theological grounds for years, had only just been wrung — at last — from the reluctant hands of a governing body which contained Canon Liddon and Dr Pusey.

To my father, on his settlement in Oxford, Jowett had been a kind and helpful friend; he had a very quick sympathy with my mother; and as I grew up he became my friend too, so that as I look back upon my Oxford years both before and after my marriage, the dear Master — he became Master 1870 — plays a very marked part in the Oxford scene as I shall ever remember it.

It was not however till two years later that I left school, and slipped into the Oxford life as a fish into water. I was sixteen, beginning to be conscious of all sorts of rising needs and ambitions, keenly alive to the spell of Oxford, and to the good fortune which had brought me to live her streets. There was in me, I think, a real hunger to learn, and a very quick sense of romance in things or people. But after sixteen, except in music, I had no definite teaching, and everything I learnt came to me from persons — and books — sporadically, without any general guidance or plan. It was all a great voyage of discovery, organised mainly by myself, on the advice of a few men and women very much older, who took an interest in me, and were endlessly kind to the shy and shapeless creature I must have been.

It was '68 or '69 — I think I was seventeen — that I remember my first sight of a college garden lying cool and shaded between grey college walls, and on the grass a figure that held me fascinated — a lady in a green brocade dress, with a belt and chatelaine of Russian Silver, who was playing croquet, then a novelty in Oxford, and seemed to me, as I watched her, a perfect model of grace and vivacity. A man nearly thirty years older than herself whom I knew to be her husband was standing near her, and a handful of undergraduates made an amused and admiring court round the lady. The elderly man — he was then fifty-three — was Mark Pattison, Rector of Lincoln College, and the croquet-player had been his wife about seven years. After the Rector's death in 1884, Mrs Pattison married Sir Charles Dilke in the very midst of the divorce proceedings which were to wreck in full stream a brilliant political career; and she showed him a proud devotion till her death in 1904. None of her early friends who remember her later history can ever think of the 'Frances Pattison' of Oxford days without a strange stirring of heart. I was much at Lincoln in the years before I married, and derived an impression from the life lived there that has never left me. Afterwards I saw much less of Mrs Pattison who was generally on the Riviera in the winter; but from 1868 to 1872, the Rector, learned, critical, bitter, fastidious, and 'Mrs Pat', with her gaiety, her picturesqueness, her impatience of the Oxford solemnities and decorums, her sharp restless wit, her determination *not* to be academic, to hold on to the greater world of affairs outside — mattered more to me perhaps than anybody else. They were very good to me, and I was never tired of going there: though I was much puzzled by their ways, and — while my Evangelical phase lasted — much scandalised often by the speculative freedom of the talk I heard. Sometimes my rather uneasy conscience protested in ways which I think must have amused my hosts, though they never said a word. They were fond of asking me to come to supper at Lincoln on Sundays. It was a gay, unceremonious meal, at which Mrs Pattison appeared in the kind of gown which at a much later date began to be called a tea-gown. It was generally white or grey, with various ornaments and accessories which always seemed to me, accustomed for so long to the rough-and-tumble of school life, marvels of delicacy and prettiness; so that I was sharply conscious, on these occasions, of the graceful figure made by the young mistress of the old house. But some last stubborn trace in me of the Evangelical view of Sunday declared that while one might talk — and one *must* eat! — on Sunday, one mustn't put on evening dress, or behave as though it were just like a weekday. So while everyone else was in evening dress, I more than once — at seventeen — came to these Sunday gatherings on a winter evening, purposely, in a high woollen frock, sternly but uncomfortably conscious of being sublime — if only one were not ridiculous! The Rector, 'Mrs Pat', Mr Bywater, myself, and perhaps a couple of undergraduates — often a bewildered and silent couple — I see that little vanished company in the far past, so plainly! Three of them are dead — and for me, the grey walls of Lincoln must always be haunted by their ghosts.

The historian of French painting and French decorative art was already in those days unfolding in Mrs Pattison. Her drawing-room was French, sparely furnished with a few old girandoles and mirrors on its white panelled walls, and a Persian carpet with a black centre, on which both the French furniture and the living inmates of the room looked their best. And upstairs, in 'Mrs Pat's' own working-room, there were innumerable things that stirred my curiosity — old French drawings and engravings, masses of foreign books that showed the young and brilliant owner of the room to be already a scholar, even as her husband courted scholarship; together with the tools and materials for etching, a mysterious process in which I was occasionally allowed to lend a hand, and which, as often as not, during the application of the acid to the plate, ended in dire misfortune to the etcher's fingers or dress, and in the helpless laughter of both artist and assistant.

The Rector himself was an endless study to me — he and his frequent companion, Ingram Bywater, afterwards the distinguished Greek Professor. To listen to these two friends as they talked of foreign scholars in Paris, or Germany, of Renan, or Ranke, or Curtis; as they poured scorn on Oxford scholarship, or the lack of it, and on the ideals of Balliol, which aimed at turning out public officials, as compared with the researching ideals of the German universities, which seemed to the Rector the only ideals worth calling academic; or as they flung gibes at Christ Church whence Pusey and Liddon still directed the powerful Church party of the University: — was to watch the doors of new worlds gradually opening before a girl's questioning intelligence. The Rector would walk up and down, occasionally taking a book from his crowded shelves, while Mr Bywater and Mrs Pattison smoked, with the after-luncheon coffee, — and in those days a woman with a cigarette was a rarity in England — and sometimes at a caustic *mot* of the former's there would break out the Rector's cackling laugh, which was ugly no doubt, but when he was amused and at ease, extraordinarily full of mirth. To me he was from the beginning the kindest friend. He saw that I came of a literary stock and had literary ambitions; and he tried to direct me. 'Get to the bottom of something' — he would say — 'Chose a subject, and know *everything* about it!' I eagerly followed his advice, and began to work at early Spanish in the Bodleian. But I think he was wrong — I venture to think so! —though as his half melancholy, half satirical look comes back to me, I realise how easily he would defend himself, if one could tell him so now. I think I ought to have been told to take a history examination and learn Latin properly. But if I had, half the exploring joy of those early years would no doubt have been cut away.

Later on, in the winters when Mrs Pattison, threatened with rheumatic gout, disappeared to the Riviera, I came to know a sadder and lonelier Rector. I used to go to tea with him then in his own book-lined sanctum, and we mended the blazing fire between us and talked endlessly. Presently I married, and his interest in me changed; though our friendship never lessened, and I shall always remember with emotion my last sight of him lying a white and dying man on his sofa in London — the clasp of the wasted hand, the sad haunted eyes. When his 'Memoirs' appeared, after his death, a book of which Mr Gladstone once said to me that he reckoned it as among the most tragic and the most memorable books of the nineteenth century, I understood him more clearly, and more tenderly, than I could have done as a girl. Particularly, I understood why in that sceptical and agnostic talk which never spared the Anglican ecclesiastics of the moment, or such a later Catholic convert as Manning, I cannot remember that I ever heard him mention the great name of John Henry Newman with the slightest touch of disrespect. On the other hand, I once saw him receive a message that some friend brought him from Newman with an eager look and a start of pleasure. He had been a follower of Newman's in the Tractarian days, and no one who ever came near to Newman could afterwards lightly speak ill of him. It was Stanley and not the Rector, indeed, who said of the famous Oratorian that the whole course of English religious history might have been different if Newman had known German. But Pattison might have said it, and if he had, it would have been without the smallest bitterness as the mere expression of a sober and indisputable truth. Alas! — merely to quote it, nowadays, carries one back to a Germany before the Flood — a Germany of small States, a land of scholars and thinkers; a Germany that would surely have recoiled in horror from any prevision of that deep and hideous abyss which her descendants, maddened by wealth and success, were one day to dig between themselves and the rest of Europe.

One of my clearest memories connected with the Pattisons and Lincoln is that of meeting George Eliot and Mr Lewes there, in the spring of 1870, when I was eighteen. It was at one of the Sunday suppers. George Eliot sat at the Rector's right hand. I was opposite her; on my left was George Henry Lewes, to whom I took a prompt and active dislike. He and Mrs Pattison kept up a lively conversation in which Mr Bywater, on the other side of the table played full part. George Eliot talked very little, and I not at all. The Rector was shy or tired, and George Eliot was in truth entirely occupied in watching or listening to Mr Lewes. I was disappointed that she was so silent, and perhaps her quick eye may have divined it, for after supper, as we were going up the interesting old staircase, made in the thickness of the wall, which led direct from the dining-room to the drawing-room above, she said to me: 'The Rector tells me that you have been reading a good deal about Spain. Would you care to hear something of our Spanish journey?' — the journey which had preceded the appearance of 'The Spanish Gypsy', then newly published. My reply is easily imagined. The rest of the party passed through the dimly lit drawing-room to talk and smoke in the gallery beyond. George Eliot sat down in the darkness and I beside her. Then she talked for about twenty minutes, with perfect ease and finish, without misplacing a word or dropping a sentence, and I realised at last that I was in the presence of a great writer. Not a great *talker*. It is clear that George Eliot never was that. Impossible for her to 'talk' her books, or evolve her books from conversation, like Madame de Stael. She was too self-conscious, too desperately reflective, too rich in second-thoughts for that. But in tète-á-tète, and with time to choose her words, she could — in monologue, with just enough stimulus from a companion to keep it going — produce on a listener exactly the impression of some of her best work. As the low clear voice flowed on, in Mrs Pattison's drawing-room, I *saw* Saragossa, Granada, the Escorial, and that survival of the old Europe in the new, which one must go to Spain to find. Not that the description was particularly vivid — in talking of famous places John Richard Green could make words tell and paint with far greater success; but it was singularly complete and accomplished. When it was done the effect was there — the effect she had meant to produce. I shut my eyes, and it all comes back:

— the darkened room, the long, pallid face, set in black lace, the evident wish to be kind to a young girl.

Two more impressions of her let me record. The following day, the Pattisons took their guests to see the 'eights' races from Christ Church meadow. A young Fellow of Merton, Mandell Creighton, afterwards the beloved and famous Bishop of London, was among those entertaining her on the barge, and on the way home he took her and Mr Lewes through Merton garden. I was of the party, and I remember what a carnival of early summer it was in that enchanting place. The chestnuts were all out, one splendour from top to toe; the laburnums, the lilacs, the hawthorns red and white, the new-mown grass spreading its smooth and silky carpet round the college walls, a May sky overhead, and through the trees glimpses of towers and spires, silver grey, in the sparkling summer air; — the picture was one of those that Oxford throws before the spectator, at every turn, like the careless beauty that knows she has only to show herself, to move, to breathe, to give delight. George Eliot stood on the grass, in the bright sun, looking at the flower-laden chestnuts, at the distant glimpses on all sides, of the surrounding city, saying little — that she left to Mr. Lewes! But drinking it in, storing it in that rich, absorbent mind of hers. And afterwards when Mr Lewes — Mr Creighton, she and I walked back to Lincoln, I remember another little incident throwing light on the ever-ready instinct of the novelist. As we turned into the quadrangle of Lincoln — suddenly, at one of the upper windows of the Rector's lodgings, which occupied the far right-hand corner of the quad, there appeared the head and shoulders of Mrs Pattison, as she looked out and beckoned smiling to Mrs Lewes. It was a brilliant apparition, as though a French portrait by Greuze or Perronneau had suddenly slipped into a vacant space in the old college wall. The pale, pretty head, *blond-cendrée*; the delicate smiling features and white throat; a touch of black, a touch of blue; a white dress; a general eighteenth-century impression as though of powder and patches: — Mrs Lewes perceived it in a flash, and I saw her run eagerly to Mr Lewes and draw his attention to the window and its occupant. She took his arm, while she looked and waved. If she had lived longer, some day, and somewhere in her books, that vision at the window, and that flower-laden garden would have reappeared. I seemed to see her consciously and deliberately committing them both to memory.

But I do not believe that she ever meant to describe the Rector in 'Mr Casaubon'. She was far too good a scholar herself to have perpetrated a caricature so flagrantly untrue. She knew Mark Pattison's quality, and could never have meant to draw the writer of some of the most fruitful and illuminating of English essays, and one of the most brilliant pieces of European biography, in the dreary and foolish pedant who over-shadows 'Middlemarch'. But the fact that Mark Pattison was an elderly scholar with a young wife, and that George Eliot knew him, led later on to a legend which was, I am sure, unwelcome to the writer of 'Middlemarch', while her supposed victim passed it by with amused indifference.

As to the relation between the Rector and the Squire of 'Robert Elsmere' which has been often assumed, it was confined, as I have already said (in the introduction to the library edition of 'Robert Elsmere' published in 1909) to a likeness in outward aspect —'a few personal traits, and the two main facts of great learning and a general impatience of fools'. If one could imagine Mark Pattison a landowner, he would certainly never have neglected his estates, or tolerated an inefficient agent.

Only three years intervened between my leaving school and my engagement to Mr T. Humphry Ward, Fellow and Tutor of Brasenose College, Oxford. But those three years seem to me now to have been extraordinarily full. Lincoln and the Pattisons, Balliol and Mr Jowett, and the Bodleian Library, outside the influences and affections of my own home, stand in the forefront of what memory looks back on as a broad and animated scene. The great Library, in particular, became to me a living and inspiring presence. When I think of it, as it then was, I am aware of a medley of beautiful things — pale sunlight on book-lined walls, or streaming through old armorial bearings on Tudor windows; spaces and distances, all books, beneath a painted roof from which gleamed the motto of the University — 'Dominus illuminato mea'; gowned figures moving silently about the spaces; the faint scents of old leather and polished wood; and fusing it all, a stately dignity and benignant charm, through which the voices of the bells outside, as they struck each successive quarter from Oxford's many towers, seemed to breathe a certain eternal reminder of the past and the dead.

But regions of the Bodleian were open to me then that no ordinary reader sees now. Mr Coxe — the well-known, much loved Bodley's Librarian of those days — took kindly notice of the girl-reader, and very soon, probably on the recommendation of Mark Pattison, who was a Curator, made me free of the lower floors, where was the 'Spanish room', with its shelves of seventeenth and eighteenth century volumes in sheepskin or vellum, with their turned-in edges and leathern strings. Here I might wander at will, absolutely alone, save for the visit of an occasional librarian from the upper floor, seeking a book. To get to the Spanish Room one had to pass through the Douce Library, the home of treasures beyond price; on one side half the precious things of Renaissance printing, French or Italian or Elizabethan, on the other, stands of illuminated Missals and Hour Books, many of them rich in pictures and flower-work, that shone like jewels in the golden light of the room. That light was to me something tangible and friendly. It seemed to be the mingled product of all the delicate browns and yellows and golds in the binding of the books, of the brass latticework that covered them, and of reflections from the beautiful stonework of the Schools Quadrangle outside. It was in these noble surroundings that, with far too little, I fear, of positive reading, and with much undisciplined wandering from shelf to shelf and subject to subject, there yet sank deep into me the sense of history, and of that vast ocean of the recorded past, from which the generations rise, and into which they fall back. And that in itself was a great boon — almost, one might say, a training, of a kind.

But a girl of seventeen is not always thinking of books, especially in the Oxford summer term.

In 'Miss Bretherton', my earliest novel, and in 'Lady Connie', so far my latest,[1] will be found by those who care to look for it, the reflection of that other life of Oxford, the life which takes its shape not from age, but from youth, not from the past which created Oxford, but from the lively laughing present which every day renews it. For six months of the year Oxford is a city of young men, for the most part between the ages of eighteen and twenty-two. In my maiden days it was not also a city of

---

[1] These chapters were written before the appearance of '*Missing*' in the autumn of 1917

young women, as it is today. Women — girls especially — comparatively on sufferance. The Heads of Houses were married; the Professors were mostly married; but married tutors had scarcely begun to be. Only at two seasons of the year was Oxford invaded by women — by bevies of maidens who came, in early May and middle June, to be made much of by their brothers and their brothers' friends, to be danced with and flirted with, to know the joys of coming back on a summer night from Nuneham up the long fragrant reaches of the lower river, or of 'sitting out' in historic gardens where Philip Sidney or Charles I had passed.

At the Eights and 'Commem', the old, old place became a mere background for pretty dresses, and college luncheons, and river picnics. The seniors groaned often, as well they might; for there was little work done in my day in the summer term. But it is perhaps worth while for any nation to possess such harmless festivals in so beautiful a setting as these Oxford gatherings. How many of our national festivals are spoilt by ugly and sordid things — betting and drink, greed and display! Here, all there is to see is a competition of boats, manned by England's best youth, upon a noble river, flowing, in Virgilian phrase, 'under ancient walls'; a city of romance, given up for a few days to the pleasure of the young, and breathing into that pleasure her own refining, exalting note; a stately ceremony — the Encćnia — going back to the infancy of English learning; and the dancing of young men and maidens in Gothic or classical halls built long ago by the 'fathers who begat us'. My own recollection of the Oxford summer, the Oxford river and hayfields, the dawn on Oxford streets, as one came out from a Commemoration ball, or the evening under Nuneham woods where the swans on that still water, now, as always, 'float double, swan and shadow' — these things I hope will be with me to the end. To have lived through them is to have tasted youth and pleasure from a cup as pure, as little alloyed with baser things, as the high gods allow to mortals.

Let me recall one more experience before I come to the married life which began in 1872; — my first sight of Taine, the great French historian, in the spring of 1871. He had come over at the invitation of the Curators of the Taylorian Institution to give a series of lectures on Corneille and Racine. The lectures were arranged immediately after the surrender of Paris to the German troops, when it might have been hoped that the worst calamities of France were over. But before M. Taine crossed to England the insurrection of the Commune had broken out, and while he was actually in Oxford delivering his six lectures, the terrible news of the last days of May, the burning of the Tuileries, the Hotel de Ville and the Cour des Comptes, all the savagery of the beaten revolution let loose on Paris itself, came crashing, day by day and hour by hour, like so many horrible explosions in the heavy air of Europe, still tremulous with the memories and agonies of recent war.

How well I remember the effect in Oxford! — the newspaper cries in the streets, the fear each morning as to what new calamities might have fallen on civilisation, the intense fellow-feeling in a community of students and scholars for the students and scholars of France!

When M. Taine arrived, he himself bears witness (see his published Correspondence, vol. II) that Oxford could not do enough to show her sympathy with a distinguished Frenchman. He writes from Oxford on May 25: —

I have no courage for a letter today. I have just heard of the horrors of Paris, the burning of the Louvre, the Tuileries, the Hotel de Ville, etc. My heart is wrung. I have energy for nothing. I cannot go out and see people. I was in the Bodleian when the Librarian told me this and showed me the newspapers. In presence of such madness and such disasters, they treat a Frenchman here with a kind of pitying sympathy.

Oxford residents indeed, inside and outside the colleges, crowded the first lecture to show our feeling not only for M. Taine, but for a France wounded and trampled on by her own children. The few dignified and touching words with which he opened his course, his fine dark head, the attractiveness of his subject, the lucidity of his handling of it, made the lecture a great success; and a few nights afterwards at dinner at Balliol, I found myself sitting next the great man. In his published correspondence there is a letter describing this dinner which shows that I must have confided in him not a little — as to my Bodleian reading, and the article on the *Poema del Cid* that I was writing. He confesses, however, that he did his best to draw me — examining the English girl as a new specimen for his psychological collection. As for me, I can only perversely remember a passing phrase of his to the effect that there was too much magenta in the dress of English women, and too much pepper in the English *cuisine*. From English cooking — which showed ill in the Oxford of those days — he suffered indeed a good deal. Nor, in spite of his great literary knowledge of England and English, was his spoken English clear enough to enable him to grapple with the lodging-house cook. Professor Max Müller, who had induced him to give the lectures, and watched over him during his stay, told me that on his first visit to the historian in his Beaumont Street rooms, he found him sitting bewildered before the strangest of meals. It consisted entirely of a huge beefsteak, served in the unappetising, slovenly English way — and, a large plate of buttered toast. Nothing else. 'But I ordered bif-tek and pot-a-toes!' cried the puzzled historian, to his visitor!

Another guest of the Master's on that night was Mr Swinburne, and of him too I have a vivid recollection as he sat opposite to me on the side next to the fire, his small lower features and slender neck over-weighted by his thick reddish hair and capacious brow. I could not think why he seemed so cross and uncomfortable. He was perpetually beckoning to the waiters, then, when they came, holding peremptory conversation with them; while I from my side of the table could see them going away, with a whisper or a shrug to each other, like men asked for the impossible. At last with a kind of bound, Swinburne leapt from his chair and seized a copy of *The Times*, which he seemed to have persuaded one of the men to bring him. As he got up I saw that the fire behind him, and very close to him, must indeed have been burning the very marrow out of a long-suffering poet. And alack, in that house without a mistress, the small conveniences of life, such as fire-screens, were often overlooked. The Master did not possess any. In a pale exasperation Swinburne folded *The Times* over the back of his chair, and sat down again. Vain was the effort! The room was narrow, the party large, and the servants pushing by, had soon dislodged *The Times*. Again and again did Swinburne in a fury replace it; and was soon reduced to sitting silent and wild-eyed, his back firmly pressed against the chair and the newspaper, in a concentrated struggle with fate.

Matthew Arnold was another of the Party, and I have a vision of my uncle standing talking with M. Taine, with whom he then and there made a lasting friendship. The Frenchman was not, I trust, aware at that moment of the heresies of the English critic who had ventured only a few years before to speak of 'the exaggerated French estimate of Racine', and even to endorse the judgement of Joubert — 'Racine est le Virgile des ignorants'! Otherwise M. Taine might have given an even sharper edge than he actually did to his remarks, in his letters home, on the critical faculty of the English. 'In all that I read and hear' — he says to Madame Taine — 'I see nowhere the fine literary sense which means the gift — or the art — of understanding the souls and passions of the past'. And again, 'I have had infinite trouble today to make my audience appreciate some *finesses* of Racine'. There is a note of resigned exasperation in these comments which reminds me of the passionate feeling of another French critic — Edmond Scherer, Sainte-Beuve's best successor — ten years later. A *propos* of some judgement of Matthew Arnold — whom Scherer delighted in — on Racine, of the same kind as those I have already quoted, the French man of letters once broke out to me, almost with fury, as we walked together at Versailles. But, after all, was the Oxford which contained Pater, Pattison, and Bywater, which had nurtured Matthew Arnold and Swinburne — Swinburne with his wonderful knowledge of the intricacies and subtleties of the French tongue, and the French literature — merely 'solide and positif', as Taine declares? The judgement is, I think, a characteristic judgement of that man of formulas — often so brilliant, and so often so mistaken — who in the famous 'History of English Literature', taught his English readers as much by his blunders as by his merits. He provoked us into thinking. And what critic does more? Is not the whole fraternity like so many successive 'Penelopes', each unravelling the web of the one before? The point is that the web should be eternally re-made and eternally unravelled.

II

I married Mr Thomas Humphry Ward, Fellow and Tutor of Brasenose College, on April 6, 1872, the knot being tied by my father's friend, my grandfather's pupil and biographer, Dean Stanley. For nine years, till the spring of 1881, we lived in Oxford, in a little house, north of the Parks, in what was then the newest quarter of the University town. They were years, for both of us, of great happiness and incessant activity. Our children, two daughters and son, were born in 1874, 1876 and 1879. We had many friends, all pursuing the same kind of life as ourselves, and interested in the same kind of things. Nobody under the rank of a Head of a College, except a very few privileged Professors, possessed as much as a thousand a year. The average income of the new race of married tutors was not much more than half that sum. Yet we all gave dinner-parties and furnished our houses with Morris papers, old chests and cabinets, and blue pots. The dinner-parties were simple and short. At our own early efforts of the kind, there certainly was not enough to eat. But we all improved with time; and on the whole I think we were very fair housekeepers and competent mothers. Most of us were very anxious to be up-to-date, and in the fashion, whether in aesthetics, in housekeeping, or education. But our fashion was not that of Belgravia or Mayfair, which indeed we scorned! It was the fashion of the movement which sprang from Morris and Burne-Jones. Liberty stuffs very plain in line, but elaborately 'smocked', were greatly in vogue, and evening dresses, 'cut square', or with 'Watteau pleats', were generally worn, and often in conscious protest against the London 'low dress', which Oxford — young married Oxford — thought both ugly and 'fast'. And when we had donned our Liberty gowns we went out to dinner, the husband walking, the wife in a bath chair, drawn by an ancient member of an ancient and close fraternity — the 'chairman' of old Oxford.

Almost immediately opposite to us in the Bradmore Road, lived Walter Pater and his sisters. The exquisiteness of their small house, and the charm of the three people who lived in it will never be forgotten by those who knew them well in those days when by the publication of the 'Studies in the Renaissance' (1873) their author had just become famous. I recall very clearly the effect of that book, and of the strange and poignant sense of beauty expressed in it; of its entire aloofness also from the Christian tradition of Oxford, its glorification of the higher and intenser forms of aesthetic pleasure, of 'passion' in the intellectual sense — as against the Christian doctrine of self-denial and renunciation. It was a gospel that both stirred and scandalised Oxford. The bishop of the diocese thought it worthwhile to protest. There was a cry of 'Neo-paganism', and various attempts at persecution. The author of the book was quite unmoved. In those days Walter Pater's mind was still full of revolutionary ferments which were just as sincere, just as much himself as that later hesitating and wistful return towards Christianity, and Christianity of the Catholic type, which is embodied in 'Marius the Epicurean', the most beautiful of the spiritual romances of Europe since the 'Confessions'. I can remember a dinner-party at his house, where a great tumult arose over some abrupt statement of his made to the High Church wife of a well-known professor. Pater had been in some way pressed controversially beyond the point of wisdom, and had said suddenly that no reasonable person could govern their lives by the opinions or actions of a man who died eighteen centuries ago. The Professor and his wife — I look back to them both with the warmest affection — departed hurriedly, in agitation; and the rest of us only gradually found out what had happened.

But before we left Oxford in 1881, this attitude of mind had, I think, greatly changed. Mr Gosse in the memoir of Walter Pater contributed to the Dictionary of National Biography says that before 1870, he had gradually relinquished all belief in the Christian religion — and leaves it there. But the interesting and touching thing to watch was the gentle and almost imperceptible flowing back of the tide over the sands it had left bare. It may be said, I think, that he never returned to Christianity in the orthodox, or intellectual sense. But his heart returned to it. He became once more endlessly interested in it, and haunted by the 'something' in it, which he thought inexplicable. A remembrance of my own shows this. In my ardent years of exploration and revolt, conditioned by the historical work that occupied me during the later seventies, I once said to him in tête-à-tête, reckoning confidently on his sympathy, and with the intolerance and certainty of youth, that orthodoxy could not possibly maintain itself long against its assailants, especially from the historical and literary camps, and that we should live to see it break down. He shook his head and looked rather troubled. 'I don't think so —' he said. Then, with hesitation — 'And we don't altogether agree. You think it's all plain. But I can't. There are such mysterious things. Take that saying "Come unto me, all ye that are weary and heavy laden". How can you explain that? There is a mystery in it — something supernatural.'

A few years later, I should very likely have replied that the answer of the modern critic would be: 'The words you quote are in all probability from a lost Wisdom book; there are very close analogies in Proverbs and in the Apocrypha. They are a fragment without a context, and may represent on the Lord's lips, either a quotation, or the text of a discourse. Wisdom is speaking — the Wisdom "which is justified of her children"'. But if anyone had made such a reply, it would not have affected the mood in Pater of which this conversation gave me my first glimpse, and which is expressed again and again in the most exquisite passages of 'Marius'. Turn to the first time when Marius — under Marcus Aurelius — is present at a Christian ceremony, and sees, for the first time, the wonderful spectacle of those who believed'.

> The people here collected might have figured as the earliest handsel or pattern of a new world, from the very face of which discontent had passed away . . . . They had faced life and were glad, by some science or light of knowledge they had, to which there was certainly no parallel in the older world. Was some credible message from beyond 'the flaming rampart of the world' — a message of hope . . . . already moulding their very bodies and looks and voices, now and here ?

Or again, to the thoughts of Marius at the approach of death: —

> At this moment, his unclouded receptivity of soul, grown so steadily through all those years, from experience to experience, was at its height; the house was ready for the possible guest, the tablet of the mind white and smooth, for whatever divine fingers might choose to write there.

'Marius' was published twelve years after the 'Studies in the Renaissance', and there is a world between the two books. Some further light will be thrown on this later phase of Mr Pater's thought by a letter he wrote to me in 1885 on my translation of Amiel's from 'Journal Intime'. Here it is rather the middle days of his life that concern me, and the years of happy friendship with him and his sisters, when we were all young together. Mr Pater and my husband were both fellows and tutors of Brasenose, though my husband was much the younger; a fact which naturally brought us into frequent contact. And the beautiful little house across the road, with its two dear mistresses drew me perpetually, both before and after my marriage. The drawing-room which runs the whole breadth of the house from the road to the garden behind was 'Paterian' in every line and ornament. There was a Morris paper; spindle-legged tables and chairs; a sparing allowance of blue plates and pots, bought, I think, in Holland, where Oxford residents in my day were always foraging, to return, often, with treasures of which the very memory now stirs a half-amused envy of one's own past self, that had such chances and lost them; framed embroidery of the most delicate design and colour, the work of Mr Pater's elder sister; engravings, if I remember right, from Botticelli or Luini, or Mantegna; a few mirrors, and a very few flowers, chosen and arranged with a simple yet conscious art. I see that room always with the sun in it, touching the polished surfaces of wood and brass and china, and bringing out its pure, bright colour. I see it too pervaded by the presence of the younger sister Clara, — a personality never to be forgotten by those who loved her. Clara Pater, whose grave and noble beauty in youth has been preserved in a drawing by Mr Wirgman, was indeed a 'rare and dedicated spirit'. When I first knew her, she was four or five and twenty, intelligent, alive, sympathetic, with a delightful humour, and a strong judgement, but without much positive acquirement. Then after some years, she began to learn Latin and Greek with a view to teaching; and after we left Oxford she became Vice-President of the new Somerville College for Women. Several generations of girl-students must still preserve the tenderest and most grateful memories of all that she was there, as woman, teacher, and friend. Her point of view, her opinion had always the crispness, the savour that goes with perfect sincerity. She feared no one, and she loved many, as they loved her. She loved animals too, as all the household did. How well I remember the devoted nursing given by the brother and sisters to a poor little paralytic cat, whose life they tried to save — in vain! When, later, I came across in 'Marius' the account of Marcus Aurelius carrying away the dead child Annius Verus — 'pressed closely to his bosom, as if yearning just then for one thing only, to be united, to be absolutely one with it, in its obscure distress' — I remembered the absorption of the writer of those lines, and of his sisters, in the suffering of that poor little creature, long years before. I feel tolerably certain that in writing the words Walter Pater had that past experience in mind.

After Walter Pater's death, Clara, with her elder sister, became the vigilant and joint guardians of their brother's books and fame, till, four years ago, a terrible illness cut short her life, and set free, in her brother's words, the 'unclouded and receptive soul'.

CHAPTER VII

Balliol and Lincoln

When the Oxford historian of the future comes across the name and influence of Benjamin Jowett, the famous Master of Balliol, and Greek professor, in the mid-current of the nineteenth century, he will not be without full means of finding out what made that slight figure (whereof he will be able to study the outward and visible presence in some excellent portraits, and in many caricatures) so significant and so representative. The 'Life' of the Master, by Evelyn Abbott and Lewis Campbell, is to me one of the most interesting biographies of our generation. It is long — for those who have no Oxford ties, no doubt, too long; and it is cumbered with the echoes of old controversies, theological and academic, which have mostly, though by no means wholly, passed into a dusty limbo. But it is one of the rare attempts that English biography has seen to paint a man as he really was; and to paint him not with the sub-malicious strokes of a Purcell, but in love, although in truth.

The Master, as he fought his many fights, with his abnormally strong will, and his dominating personality; the Master, as he appeared, on the one hand, to the upholders of 'research', of learning that is, as an end in itself apart from teaching and, on the other, to the High Churchmen encamped in Christ Church, to Pusey, Liddon, and all their clan — pugnacious, formidable, and generally successful — here he is to the life. This is the Master whose personality could never be forgotten in any room he chose to enter; who brought restraint rather than ease to the gatherings of his friends, mainly because, according to his own account, of a shyness he could never overcome; whose company on walk was too often more of a torture than an honour to the undergraduate selected for it, whose lightest words were feared, quoted, chuckled over, or resented, like those of no one else.

Of this Master, I have many remembrances. I see, for instance, a drawing-room full of rather tongue-tied embarrassed guests, some Oxford residents, some Londoners; and the Master among them, as a stimulating — but disintegrating! — force, of whom every one was uneasily conscious. The circle was wide, the room bare, and the Balliol arm chairs were not placed for conversation. On a high chair against the wall, sat a small boy of ten — we will call him Arthur — oppressed by his surroundings. The talk languished and dropped. From one side of the large room, the Master, raising his voice, addresses the small boy on the other side.

'Well, Arthur, so I hear you've begun Greek. How are you getting on?'

To the small boy looking round the room it seemed as though twenty awful grown-ups were waiting in a dead silence to eat him up. He rushed upon his answer.

'I — I'm reading the Anabásis,' he said desperately.

The false quantity sent a shock through the room. Nobody laughed, out of sympathy with the boy, who already knew that something dreadful had happened. The boy's miserable parents, Londoners, who were among the twenty, wished themselves under the floor. The Master smiled.

'Anábasis, Arthur,' he said cheerfully. 'You'll get it right next time.'

And he went across to the boy, evidently feeling for him, and wishing to put him at ease. But after thirty years, the boy and his parents still remember the incident with a shiver. It could not have produced such an effect, except in an atmosphere of tension; and that, alas! too often, was the atmosphere which surrounded the Master.

I can remember, too, many proud yet anxious half-hours in the Master's study — such a privilege, yet such an ordeal! — when, after our migration to London, we became, at regular intervals, the Master's weekend visitors. 'Come and talk to me a little in my study,' the Master would say pleasantly. And there in the room where he worked for so many years, as the interpreter of Greek thought to the English world, one would take a chair beside the fire, with the Master opposite. I have described my fireside *têtes-à-tête*, as a girl, with another head of a College — the Rector of Lincoln, Mark Pattison. But the Master was a far more strenuous companion. With him, there were no diversions, none! — no relief from the breathless adventure of trying to please him, and doing one's best. The

Rector once, being a little invalidish, allowed me to make up the fire, and after watching the process sharply, said — 'Good! Does it drive *you* distracted, too, when people put on coals the wrong way? An interruption, which made for human sympathy! The Master, as far as I can remember, had no nerves'; are a bond between many. But he occasionally had sudden returns upon himself. I remember once after we had been discussing a religious book which had interested us both, he abruptly drew himself up, in the full tide of talk, and said with a curious impatience — 'But one can't be always thinking of these things!' — and changed the subject.

So much for the Master, the stimulus of whose mere presence was, according to his biographers, 'often painful'. But there were at least two other Masters in the 'Mr Jowett' we reverenced. And they too are fully shown in this biography. The Master who loved his friends and thought no pains too great to take for them; including the very rare pains of trying to mend their characters by faithfulness and plain speaking, whenever he thought by faithfulness and plain speaking, whenever he thought they wanted it. The Master, again, whose sympathies were always with social reform, and with the poor, whose hidden life was full of deeds of kindness and charity, who, in spite of his difficulties of manner, was loved by all sorts and conditions of men — and women — in all circles of life; by politicians and great ladies; by diplomats and scholars and poets; by his secretary and his servants: — there are many traits of this good man and useful citizen, recorded by his biographers.

And, finally, there was the Master who reminded his most intimate friends of a sentence of his about Greek literature, which occurs in the Introduction to the 'Phaedrus'. 'Under the marble exterior of Greek literature was concealed a soul thrilling with spiritual emotion,' says the Master. His own was not exactly a marble exterior; but the placid and yet shrewd cheerfulness of his delicately rounded face, with its small mouth and chin, its great brow, and frame of snowy hair, gave but little clue to the sensitive and mystical soul within. If ever a man was *Gottbetrunken*, it was the Master, many of whose meditations and passing thoughts, withdrawn, while he lived, from all human ken, yet written down — in thirty or forty volumes! — for his own discipline and remembrance, can now be read, thanks to his biographers, in the pages of the Life. They are extraordinarily frank and simple; startling often, in their bareness and truth. But they are, above all, the thoughts of a mystic, moving in a divine presence. An old and intimate friend of the Master's once said to me that he believed 'Jowett's inner mind, especially towards the end of his life, was always in an attitude of Prayer. One would go and talk to him on University or College business in his study, and suddenly see his lips moving, slightly and silently, and know what it meant.' The records of him which his death revealed — and his closest friends realised it in life — show a man perpetually conscious of a mysterious and blessed companionship; which is the mark of the religious man, in all faiths and all churches. Yet this was the man who, for the High Church party at Oxford, with its headquarters at Christ Church, under the flag of Dr Pusey and Canon Liddon, was the symbol and embodiment of all heresy; whose University salary as Greek professor, which depended on a Christ Church subsidy, was withheld for years by the same High Churchmen, because of their inextinguishable wrath against the Liberal leader who contributed so largely to the test-abolishing legislation of 1870 — legislation by which Oxford, in Liddon's words, was 'logically lost to the Church of England'.

Yet no doubt they had their excuses! For this, too, was the man who, in a city haunted by Tractarian shades, once said to his chief biographer that 'Voltaire had done more good than all the Fathers of the Church put together!' — who scornfully asks himself in his diary, à *propos* of the Bishops' condemnation of 'Essays and Reviews', 'What is Truth against an *esprit de corps*?' — and drops out the quiet dictum: 'Half the books that are published are religious books, and what trash this religious literature is!' Nor did the Evangelicals escape. The Master's dislike for many well-known hymns specially dear to that persuasion was never concealed. 'How cocky they are!' he would say contemptuously. '"When upwards I fly — Quite justified I" — who can repeat a thing like that?'

How the old war-cries ring again in one's ears as one looks back! Those who have only known the Oxford of the last twenty years can never, I think, feel towards that 'august place' as we did in the seventies of the last century; we who were still within sight and hearing of the great fighting years of an earlier generation, and still scorched by their dying fires. Balliol, Christ Church, Lincoln: — the Liberal and utilitarian camp, the Church camp, the researching and pure scholarship camp — with Science and the Museum hovering in the background, as the growing aggressive powers of the future seeking whom they might devour: — they were the signs and symbols of mighty hosts, of great forces still visibly incarnate, and in marching array. Balliol versus Christ Church — Jowett versus Pusey and Liddon — while Lincoln despised both, and the new scientific forces watched and waited: — that was how we saw the field of battle, and the various alarms and excursions it was always providing.

But Balliol meant more to me than the Master. Professor Thomas Hill Green — 'Green of Balliol' — was no less representative in our days of the spiritual and liberating forces of the great college; and the time which has now elapsed since his death has clearly shown that his philosophic work and influence hold a lasting and conspicuous place in the history of nineteenth-century thought. He and his wife became our intimate friends, and in the 'Grey' of 'Robert Elsmere' I tried to reproduce a few of those traits — traits of a great thinker and teacher, who was also one of the simplest, sincerest, and most practical of men — which Oxford will never forget, so long as high culture and noble character are dear to her. His wife — so his friend and biographer, Lewis Nettleship, tells us — once compared him to Sir Bors in 'The Holy Grail':

> A square-set man and honest; and his eyes,
> An out-door sign of all the wealth within,
> Smiled with his lips, a smile beneath a cloud,
> But haven had meant it for a sunny one!

A quotation in which the mingling of a cheerful, practical, humorous temper, the temper of the active citizen and politician, with heavy tasks of philosophic thought, is very happily suggested. As we knew him, indeed, before his growing reputation, confirmed by the Introduction to the Clarendon Press edition of Hume, had led to his appointment as

Whyte's Professor of Moral Philosophy, Mr Green was not only a leading Balliol tutor, but an energetic Liberal, a member both of the Oxford Town Council and of various University bodies; a helper in all the great steps taken for the higher education of women at Oxford, and keenly attracted by the project of a High School for the town boys of Oxford — a man, in other words, preoccupied, just as the Master was, and for all his philosophic genius, with the need of leading 'a useful life'.

Let me pause to think how much that phrase meant in the mouths of the best man whom Balliol produced, in the days when I knew Oxford. The Master, Green, Toynbee — their minds were full, half a century ago, of the 'condition of the people' question, of temperance, housing, wages, electoral reform; and within the University, and by the help of the weapons of thought and teaching, they regarded themselves as the natural allies of the Liberal party which was striving for these things through politics and Parliament. 'Usefulness', 'social reform', the bettering of daily life for the many — these ideas are stamped on all their work and on all the biographies of them that remain to us.

And the significance of it is only to be realised when we turn to the rival group, to Christ Church, and the religious party which that name stood for. Read the lives of Liddon, of Pusey, or — to go further back — of the great Newman himself. Nobody will question the personal goodness and charity of any of the three. But how little the leading ideas of that seething time of social and industrial reform, from the appearance of *Sybil* in 1843 to the Education Bill of 1870, mattered either to Pusey or Liddon, compared with the date of the book of Daniel, or the attention of the Athanasian Creed! Newman, at a time when national drunkenness was an overshadowing terror in the minds of all reformers, confesses with a pathetic frankness that he had never considered 'whether there were too many public-houses in England or no'; and in all his religious controversies of the thirties and the forties, you will look in vain for any word of industrial or political reform. So also in the 'Life' of that great rhetorician and beautiful personality, Canon Liddon, you will scarcely find a single letter that touches on any question of social betterment. How to safeguard the 'principle of authority', how to uphold the traditional authorship of the Pentateuch, and of the Book of Daniel, against 'infidel' criticism; how to stifle among the younger High Churchmen like Mr (now Bishop) Gore, then head of the Pusey House, the first advances towards a reasonable freedom of thought; how to maintain the doctrine of Eternal Punishment against the protest of the religious consciousness itself — it is on these matters that Canon Liddon's correspondence turns, it was to them his life was devoted.

How vainly! Who can doubt now which type of life and thought had in it the seeds of growth and permanence — the Balliol type, or the Christ Church type? There are many High Churchmen, it is true, at the present day, and many Ritualist Churches. But they are alive today, just in so far as they have learnt the lesson of social pity, and the lesson of a reasonable criticism, from the men whom Pusey and Liddon and half the bishops condemned and persecuted in the middle years of the nineteenth century.

When we were living in Oxford, however, this was not exactly the point of view from which the great figure of Liddon presented itself, to us of the Liberal camp. We were constantly aware of him, no doubt, as the rival figure to the Master of Balliol, as the arch wire-puller and ecclesiastical intriguer in University affairs, leading the Church forces with a more than Roman astuteness. But his great mark was made, of course, by his preaching, and that not so much by the things said as by the man saying them. Who now would go to Liddon's famous Bamptons, for all their learning, for a still valid defence of the orthodox doctrine of the Incarnation? Those wonderful paragraphs of subtle argumentation from which the great preacher emerged, as triumphantly as Mr Gladstone from a Gladstonian sentence in a House of Commons debate — what remains of them? Liddon wrote of Stanley that he — Stanley — was 'more entirely destitute of the logical faculty' than any educated man he knew. In a sense it was true. But Stanley, if he had been aware of the criticism, might have replied that, if he lacked logic, Liddon lacked something much more vital — i.e. the sense of history — and of the relative value of testimony!

Newman, Pusey, Liddon — all three, great schoolmen, arguing from an accepted brief; the man of genius, the man of a vast industry, intense but futile, the man of captivating presence and a perfect rhetoric: — history, with its patient burrowings, has surely undermined the work of all three; sparing only that element in the work of one of them — Newman — which is the preserving salt of all literature — i.e. the magic of personality. And some of the most efficacious burrowers have been their own spiritual children. As was fitting! For the Tractarian movement, with its appeal to the primitive church, was in truth and quite unconsciously, one of the agencies in a great process of historical enquiry, which is still going on, and of which the end is not yet.

But to me, in my twenties, these great names were not merely names or symbols, as they are to the men and women of the present generation. Newman I had seen in my childhood, walking about the streets of Edgbaston, and had shrunk from him in a dumb childish resentment as from someone whom I understood to be the author of our family misfortunes. In those days, as I have already recalled in an earlier chapter, the daughters of a 'mixed marriage' were brought up in the mother's faith and the sons in the father's. I, therefore, as a schoolgirl under Evangelical influence, was not allowed to make friends with any of my father's Catholic colleagues. Then, in 1880, twenty years later, Newman came to Oxford, and on Trinity Monday there was a great gathering at Trinity College, where the Cardinal in his red, a blanched and spiritual presence, received the homepage of a new generation who saw in him a great soul and a great master of English, and cared little or nothing for the controversies in which he had spent his prime. As my turn came to shake hands, I recalled my father to him and the Edgbaston days. His face lit up — almost mischievously. 'Are you the little girl I remember seeing sometimes — in the distance?' he said to me, with a smile and look that only he and I understood.

On the Sunday preceding that gathering I went to hear his last sermon in the city he loved so well, preached at the new Jesuit church in the suburbs; while little more than a mile away, Bidding Prayer and sermon were going on as usual in the University Church where in his youth, week by week, he had so deeply stirred the hearts and consciences of men. The sermon in St Aloysius was preached with great difficulty, and was almost incoherent from the physical weakness of the speaker. Yet who that was present on that Sunday will ever forget the great ghost that fronted them, the faltering accents, the words from which the life blood had departed yet not the charm?

Then — Pusey! There comes back to me a bowed and uncouth figure, whom one used to see both in the Cathedral procession on a Sunday, and — rarely — in the University pulpit. One sermon on Darwinism, which was preached, if I remember right, in the early seventies, remains with me, as the appearance of some modern Elijah, returning after long silence and exile to protest against an unbelieving world. Sara Coleridge had years before described Pusey in the pulpit with a few vivid strokes.

> He has not one of the graces of oratory (she says). His discourse is generally a rhapsody describing with infinite repetition the wickedness of sin, the worthlessness of earth, and the blessedness of heaven. He is as still as a statue all the time he is uttering it, looks as white as a sheet, and is as monotonous in delivery as possible.

Nevertheless Pusey wielded a spell which is worth much oratory — the spell of a soul dwelling spiritually on the heights; and a prophet moreover may be as monotonous or as incoherent as he pleases, while the world is still in tune with his message. But in the seventies, Oxford, at least, was no longer in tune with Pusey's message, and the effect of the veteran leader, trying to come to terms with Darwinism, struggling that is with new and stubborn forces he had no further power to bind, was tragic, or pathetic, as such things must always be. New Puseys arise in every century. The 'sons of authority' will never perish out of the earth. But the language changes, and the argument changes; and perhaps there are none more secretly impatient with the old prophet than those younger spirits of his own kind who are already stepping into his shoes

Far different was the effect of Liddon, in those days, upon us younger folk! The grace and charm of Liddon's personal presence were as valuable to his party in the seventies as that of Dean Stanley had been to Liberalism at an earlier stage. There was indeed much in common between the aspect and manner of the two men, though no likeness, in the strict sense, whatever. But the exquisite delicacy of feature, the brightness of eye, the sensitive play of expression, were alike in both. Saint Simon says of Fenelon: —

> He was well made, pale, with eyes that showered intelligence and fire — and with a physiognomy that no one who had seen it once could forget. It had both gravity and

polish, seriousness and gaiety; it spoke equally of the scholar, the bishop and the *grand seigneur*, and the final impression was one of intelligence, subtlety, grace, charm; above all, of dignity. One had to tear oneself from looking at him.

Many of those who knew Liddon, best could, I think, have adapted this language to him; and there is much in it that fitted Arthur Stanley.

But the love and gift for managing men was of course a secondary thing in the case of our great preacher. The University politics of Liddon and his followers are dead and gone; and as I have ventured to think, the intellectual force of Liddon's thoughts and arguments, as they are presented to us now on the printed page, is also a thing of the past. But the vision of the preacher, in those who saw it, is imperishable. The scene in St. Paul's has been often described, by none better than by Dr Liddon's colleague, Canon Scott Holland. But the Oxford scene, with all its old-world setting, was more touching, more interesting. As I think of it, I seem to be looking out from those dark seats under the undergraduates' gallery — where sat the wives of the Masters of Arts — at the crowded church, as it waited for the preacher. First, came the stir of the procession; the long line of Heads of Houses, in their scarlet robes as Doctors of Divinity, all but the two heretics, Pattison and Jowett, who walked in their plain black, and warmed my heart always thereby! And then, the Vice-Chancellor, with the 'pokers', and the preacher. All eyes were fixed on the slender willowy figure, and the dark head touched with silver. The bow to the Vice-Chancellor as they parted at the foot of the pulpit stairs, the mounting of the pulpit, the quiet look out over the Church, the Bidding Prayer, the voice — it was all part of an incomparable performance, which cannot be paralleled today.

The voice was high and penetrating, without much variety as I remember it; but of beautiful quality, and at times wonderfully moving. And what was still more appealing was the evident strain upon the speaker of his message. It wore him out visibly as he delivered it. He came down from the pulpit white and shaken, dripping with perspiration. Virtue had gone out of him. Yet his effort had never for a moment weakened his perfect self-control, the flow and finish of the long sentences, or the subtle inter-connection of the whole! One Sunday I remember in particular. Oxford had been saddened the day before by the somewhat sudden death of a woman whom everybody loved and respected, — Mrs Acland, the wife of the well-known doctor and professor. And Liddon with a wonderfully happy instinct, had added to his sermon a paragraph dealing with Mrs Acland's death, which held us all spellbound till the beautiful words died into silence. It was done with a fastidious literary taste that is rather French than English; and yet it came from the very heart of the speaker. Looking back through my many memories of Dr Liddon as a preacher, that tribute to a noble woman in death remains with me as the finest and most lasting of them all.

CHAPTER VIII

Early Married Life

How many other figures in that vanished Oxford world I should like to draw! — Mandell or 'Max' Creighton, our life-long friend, then just married to the wife who was his best comrade, while he lived, and since his death has made herself an independent force in English life. I first remember the future Bishop of London when I was fifteen, and he was reading history with my father on a Devonshire reading party. The tall, slight figure in blue serge, the red-gold hair, the spectacles, the keen features, and quiet commanding eye — I see them first against a background of rocks on Lynton shore. Then again a few years later, in his beautiful Merton rooms, with the vine-tendrils curling round the windows, the Morris paper, and the blue willow-pattern plates upon it, that he was surely the first to collect in Oxford. A luncheon party returns upon me — in Brasenose — where the brilliant Merton fellow and tutor, already a power in Oxford, first met his future wife; afterwards, their earliest married home in Oxford so near to ours, in the new region of the Parks; then the Vicarage on the Northumberland coast where Creighton wrestled with the north-country folk, with their virtues and their vices, drinking deep draughts thereby from the sources of human nature; where he read and wrote history, preparing for his *magnum opus*, the history of the Renaissance Popes; where he entertained his friends, brought up his children, and took mighty walks — always the same restless, energetic, practical pondering spirit, his mind set upon the Kingdom of God, and convinced that in and through the English Church a man might strive for the Kingdom as faithfully and honestly as anywhere else. The intellectual doubts and misgivings on the subject of taking orders, so common in the Oxford of his day, Creighton had never felt. His life had ripened to a rich maturity without — apparently — any of those fundamental conflicts which had scarred the lives of other men.

The fact set him strong contrast with another historian who was also our intimate friend — John Richard Green. When I first knew him, during my engagement to my husband, and seven years before the 'Short History' was published, he had just practically — through not formally — given up his orders. He had been originally curate to my husband's father, who held a London living, and the bond between him and his Vicar's family was singularly close and affectionate. After the death of the dear mother of the flock, a saintly and tender spirit, to whom Mr Green was much attached, he remained the faithful friend of all her children. How much I heard of him before I saw him! The expectation of our first meeting filled with trepidation. Should I be admitted too into that large and generous heart? — would he 'pass' the girl who had dared to be his 'boy's' fiancée? But after ten minutes all was well, and he was my friend no less than my husband's, to the last hour of his fruitful, suffering life.

And how much it meant, his friendship! It became plain very soon after our marriage that ours was to be a literary partnership. My first published story, written when I was eighteen, had appeared in the *Churchmen's Magazine* in 1870, and an article on the 'Poema del Cid', the first fruits of my Spanish browsings in the Bodleian, appeared in *Macmillan* early in 1872. My husband was already writing in the *Saturday Review* and other quarters, and had won his literary spurs as one of the three authors of that *jeu d'espirit* of no small fame in its day, the *Oxford Spectator*. Our three children arrived in 1874, 1876, and 1879, and all the time I was reading, listening, talking, and beginning to write in earnest — mostly for the Saturday Review. 'J.R.G.', as we loved to call him, took up my efforts with the warmest encouragement, tempered indeed by constant fears that I should become a hopeless bookworm and Dryasdust, yielding day after day to the mere luxury of reading, and putting nothing into shape!

Against this supposed tendency in me he railed perpetually. 'Anyone can read!' he would say; — 'anybody of decent wits can accumulate notes and references — the difficulty is to *write* — to make something!' And later on, when I was deep in Spanish chronicles, and thinking vaguely of a History of Spain, early Spain at any rate, he wrote almost impatiently — '*Begin* — and begin your *book*. Don't do "studies" and that sort of thing — one's book teaches one everything as one writes it'. I was reminded of that letter years later when I came across in Amiel's journal a passage almost to the same effect. 'It is by writing that one learns — it is by pumping that one draws water into one's well'. But in J.R.G.'s case the advice he gave his friend was carried out by himself through every hour of his short, concentrated life. 'He died learning', as the inscription on his grave testifies; but he also died *making*. In other words, the shaping, creative instinct wrestled in him with the powers of death through long years, and never deserted him to the very end. Who that has ever known the passion of the writer and the student can read without tears the record of his last months? He was already doomed when I first saw him 1871, for signs of tuberculosis had been discovered in 1869, and all through the seventies and till he died, in 1883, while he was writing the 'Short History', the expanded Library Edition in four volumes, and the two brilliant monographs on 'The Making of England' and 'The Conquest of England', the last of which was put together from his notes, and finished by his devoted wife and secretary after his death, he was fighting for his life, in order that he might finish his work. He was a dying man from January 1881, but he finished and published 'The Making of England' in 1882, and began 'The Conquest of England'. On February 25, ten days before his death, his wife told him that the end was near. He thought a little, and said that he had still something to say in his book 'which is worth saying. I will make a fight for it. I will do what I can, and I must have sleeping draughts for a week. After that it will not matter if they lose their effect.' He worked on a little longer — but on March 7 all was over. My husband had gone out to see him in February, and came home marvelling at the miracle of such life in death.

I have spoken of the wonderful stimulus and encouragement he could give to the young student. But he was no flatterer. No one could strike harder or swifter than he, when he chose.

It was to me — in his eager friendship for 'Humphry's' young wife — he first entrusted the task to that primer of English literature which afterwards Mr Stopford Brooke carried out with such astonishing success. But I was far too young for such a piece of work, and knew far too little. I wrote a beginning, however, and took it up to him when he was in rooms in Beaumont Street. He was entirely dissatisfied with it, and as gently and kindly as possible told me it wouldn't do, and that I must give it up.[1] Then throwing it aside, he began to walk up and down his room, sketching out how such a general outline of English Literature might be written and should be written. I sat by enchanted, all my natural disappointment charmed away. The knowledge, the enthusiasm, the *shaping* power of the frail human being moving there before me — with the slight emaciated figure, the great brow, the bright eyes; all the physical presence, instinct, aflame, with the intellectual and poetic passion which grew upon him as he traced the mighty stream of England's thought and song: — it was an experience never forgotten, one of those by which mind teaches mind, and the endless succession is carried on.

There is another memory from the early time, which comes back to me — of J.R.G. in Notre Dame. We were on our honeymoon journey, and we came across him in Paris. We went together to Notre Dame and there as we all lingered at the western end, looking up to the gleaming colour of the distant apse, the spirit came upon him. He began to describe what the Church had seen; coming down through the generations, from vision to vision. He spoke in a low voice, but without a pause or break, standing in deep shadow close to the western door. One scarcely saw him, and I almost lost the sense of his individuality. It seemed to be the very voice of History — Life telling of itself.

Liberty and the passion for liberty were the very breath of his life. In 1871 just after Commune, I wrote him a cry of pity and horror about the execution of Rossel, the 'heroic young Protestant', who had fought the Versaillais because they had made peace and prevented him from fighting the Prussians. J.R.G. replied that the only defence of a man who fo-

---

[1] Since writing these lines, I have been amused to discover the following reference in the brilliant biography of Stopford Brooke, by his son-in-law, Principal Jacks, to my unlucky attempt. 'The only advantage,' says Mr Brooke in his diary for May 8, 1889, 'the older writer has over the younger is that he knows what to leave out and has a juster sense of proportion. I remember that when Green wanted the Primer of English Literature to be done, Mrs —— asked if she might try her hand at it. He said "Yes," and she set to work. She took a fancy to *Beowulf*, and wrote twenty pages on it! At this rate the book would have run to a thousand pages.'

ught for the Commune was that he believed in it, which Rossel, by his own statement, did not.

> People like old Delescluze are more to my mind, men who believe, rightly or wrongly (in the ideas of '93), and cling to their faith through thirteen years of the hulks and Cayenne, who get their chance at last, fight, work, and then all is over know how to die — as Delescluze, with that grey head bared, and the old threadbare coat thrown open, walked quietly and without a word up to the fatal barricade.

His place in the ranks of history is high and safe. That was abundantly shown by the testimony of the large gathering of English scholars and historians at the memorial meeting held in his own college some years ago. He remains as one of the leaders of that school (there is of course another and strong one!) which holds that without imagination and personality a man had better not write history at all; since no recreation of the past is really possible without the kindling and welding force that a man draws from his own spirit.

But it is a friend that I desire — with undying love and gratitude — to commemorate him here. To my husband, to all the motherless family he had taken to his heart, he was affection and constancy itself. And as for me, just before the last visit that we paid him at Mentone in 1882, a year before he died, he was actually thinking out schemes for that history of early Spain which it seemed, both to him and me, I must at last begin, and was enquiring what help I could get from libraries on the Riviera during our stay with him. Then, when we came, I remember our talks in the little Villa St Nicholas — his sympathy, his enthusiasm, his unselfish help; while all the time he was wrestling with death for just a few more months in which to finish his own work. Both Lord Bryce and Sir Leslie Stephen have paid their tribute to this wonderful talk of his later years. 'No such talk,' says Lord Bryce, 'has been heard in our generation.' Of Madame de Stael it was said that she wrote her books out of the talk of the distinguished men who frequented her salon. Her own conversation was directed to evoking from the brains of others what she afterwards, as an artist, knew how to use better than they. Her talk — small blame to her! was plundering and acquisitive. But J.R.G.'s talk *gave* perpetually — admirable listener though he was. All that he had, he gave; so that our final thought of him is not that of the suffering invalid, the thwarted workman, the life cut short, but rather that of one who had richly done his part, and left in his friends' memories no mere pathetic appeal, but much more a bracing message for their own easier and longer lives.

Of the two other historians with whom my youth threw me into contact, Mr Freeman and Bishop Stubbs, I have some lively memories. Mr Freeman was first known to me, I think through 'Johnny', as he was wont to call J.R.G., whom he adored. Both he and J.R.G. were admirable letter-writers, and a small volume of their correspondence — much of it already published separately — if it could be put together — like that of Flaubert and George Sand — would make excellent reading for a future generation. In 1877 and 1878, when I was plunged in the history of West Gothic Kings, I had many letters from Mr Freeman, and never were letters about grave matters less grave. Take this outburst about a lady who had sent him some historical work to look at. He greatly liked and admired the lady; but her work drove him wild. 'I never saw anything like it for missing the point of everything . . . .

Then she has no notion of putting a sentence together, so that she said some things which I fancy she did not mean to say — as that "the beloved Queen Louisa of Prussia" was the mother of M. Theirs. When she said that the Duke of Orleans' horses an away "leaving two infant sons", it may have been so: I have no evidence either way.'

Again — 'I am going to send you the Spanish part of my Historical Geography. It will be very bad, but — when I don't know a thing I believe I generally know that I don't know it, and so manage to wrap it up in some vague phrase which if not right, may at least not be wrong. Thus I have always held that the nursery account of Henry VIII —

And Henry the Eighth was as fat as a pig —

is to be preferred to Froude's version. For, through certainly an inadequate account of the reign, it is true as far as it goes.

Once, certainly, we stayed at Somerleaze, and I retain the impression of a very busy, human, energetic man of letters, a good Churchman, and a good citizen, brimful of likes and dislikes, and waving his red beard often as a flag of battle in many a hot skirmish, especially with J.R.G., but always warm-hearted and generally placable — except in the case of James Anthony Froude. The feud between Freeman and Froude was, of course, a standing dish in the educated world of half a century ago. It may be argued that the Muse of History has not decided the quarrel quite according to justice; that Clio has shown herself something of a jade in the matter, as easily influenced by fair externals as a certain Helen was long ago. How many people now read the 'Norman Conquest' —except the few scholars who devote themselves to the same period? Whereas Froude's History, with all its sins, lives, and in my belief will long live, because the man who wrote it was a *writer*, and understood his art.

Of Bishop Stubbs, the greatest historical name surely in the England of the last half of the nineteenth century, I did not personally see much while we lived in Oxford and he was Regius Professor. He had no gifts — it was his chief weakness as a teacher — for creating a young school around him, setting one man to work on this job, and another on that, as has been done with great success in many instances abroad. He was too reserved, too critical, perhaps too sensitive. But he stood as a great influence in the background, felt if not seen. A word of praise from him meant everything; a word of condemnation, in his own subjects, settled the matter. I remember well, after I had written a number of articles on early Spanish Kings and Bishops, for a historical Dictionary, and they were already in proof, how on my daily visits to the Bodleian I began to be puzzled by the fact that some of the very obscure books I had been using were 'out' when I wanted them, or had been abstracted from my table by one of the sub-librarians. 'Joannes Biclarensis' — he was missing! Who in the world could want that obscure chronicle of an obscure period but myself? I began to envisage some hungry German *Privatdozent*, on his holiday, raiding my poor little subject, and my books, with a view to his Doctor's thesis. Then one morning, as I went in, I came across Dr Stubbs, with an ancient and portly volume under his arm. Joannes Biclarensis himself! — I knew it at once. The Professor gave me a friendly nod, and I saw a twinkle in eye as we passed. Going to my desk, I found another volume gone — this time the 'Acts of the Councils of Toledo'. So far as I knew, not the most ardent Churchman in Oxford felt at that time any absorbing interest in the Councils of Toledo. At any rate, I had been left in undisturbed possession of them for months. Evidently something was happening, and sat down to my work in bewilderment.

Then, on my way home, I ran into a fellow-worker for the Dictionary — a well-known don, and history tutor. 'Do you know what's happened?' he said in excitement: —'*Stubbs* has been going through our work! The Editor wanted his imprimatur before the final printing. Can't expect anybody but Stubbs to know all these things! My books are gone too.' We walked up to the Parks together in a common anxiety, like a couple of schooldays in for Smalls. Then in a few days the tension was over; my books were on my desk again; the Professor stopped me in the Broad with a smile, and the remark that Joannes Biclarensis was really quite an interesting fellow and I received a very friendly letter from the Editor of the Dictionary.

And, perhaps, I may be allowed, after these forty years, one more recollection, through I am afraid a proper reticence would suppress it! A little later, 'Mr Creighton' came to visit us, after his immigration to Embleton and the north; and I timidly gave him some lives of West Gothic Kings and Bishops to read. He read them — they were very long, and terribly minute — and put down the proofs, without saying much. Then he walked down to Oxford with my husband, and sent me back a message by him — 'Tell M. to go on. There is nobody but Stubbs doing such work in Oxford now.' The impulse given by such words may be imagined. But there were already causes at work why I should not 'go on'.

I shall have more to say presently about the work on the origins of modern Spain. It was the only thorough 'discipline' I ever had; it lasted about two years — years of incessant arduous work, and it led directly to the writing of 'Robert Elsmere'. But before and after, how full life was of other things! The joys of one's new home, of the children that began to patter about it, of every bit of furniture and blue pot it contained, each representing some happy *chasse* or special earning — of its garden of half an acre, where I used to feel as Hawthorne felt in the garden of the Concord Manse — amazement that Nature should take the trouble to produce things as big as vegetable marrows, or as surprising as scarlet runners that topped one's head, just that we might own and eat them. Then the life of the University town, with all those marked antagonisms I have described, those intellectual and religious movements, that were like the meeting currents of rivers in a lake; and the pleasure of new friendships, where everybody was equal, nobody was rich, and the intellectual average was naturally high. In those days too, a small group of women of whom I was one, were laying the foundations of the whole system of women's education in Oxford. Mrs Creighton and I, with Mrs Max Miller, were the secretaries and founders of the first organised series of lectures for women in the University town; I was the first secretary of Somerville Hall, and it fell to me, by chance, to suggest the name of the future college. My friends and I were all on fire for women's education, including women's medical education, and very emulous of Cambridge, where the movement was already far advanced.

But hardly any of us were at all on fire for women's suffrage, wherein the Oxford educational movement differed greatly from the Cambridge movement. The majority, certainly, of the group to which I belonged at Oxford were at that time persuaded that the development of women's power in the State — or rather, in such a state as England, with its far-reaching and Imperial obligations, resting ultimately on the sanction of war — should be on lines of its own. We believed that growth through Local Government, and perhaps through some special machinery for bringing the wishes and influence of women of all classes to bear on Parliament, other than the Parliamentary vote, was the real line of progress. However, I shall return to this subject on some future occasion, in connection with the intensified suffragist campaign which began about ten years ago (1907-8) and in which I took some part. I will only note here my first acquaintance with Mrs Fawcett. I see her so clearly as a fresh picturesque figure — in a green silk dress, and a necklace of amber beads, when she came down to Oxford in the mid-seventies to give a course of lectures in the series that Mrs Creighton and I were organising, and I remember well the atmosphere of sympathy and admiration which surrounded her, as she spoke to an audience in which many of us were well acquainted with the heroic story of Mr Fawcett's blindness, and of the part played by his wife in enabling him to continue his economic and Parliamentary work.

But life then was not all lectures! — nor was it all Oxford. There were vacations, and vacations generally meant for us some weeks at least of travel, even when pence were fewest. The Christmas vacation of 1874 we were in Paris. The weather was bitter, and we were lodged, for cheapness' sake, in an old-fashioned hotel, where the high-canopied beds with their mountainous duvets were very difficult to wake up in on a cold morning. But in spite of snow and sleet we filled our days to the brim. We took with us some introductions from Oxford — to Madame Mohl, the Renans, the Gaston Paris, the Boutmys, the Ribots, and from my Uncle Matthew, to the Scherers at Versailles. Monsieur Taine was already known to us, and it was at their house, on one of Madame Taine's Thursdays, that I first heard French conversation at its best. There was a young man there, dark-eyed, dark-haired, to whom I listened — not always able to follow the rapid French in which he and two other men were discussing some literary matter of the moment, but conscious, for the first time, of what the conversation of intellectual equals might be, if it were always practised as the French are trained to practise it from their mother's milk, by the influence of a long tradition. The young man was M. Paul Bourget, who had not yet begun to write novels, while his literary and philosophical essays seemed rather to mark him out as the disciple of M. Taine than as the Catholic protagonist he was soon to become. M. Bourget did not then speak English, and my French conversation, which had been wholly learnt from books, had a way at that time — and alack, has still — of breaking down under me, just as one reached the thing one really wanted to say. So that I did not attempt to do more than listen. But I seem to remember that those with whom he talked were M. Francis Charmes, then a writer on the staff of the *Débats*, and afterwards the editor of the *Revue des deux Mondes* in succession to M. Brunetière; and M. Gaston Paris, the brilliant head of French philology at the Collège de France. What struck me then, and through all the new experiences, and new acquaintanceships of our

Christmas fortnight, was that strenuous and passionate intensity of the French temper, which foreign nations so easily lose sight of, but which, in truth, is as much part of the French nature as their gaiety, or as what seems to us their frivolity. The war of 1870, the Commune, were but three years behind them. Germany had torn from them Alsace-Lorraine; she had occupied Paris; and their own Jacobins had ruined and burnt what even Germany had spared. In the minds of the intellectual class there lay deep, on the one hand, a determination to rebuild France, on the other to avenge her defeat. The blackened ruins of the Tuileries and of the Cour des Comptes still disfigured a city which grimly kept them there as a warning against anarchy; while the statue of the Ville de Strasbourg in the Place de la Concorde had worn for three years the funeral garlands, which, as France confidently hopes from the peace that must end this war, will soon, after nearly half a century, give way to the rejoicing tricolour. At the same time reconstruction was everywhere beginning — especially in the field of education. The corrupt, political influence of the Empire, which had used the whole educational system of the country for the purpose of keeping itself and its supporters in power, was at an end. The reorganised 'Ecole Normale' was becoming a source of moral and mental strength among thousands of young men and women; and the École des Sciences Politiques', the joint work of Taine, Renan, and M. Boutmy, its first director, was laying foundations, whereof the results are to be seen conspicuously today, French character, French resource, French patience, French science, as this hideous war has revealed them.

I remember an illuminating talk with M. Renan himself on this subject during our visit. We had never yet seen him, and we carried an introduction to him from Max Müller, our neighbour and friend in Oxford. We found him alone, in a small working room crowded with books, at the Collège de France. Madame Renan was away, and he had abandoned his large library for something more easily warmed. My first sight of him was something of a shock — of the large ungainly figure, the genial face, with its spreading cheeks and humorous eyes, the big head, with its scanty locks of hair. I think he felt an amused and kindly interest in the two young folk from Oxford, who had come as pilgrims to his shrine, and realising that our French was not fluent and our shyness great, he filled up the time — and gaps — by a monologue, lit up by many touches of Renanesque humour, on the situation in France.

First, as to literature — 'No — we have no genius, no poets or writers of the first rank just now — at least so it seems to me. But we *work* — *nous travaillons beaucoup! Ce sera notre salut.*' It was the same as to politics. He had no illusions and few admirations. 'The Chamber is full of mediocrities. We are governed by *avocats* and *pharmaciens*. But at least *ils ne feront pas la guerre!*'

He smiled, but there was that in the smile and the gesture which showed the smart within; from which not even his scholar's philosophy, with its ideal of a world of cosmopolitan science, could protect him. At that moment he was inclined to despair of his country. The mad adventure of the Commune had gone deep into his soul; and there were still a good many pacifying years to run, before he could talk of his life as 'cette charmante promenade / travers la realité' — for which, with all it had contained of bad and good, he yet thanked the Gods. At that time he was fifty-one; he had just published 'L'Antichrist', the most brilliant of all the volumes of the 'Origines'; and he was not yet a member of the French Academy.

I turn to a few other impressions from that distant time. One night we were in the 'Theatre Francais', and Racine's 'Phãdre' was to be given. I at least had never been in the Maison de Moliãre before, and in such matters as acting I possessed, at twenty-three, only a very raw and country-cousinish judgement. There had been a certain amount of talk in Oxford of a new and remarkable French actress, but neither of us had really any idea of what was before us. Then the play began. And before the first act was over, we were sitting bent forward, gazing at the stage in an intense and concentrated excitement, such as I can scarcely remember ever feeling again, except perhaps when the same actress played 'Hernani' in London for the first time in 1884. Sarah Bernhardt was then — December 1874 — in the first full tide of her success. She was of a ghostly and willowy slenderness. Each of the great speeches seemed actually to rend the delicate frame. When she fell back after one of them, you felt an actual physical terror lest there should not be enough life left in the slight dying woman to let her speak again. And you craved for yet more and more of the *voix d'or* which rang in one's ears as the frail yet exquisite instrument of a mighty music. Never before had it been brought home to me what dramatic art might be, or the power of the French Alexandrine. And never did I come so near quarrelling with 'Uncle Matt', as when, on our return, after having heard my say about the genius of Sarah Bernhardt, he patted my hand indulgently with the remark — 'But my dear child — you see — you never saw Rachel!'

As we listened to Sarah Bernhardt, we were watching the outset of a great career which had still some forty years to run. On another evening we made acquaintance with a little old woman who had been born in the first year of the Terror, who had spent her first youth in the salon of Madame Récamier, valued there, above all, for her difficult success in drawing a smile from that old and melancholy genius, Chateaubriand; and had since held a salon on her own, which deserves a special place in the history of salons. For it was held, according to the French tradition, and in Paris, by an Englishwoman. It was, I think, Max Müller, who gave us an introduction to Madame Mohl. She sent us an invitation to one of her Friday evenings, and we duly mounted to the top of the old house in the Rue du Bac, which she made famous for so long. As we entered the room I saw a small dishevelled figure, grey-headed, crouching beside a grate with a kettle in her hand. It was Madame Mohl — then eighty-one — who was trying to make the fire burn. She just raised herself to greet us, with a swift investigating glance; and then returned to her task of making the tea, in which I endeavoured to help her. But she did not like to be helped; and I soon subsided into my usual listening and watching, which, perhaps, for one who at that time was singularly immature in all social respects, was the best policy. I seem still to see the tall substantial form of Julius Mohl standing behind her, with various other elderly men, who were no doubt famous folk, if one had known their names. And in the corner was the Spartan tea-table, with its few biscuits, which stood for the plain living whereon was nourished the high thinking and high talking which had passed through these rooms. Guizot, Cousin, Ampãre, Fauriel, Mignet, Lamartine, all the great men of the middle century had talked there; not — in general, the poets and the artists, but the politicians, the historians, and the *savants*. The little Fairy Blackstick, incredibly old, kneeling on the floor, with the shabby dress and tousled grey hair, had made a part of the central scene in France, through the Revolution, the reign of the Citizen king, and the Second Empire — playing the role, through it all, of a good friend of freedom. If only one had heard her talk! But there were few people in the room, and we were none of us inspired. I must sadly put down that Friday evening among the lost opportunities of life. For Mrs Simpson's biography of Madame Mohl shows what a wealth of wit and memory there was in that small head! Her social sense, her humour never deserted her, through she lived to be ninety. When she was dying her favourite cat, a tom, leaped on her bed. Her eyes lit up as she feebly stroked him. 'He is so distinguished!' she whispered. 'But his wife is not distinguished at all. He doesn't know it. But many men are like that.' It was one of the last sayings of an expert in the human scene.

Madame Mohl was twenty-one when the Allies entered Paris in 1814. She had lived with those to whom the fall of the 'Ancien Régime', the Terror, and the Revolutionary wars had been the experience of middle life. As I look back to the salon in the Rue du Bac, which I saw in such a flash, yet where my hand rested for a moment in that of Madame Récamier's pet and protegée, I am reminded too that I once saw, at the Forsters, in 1869, when I was eighteen, the Dr Lushington who was Lady Byron's adviser and confidant when she left her husband, and who, as a young man, had stayed with Pitt, and ridden out with Lady Hester Stanhope. One night, in Eccleston Square, we assembled for dinner in the ground floor library instead of the drawing-room, which was upstairs. I slipped in late, and saw in an armchair, his hands resting on a stick, an old, white-haired man. When dinner was announced — if I remember right — he was wheeled in to the dining room, to a place beside my aunt. I was too far away to hear him talk, and he went home after dinner. But it was one of the guests of the evening, a friend of his, who said to me — with a kindly wish, no doubt, to trill the girl just 'out' — 'You ought to remember Dr Lushington! What are you? — Eighteen? — and he is eighty-six. He was in the theatre on the night when the news reached London of Marie Antoinette's execution, and he can remember, though he was only a boy of eleven, how it was given out from the stage, and how the audience instantly broke up.'

Dr Lushington of course, carries one further back than Madame Mohl. He was born in 1782, four years after the deaths of Rousseau and Voltaire, two years before the death of Diderot. He was only six years younger than Lady Hester Stanhope, whose acquaintance he made during the three years — 1803-1806 — when she was keeping house for her uncle, William Pitt.

But on my right hand at the same dinner party there sat a guest who was to mean a good deal more to me personally than Dr Lushington — young Mr George Otto Trevelyan, as he then was, Lord Macaulay's nephew, and already the brilliant author of 'A Competition Wallah', 'Ladies in Parliament', and much else. We little thought, as we talked, that after thirty-five years, his son was to marry my daughter.

CHAPTER IX

The Beginning of 'Robert Elsmere'

If these are to be recollections of a writer, in which perhaps other writers by profession, as well as the more general public, may take some interest, I shall perhaps be forgiven if I give some account of the processes of thought and work which led to the writing of my first successful novel 'Robert Elsmere'.

It was in 1878 that a new editor was appointed for one of the huge well-known volumes, in which under the égis of the John Murray of the day, the *Nineteenth Century* was accustomed to concentrate its knowledge — classical, historical, and theological — in convenient, if not exactly handy form. Dr Wace, now a Canon of Canterbury, was then an indefatigable member of *The Times* staff. Yet he undertook this extra work, and carried it bravely through. He came to Oxford to beat up recruits for Smith's 'Dictionary of Christian Biography', a companion volume to that of 'Classical Biography,' and dealing with the first seven centuries of Christianity. He had been told that I had been busying myself with early Spain, and he came to me to ask whether I would take the Spanish lives for the period, especially those concerned with the West-Goths in Spain; while at the same time he applied to various Oxford historians for work on the Ostrogoths and the Franks.

I was much tempted but I had a good deal to consider. The French and Spanish reading it involved was no difficulty. But the power of reading Latin rapidly, both the degraded Latin of the fifth and sixth centuries, and the learned Latin of the sixteenth and seventeenth was essential; and I had only learnt some Latin since my marriage, and was by no means at home in it. I had long since found out too, in working at the Spanish Literature of the eleventh to the fourteenth century, that the only critics and researchers worth following in that field were German; and though I had been fairly well grounded in German at school, and had read a certain amount, the prospect of a piece of work which meant, in the main, Latin texts and German commentaries, was rather daunting. The well-trained woman student of the present day would have felt probably no such qualms. But I had not been well trained; and the Pattison standards of what work should be stood like dragons in the way.

However, I took the plunge, and I have always been grateful to Canon Wace. The sheer, hard, brain-stretching work of the two or three years which followed I look back to now with delight. It altered my whole outlook, and gave me horizons and sympathies that I have never lost, however dim all the positive knowledge brought me by the work has long since become. The strange thing was that out of the work which seemed both to myself and others to mark the abandonment of any foolish hopes of novel writing I might have cherished as a girl, 'Robert Elsmere' should have arisen. For after my marriage I made various attempts to write fiction. They were clearly failures. J.R.G. dealt very faithfully with me on the subject; and I could only conclude that the instinct to tell stories which had been so strong in me as a child and girl, meant nothing, and was to be suppressed. I did indeed write a story for my children, which came out in 1880 — 'Milly and Olly'; but that wrote itself and was a mere transcript of their little lives.

And yet I venture to think it was, after all, the instinct for 'making out', as the Brontës used to call their own wonderful story-telling passion, which rendered this historical work so enthralling to me. Those far-off centuries became veritably alive to me — the Arian kings fighting an ever-losing battle against the ever-encroaching power of the Catholic Church, backed by the still lingering and still potent ghost of the Roman Empire; the Catholic Bishops gathering, sometimes through winter snow, to their Councils at Seville and Toledo; the centres of culture in remote corners of the peninsula, where men lived with books and holy things, shrinking from the wild life around them, and handing on the precious remnants and broken traditions of the older classical world; the mutual scorn of Goth and Roman; martyrs, fanatics, heretics, nationalists and cosmopolitans; and, rising upon, enveloping them all, as the seventh and eight centuries drew on, the tide of Islam, and the menace of that time when the great church of Cordova should be half a mosque and half a Christian cathedral.

I lived, indeed, in that old Spain, while I was at work in the Bodleian and at home. To spend hours and days over the signatures to an obscure Council, identifying each name so far as the existing materials allowed, and attaching to it some fragment of human interest, so that gradually something of a picture emerged, as of a thing lost and recovered — dredged up from the deeps of time — that, I think, was the joy of it all.

I see, in memory, the small Oxford room, as it was on a winter evening between nine and midnight, my husband in one corner preparing his college lectures, or writing a 'Saturday middle'; my books and I in another; the reading-lamp, always to me a symbol of peace and 'recollection'; the Oxford quiet outside. And yet, it was not so tranquil as it looked. For beating round us all the time were the spiritual winds of an agitated day. The Oxford of thought was not quiet; it was divided, as I have shown, by sharper antagonisms and deeper feuds than exist today. Darwinism was penetrating everywhere; Pusey was preaching against its effects on belief; Balliol stood for an unfettered history and criticism, Christ Church for authority and creeds; Renan's 'Origines' were still coming out, Strauss's last book also; my uncle was publishing 'God and the Bible' in succession to 'Literature and Dogma'; and 'Supernatural Religion' was making no small stir. And meanwhile what began to interest and absorb me were *sources-testimony*. To what — to whom — did it all go back? — This great story of early civilisation, early religion, which modern men could write and interpret so differently?

And on this question, the writers and historians of four early centuries, from the fifth to the ninth, as I lived with them, seemed to throw a partial, but yet a searching light. I have expressed it in 'Robert Elsmere'. Langham and Robert, talking in the Squire's library on Robert's plans for a history of Gaul during the breakdown of the Empire and the emergence of modern France, come to the vital question: 'History depends on *testimony*. What is the nature and virtue of testimony at given times?' In other words, did the man of the third century understand, or report, or interpret facts in the same way as the man of the sixteenth or the nineteenth? And if not, what are the differences? — and what are the deductions to be made from them?

Robert replies that his work has not yet dug deep enough to make him the question.

'It is enormously important, I grant — enormously,' he repeated reflectively.

On which Langham says to himself, though not to Elsmere, that the whole of 'orthodoxy' is in it, and depends on it.

And in a later passage, when Elsmere is mastering the 'Quellen' of his subject, he expresses himself with bewilderment to Catherine on this same subject of 'testimony'. He is immersed in the chronicles and biographies of the fifth and sixth centuries. Every history, every biography is steeped in marvel. A man divided by only a few years from the bishop or saint whose life he is writing, reports the most fantastic miracles. What is the psychology of it all? The whole age seems to Robert 'non-sane'. And, meanwhile, across and beyond the mediaeval centuries, behind the Christian era itself, the modern student looks back inevitably, involuntary, to certain Greeks and certain Latins, who 'represent a forward strain', who intellectually 'belong to a world ahead of them'. '*You* —' he says to them — '*you* are really my kindred.'

That, after all, I tried to express this intellectual experience — which was of course an experience of my own — not in critical or historical work, but in a novel, that is to say in terms of human life, was the result of an incident which occurred towards the close of our lives in Oxford. It was not long after the appearance of 'Supernatural Religion', and the rise of that newer school of Biblical criticism in Germany expressed by the once honoured name of Dr Harnack. Darwinian debate in the realm of natural science was practically over. The spread of evolutionary ideas in the fields of history and criticism was the real point of interest. Accordingly, the University pulpit was often filled by men endeavouring 'to fit a not very exacting science to a very grudging orthodoxy'; and the heat of an ever-strengthening controversy was in the Oxford air.

In 1881, as it happened, the Bampton Lectures were preached by the Rev John Wordsworth, the Fellow and Tutor of Brasenose, and, later, Bishop of Salisbury. He and my husband — who, before our marriage, was also a Fellow of Brasenose — were still tutorial colleagues, and I therefore knew him personally, and his first wife, the brilliant daughter of the beloved Bodley's Librarian of my day, Mr Coxe. We naturally attended Mr Wordsworth's first Bampton. He belonged, very strongly, to what I have called the Christ Church camp; while we belonged, very strongly, to the Balliol camp. But no one could fail to respect John Wordsworth deeply; while his connection with his great-uncle, the poet, to whom he bore a strong personal likeness, gave him always a glamour in my eyes. Still I remember going with a certain shrinking; and it was the shock of indignation excited in me by the sermon which led directly — though after seven intervening years — to 'Robert Elsmere'.

The sermon was on 'The present unsettlement in religion'; and it connected the 'unsettlement' definitely with 'sin'. The 'moral causes of unbelief,' said the preacher, 'were (1) prejudice; (2) severe claims of religion; (3) intellectual faults, especially indolence, coldness, recklessness, pride and avarice.'

The sermon expounded and developed this outline with great vigour, and every sceptical head received its due buffeting in a tone and fashion that now scarcely survives. I sat in the darkness under the gallery. The preacher's fine ascetic face was plainly visible in the middle light of the church; and while the confident priestly voice flowed on, I seemed to see, grouped around the speaker, the forms of those, his colleagues and contemporaries, the patient scholars and thinkers of the Liberal host, Stanley, Jowett, Green of Balliol, Lewis Nettleship, Henry Sidgewick, my uncle, whom he in truth — through perhaps not consciously — was attacking. My heart was hot within me. How could one show England what was really going on in her midst? Surely the only way was through imagination; through a picture of actual life and conduct; through something as 'simple, sensuous, passionate' as one could make it. Who and what were the persons of whom the preacher gave this grotesque account? What was their history? How had their thoughts and doubts come to be? What was the effect of them on conduct?

The *immediate* result of the sermon however was a pamphlet called 'Unbelief and Sin: a Protest addressed to those who attended the Bampton Lecture of Sunday, March 6th'. It was rapidly written and printed, and was put up in the windows of a well-known shop in the High Street. In the few hours of its public career, it enjoyed a very lively sale. Then an incident — quite unforeseen by its author — slit its little life! A well-known clergyman walked in to the shop and asked for the pamphlet. He turned it over, and at once pointed out to one of the partners of the firm in the shop that there was no printer's name upon it. The booksellers who had produced the pamphlet, no doubt with an eye to their large clerical *clientále*, had omitted the printer's name, and the omission was illegal. Pains and penalties were threatened, and the frightened booksellers at once withdrew the pamphlet, and sent word of what had happened to my much astonished self, who had neither noticed the omission, nor was aware of the law. But Dr Foulkes, the clergyman in question — no one that knew the Oxford of my day will have forgotten his tall militant figure, with the defiant white hair, and the long clerical coat, as it haunted the streets of the University! — had only stimulated the tare he seemed to have rooted up. For the pamphlet thus easily suppressed was really the germ of the later book; in that, without attempting direct argument, it merely sketched two types of character: that either knows no doubts or has suppressed them, and the character that fights its stormy way to truth.

The latter was the first sketch of 'Robert Elsmere'. That same evening, at a College party, Professor Green came up to me. I had sent him the pamphlet the night before, and had not yet had a word from him. His kind brown eyes smiled upon me as he said a hearty 'thank you', adding 'a capital piece of work', or something to that effect; after which my spirits were quite equal to telling him the story of Dr Foulkes' raid.

. . . .

The year 1880-81, however, was marked for me by three other events of quite a different kind: Monsieur Renan's visit to Oxford, my husband's acceptance of a post on the staff of *The Times*, and a visit that we paid to the W.E. Forsters in Ireland, in December 1880, at almost the blackest moment of the Irish land-war.

Of Renan's visit I have mingled memories — all pleasant, but some touched with comedy. Gentle Madame Renan came with her famous husband and soon won all hearts. Oxford in mid-April was then, as always, dream of gardens just coming into leaf, enchasing buildings of a silvery grey, and full to the brim of the old walls with the early blossom — almond, or cherry, or flowering currant. M. Renan was delivering the Hibbert Lectures in London, and came down to stay for a long weekend with our neighbours, the Max Müllers. Dr Hatch was then preaching the Bampton Lectures, that first admirable series of his on the debt of the Church to Latin organisation, and M. Renan attended one of them. He had himself just published 'Marc Aurele', and Dr Hatch's subject was closely akin to that of his own Hibbert Lectures. I remember seeing him emerge from the porch of St Mary's his strange triangular face pleasantly dreamy. 'You were interested?' Said someone at his elbow. '*Mais oui!*' said M. Renan, smiling, 'he might have given my lecture, and I might have preached his sermon! (*Nous aurions du changer de cahiers!*)' Renan in the pulpit of Pusey, Newman, and Burgon, would indeed have been a spectacle of horror to the ecclesiastical mind. I remember once, many years after, following the *parroco* of Castel Gandolfo, through the dreary and deserted rooms of the Papal villa, where, before 1870, the Popes used to make villegiatura, on that beautiful ridge overlooking the Alban lake. All the decoration of the villa seemed to me curiously tawdry and mean. But suddenly my attention was arrested by a great fresco covering an entire wall. It represented the triumph of the Papacy over the infidel of all dates. A Pope sat enthroned, wearing the triple crown, with angels hovering overhead; and in a huge brazier at his feet, burnt the writings of the world's heretics. The blazing volumes were inscribed — Arius — Luther — Voltaire — *Renan!*

We passed on through the empty rooms, and the *parroco* locked the door behind us. I thought, as we walked away, of the summer light fading from the childish picture, painted probably not long before the entry of the Italian troops into Rome, and of all that was symbolised by it and the deserted villa, to which the 'prisoner of the Vatican' no longer returns. But at least Rome had given Ernest Renan no mean place among her enemies — Arius, Luther, Voltaire — *Renan!*

But in truth, Renan, personally, was not the enemy of any church, least of all the great Church which had trained his youth. He was a born scholar and thinker, in temper extremely gentle and scrupulous, and with a sense of humour, or rather irony, not unlike that of Anatole France, who has learnt much from him. There was of course a streak in him of that French paradox, that impish trifling with things fundamental, which the English temperament dislikes and resents; as when he wrote the 'Abbesse de Jouarre', or threw out the whimsical doubt in a passing sentence of one of his latest books, whether, after all, his life of labour and self-denial had been worthwhile, and whether, if he had lived the life of an Epicurean, like Théophile Gautier, he might not have got more out of the existence. 'He was really a good and great man,' said Jowett, writing after his death. But 'I regret that he wrote at the end of his life that strange drama about the Reign of Terror.'

There are probably few of M. Renan's English admirers who do not share the regret. At the same time, there, for all to see, is the long life as it was lived — of the ever-toiling scholar and thinker, the devoted husband and brother, the admirable friend. And certainly, during the Oxford visit I remember, M. Renan was at his best. He was in love — apparently! — with Oxford, and his charm, his gaiety played over all that we presented to him. I recall him at Wadham Gardens, wandering in a kind of happy dream —'Ah, if one had only such places as this to work in, in France! What pages — and how perfect! — one might write here!' Or again, in a different scene, at luncheon in our little house in the Parks, when Oxford was showing, even more than usual, its piteous inability to talk decently to the great man in his own tongue. It is true that he neither understood ours — in conversation — nor spoke a word of it. But that did not at all mitigate our own shame — and surprise! For at that time, in Oxford world proper, everybody, probably, read French habitually and many of us thought we spoke it. But a mocking spirit suggested to one of the guests at this luncheon party — an energetic historical tutor — the wish to enlighten M. Renan as to how the University was governed, the intricacies of Convocation, and Congregation, the

Hebdomadal Council, and all the rest. The other persons present fell at first breathlessly silent watching the gallant but quite hopeless adventure. Then, in sheer sympathy with a good man in trouble, one after another, we rushed in to help, till the constitution of the University must have seemed indeed a thing of Bedlam to our smiling but much puzzled guest; and all our cheeks were red. But M Renan cut the knot. Since he could not understand, and we could not explain, what the constitution of Oxford University *was*, he suavely took up his parable as to what it should be. He drew the ideal University, as it were, in the clouds; clothing his notion, we, he went on, in so much fun and so much charm, that his English hosts more than forgot their own defeat in his success. The little scene has always remained with me as a crowning instance of the French genius for conversation. Throw what obstacles in the way you please; it will surmount them all.

To judge however from M. Renan's letter to his friend, M. Berthelot, written from Oxford on this occasion, he was not as much pleased as we thought he was, or as we were with him. He says: 'Oxford is the strangest relic of the past, the type of living death. Each of its colleges is a terrestrial paradise, but a deserted Paradise.' (I see from the date that the visit took place in the Easter vacation!) And he describes the education given as 'purely humanist and clerical', administered to à gilded youth that comes to chapel in surplices. There is an almost total absence of the scientific spirit'. And the letter further contains a mild gibe at All Souls, for its absentee Fellows. 'The lawns are admirable, and the Fellows eat up the college revenues, hunting and shooting up and down England. Only one of them works — my kind host, Max Muller.'

At that moment the list of the Fellows of All Souls contained the names of men who have since rendered high service to England; and M. Renan was probably not aware that the drastic reforms introduced by the two great University Commissions of 1854 and 1857 had made the sarcastic picture he drew for his friend not a little absurd. No doubt a French intellectual will always feel that the mind-life of England is running at a slower pace than that of his own country. But if Renan had worked for a year in Oxford, the old priestly training in him, based so solidly on the moral discipline of St Nicolas and St Sulpice, would have become more aware of much else. I like to think that he would have echoed the verdict on the Oxford undergraduate of a young and brilliant Frenchman, who spent much time at Oxford, fifteen years later. 'There is no intellectual élite here so strong as ours (i.e. among French students),' says M. Jacques Bardoux — 'but they undoubtedly have a political élite, and a much rarer thing, a moral élite . . . . What an environment! — and how full is this education of moral stimulus and force!'

Has not every word of this been justified to the letter by the experience of the war?

After the present cataclysm, we know very well that we shall have to improve and extend our higher education. Only, in building up the new, let us not lose grip upon the irreplaceable things of the old!

It was not long after M. Renan's visit that, just as we were starting for a walk on a May afternoon, the second post brought my husband a letter which changed our lives. It contained a suggestion that my husband should take work on *The Times* as a member of the editorial staff. We read it in amazement, and I walked on to Port Meadow. It was a fine day. The river was alive with boats; in the distance rose the towers and domes of the beautiful city; and the Oxford magic blew about us in the summer wind. It seemed impossible to leave the dear Oxford life! All the drawbacks and difficulties of the new proposal presented themselves; hardly any of the advantages. As for me, I was convinced we must and should refuse, and I went to sleep in that conviction.

But the mind travels far — and mysteriously — in sleep. With the first words that my husband and I exchanged in the morning, we knew that the die was cast, and that our Oxford days were over.

The rest of the year was spent in preparation for the change; and in the Christmas vacation of 1880-81 my husband wrote his first 'leaders' for the paper. But before that we went for a week to Dublin to stay with the Forsters, at the Chief Secretary's Lodge.

A visit I shall never forget! It was the first of the two terrible winters my uncle spent in Dublin as Chief Secretary, and the struggle with the Land League was at its height. Boycotting, murder and outrage filled the news of every day. Owing to the refusal of the Liberal Government to renew the Peace Preservation Act when they took office in 1880 — a disastrous but perhaps intelligible mistake — the Chief Secretary, when we reached Dublin, was facing an agrarian and political revolt of the most determined character, with nothing but the ordinary law, resting on juries and evidence, as his instrument — an instrument which the Irish Land League had taken good care to shatter in his hands. Threatening letters were flowing in upon both himself and my godmother; and the tragedy of 1882, with the revelations as to the various murder plots of the time, to which it led, were soon to show how terrible was the state of the country, and how real the danger in which he personally stood. But none the less social life had to be carried on; entertainments had to be given; and we went over, if I remember right, for the two Christmas balls to be given by the Chief Secretary and the Viceroy. On myself, fresh from the quiet Oxford life, the Irish spectacle, seen from such a point of view, produced an overwhelming impression. And the dancing, the visits and dinner parties, the keeping up of a brave social show — quite necessary and right under the circumstances! — began to seem to me, after only twenty-four hours, like some pageant seen under a thunder-cloud.

Mr Forster had then little more than five years to live. He was on the threshold of the second year of his Chief Secretaryship. During the first year he had faced the difficulties of the position in Ireland, and the perpetual attacks of the Irish Members in Parliament, with a physical nerve and power still intact. I can recall my hot sympathy with him during 1880, while with one hand he was fighting the Land League, and with the other — a fact never sufficiently recognised — giving all the help he could to the preparation of Mr Gladstone's second Land Act. The position then was hard, sometimes heartbreaking; but it was not beyond his strength. The second year wore him out. The unlucky Protection Act — an experiment for which the Liberal Cabinet and even its Radical Members, Mr Bright and Mr Chamberlain, were every whit as chargeable as himself — imposed a personal responsibility on him for every case out of the many hundreds of prisoners made under the Act, which was in itself intolerable. And while he tried in front to dam back the flood of Irish outrage, English Radicalism at his heels was making the task impossible. What he was doing satisfied nobody, least of all himself. The official and land-owning classes in Ireland, the Tories in England, raged, because, in spite of the Act, outrage continued; the Radical party in the country, which had always disliked the Protection Act, and the Radical press were on the lookout for every sign of failure; while the daily struggle in the House with the Irish Members while Parliament was sitting, in addition to all the rest, exhausted a man on whose decision important executive Acts, dealing really with a state of revolution, were always depending. All through the second year, as it seemed to me, he was overwhelmed by a growing sense of a monstrous and insoluble problem, to which no one, through nearly another forty years — not Mr Gladstone with his Home Rule Acts, as we were soon to see, nor Mr Balfour's wonderful brainpower sustained by a unique temperament — was to find the true key. It is not found yet. Twenty years of Tory government practically solved the Land Question, and agricultural Ireland has begun to be rich. But the past year has seen an Irish rebellion; a Home Rule Act has at last, after thirty years, been passed, and is dead before its birth; while at the present moment an Irish Convention is sitting[1] Thirty-six years have gone since my husband and I walked with William Forster through the Phœnix Park, over the spot where, a year later, Lord Frederick Cavendish and Mr Burke were murdered. And still the Æschylean 'curse' goes on, from life to life, from Government to Government. When will the Furies of the past become the 'kind goddesses' of the future — and the Irish and English peoples build them a shrine of reconciliation?

With such thoughts one looks back over the past. Amid its darkness, I shall always see the pathetic figure of William Forster, the man of Quaker training, at grips with murder and anarchy; the man of sensitive, affectionate spirit, weighed down under the weight of rival appeals, now from the side of democracy, now from the side of authority; bitterly conscious, as an English Radical, of his breach with Radicalism; still more keenly sensitive, as a man responsible for the executive government of a country in which the foundations had given way, to that atmosphere of cruelty and wrong in which the Land League moved, and to the hideous instances poured every day into his ears.

He bore it for more than a year after we saw him in Ireland at his thankless work. It was our first year in London, and we were near enough to watch closely the progress of his fight. But it was a fight not to be won. The spring of 1882 saw his resignation — on May 2 — followed on May 6 by the Phoenix Park murders and the long and gradual disintegration of the powerful ministry of 1880, culminating in the Home Rule disaster of 1886. Mr Churchill in the Life of his father, Lord Randolph, says of Mr Forester's resignation, 'he passed out of the Ministry to become during the rest of Parliament one of its most dangerous and vigilant opponents.' The physical change indeed, caused by the Irish struggle, which was for a time painfully evident to the House of Commons, seemed to pass away with rest and travel. The famous attack he made on Parnell in the spring of 1883, as the responsible promoter of outrage in Ireland, showed certainly no lack of power — rather an increase. I happened to be in the House the following day, to hear Parnell's reply. I remember my uncle's taking me down with him to the House, and begging a seat for me in Mrs Brand's gallery. The figure of Parnell — the speech, nonchalant, terse, defiant, without a single grace of any kind — his hands in the pockets of his coat — and the tense silence of the crowded House, remain vividly with me. Afterwards my uncle came upstairs for me, and we descended towards Palace Yard through various side passages. Suddenly a door, communicating with the House itself, opened in front of us, and Parnell came out. My uncle pressed my arm, and we held back, while Parnell passed by, sombrely absorbed, without betraying by the smallest movement or gesture any recognition of my uncle's identity.

In other matters — Gordon, Imperial Federation, the Chairmanship of the Manchester Ship Canal, and the rest — William Forster showed,

---

[1] These words were written in the winter of 1917. At the present moment (June 1918) we have just seen the deportation of the Sinn Feiners, and are still expecting yet another Home Rule Bill.

up till 1885, what his friends fondly hoped was the promise of renewed and successful work. But in reality he never recovered Ireland. The mark of those two years had gone too deep. He died in April 1886, just before the introduction of the Home Rule Bill, and I have always on the retina of the inward eye the impression of a moment at the western door of Westminster Abbey, after the funeral service. The flower-heaped coffin had gone through. My aunt and her adopted children followed it. After them came Mr Gladstone, with other members of the Cabinet. At the threshold Mr Gladstone moved forward, and took my aunt's hand, bending over it bareheaded. Then she went with the dead, and he turned away, towards the House of Commons. To those of us who remembered what the relations of the dead and the living had once been, and how they had parted, here was a peculiar pathos in the little scene.

A few days later Mr Gladstone brought in the Home Rule Bill, and the two stormy months followed, which ended in the Liberal Unionist split, and the defeat of the Bill on June 7 by thirty votes, and were the prelude to the twenty years of Tory Government. If William Forster had lived, there is no doubt that he must have played a leading part in the struggles of that and subsequent sessions. In 1888 Mr Balfour said to my husband, after some generous words on the part played by Forster in those two terrible years — 'Forster's loss was irreparable to us (i.e. to the Unionist party). If he and Fawcett had lived, Gladstone could not have made head.'

It has been, I think, widely recognised by men of all parties in recent years that personally William Forster bore the worst of the Irish day, whatever men may think of his policy. But after all, it is not for this, primarily, that England remembers him. His monument is everywhere — in the schools that have covered the land since 1870, when his great Act was passed. And if I have caught a little picture from the moment when death forestalled that imminent partying between himself and the leader he had so long admired and followed which life could only have broadened, let me match it by an earlier and happier one, borrowed from a letter of my own, written to my father when I was eighteen, and describing the bringing-in of the Education Act.

He sat down amidst loud cheering . . . . *Gladstone pulled him down with a sort of hug of delight.* It is certain that he is very much pleased with the Bill, and, what is of great consequence, that he thinks the Government has throughout been treated with great consideration in it. After the debate he said to Uncle F., 'Well, I think our pair of ponies will run through together!'

Gladstone's 'pony' was of course the Land Act of 1870.

CHAPTER X

London in the Eighties

The few recollections of William Forster that I have put together in the preceding chapter lead naturally perhaps to some account of my friendship and working relations at this time with Forster's most formidable critic in the political press — Mr John Morley, now Lord Morley. It was in the late seventies, I think, that I first saw Mr Morley. I sat next him at the Master's dinner table, and the impression he made upon me was immediate and lasting. I trust that a great man, to whom I owed much, will forgive me for dwelling on some of the incidents of literary comradeship which followed!

My husband and I on the way home compared notes. We felt that we had just been in contact with a singular personal power combined with a moral atmosphere which had in it both the bracing and the charm, that physically, are the gift of the heights. The 'austere' Radical indeed was there. With regard to certain vices and corruptions of our life and politics, my uncle might as well have used Mr Morley's name as that of Mr Frederick Harrison, when he presented us in 'Friendship's Garland' with Mr Harrison setting up a guillotine in his back garden. There was something — there always has been something — of the sombre intensity of the prophet in Mr Morley. Burke drew, as we all remember, an ineffaceable picture of Marie Antoinette's young beauty as he saw it in 1774, contrasting it with the 'abominable scenes' amid which she perished. Mr Morley's comment is —

> But did not the protracted agonies of a nation deserve the tribute of a tear? As Paine asked, were men to weep over the plumage and forget the dying bird? . . . It was no idle abstraction, no metaphysical right of man for which the French cried, but only the practical right of being permitted, by their own toil, to save themselves and the little ones about their knees from hunger and cruel death.

The cry of the poor, indeed against the rich and tyrannous, the cry of the persecuted Liberal, whether in politics or religion, against his oppressors — it used to seem to me, in the eighties, when, to my pleasure and profit, I was often associated with Mr Morley, that in his passionate response to this double appeal lay the driving impulse of his life, and the secret of his power over others. While we were still at Oxford he had brought out most of his books: 'On Compromise' — the fierce and famous manifesto of 1874 — and the well-known volumes on the Encyclopeadists, Voltaire, Rousseau, Diderot. It was not for nothing that he had been a member of Pattison's college, and a follower of John Stuart Mill. The will to look the grimmest facts of life and destiny in the face, without flinching, and the resolve to accept no 'anodyne' from religion or philosophy, combined with a ceaseless interest in the human fate and the human story, and a natural, inbred sympathy for the many against the few, for the unfortunate against the prosperous: — it was these ardours and the burning sincerity with which he felt them, which made him so great a power among us his juniors by half a generation. I shall never lose the impression that 'Compromise', with its almost savage appeal for the sincerity in word and deed, made upon me — an impression which had its share in 'Robert Elsmere'.

But together with this tragic strenuousness there was always the personal magic which winged it and gave it power. Mr Morley has known all through his life what it was to be courted, by men and women alike, for the mere pleasure of his company; in which he resembled another man whom both he and I knew well — Sir Alfred Lyall. It is well known that Mr Gladstone was fascinated by the combination in his future biographer of the Puritan, the man of iron conviction, and the delightful man of letters. And in my own small sphere I realised both aspects of Mr Morley during the eighties. Just before we left Oxford I had begun to write reviews and occasional notes for the *Pall Mall*, which he was then editing; after we settled in London, and he had become also editor of *Macmillan*, he asked me, to my no little conceit, to write a monthly *causerie* on a book or books for that magazine. I never succeeded in writing nearly so many; but in two years I contributed perhaps eight or ten papers — until I became absorbed in 'Robert Elsmere' and Mr Morley gave up journalism for politics. During that time my pleasant task brought me into frequent contact with my editor. Nothing could have been kinder than his letters; at the same time there was scarcely one of them that did not convey some hint, some touch of the critical goad, invaluable to the recipient. I wrote him a letter of wailing when he gave up the editorship and literature, and became Member for Newcastle. Such a fall it seemed to me then! But Mr Morley took it patiently. 'Do not lament over your friend, but pray for him!' As indeed one might well do, in the case of one who for a few brief months — in 1886 — was to be Chief Secretary for Ireland, and again 1892 -1895.

It was, indeed, in connection with Ireland that I became keenly and personally aware of that other side of Mr Morley's character — the side which showed him the intransigent supporter of liberty at all costs and all hazards. It was, I suppose, the brilliant and pitiless attacks in the *Pall Mall* on Mr Forster's Chief Secretaryship, which, as much as anything else, and together with what they reflected in the Cabinet, weakened my uncle's position, and ultimately led to his resignation in the spring of 1882. Many of Mr Forster's friends and kinsfolk resented them bitterly; and among the kinsfolk, one of them, I have reason to know, made a strong private protest. Mr Morley's attitude in reply could only have been that which is well expressed by a sentence of Darmesteter's about Renan: 'So pliant in appearance, so courteous in manner, he became a bar of iron as soon as one sought to wrest from him an act or word contrary to the intimate sense of his conscience.'

But no man has monopoly of conscience. The tragedy was that here were two men, both democrats, both humanitarians, but that an executive office, in a time of hideous difficulty, had been imposed upon the one, from which the other — his critic — was free. Ten years later, when Mr Morley was Chief Secretary, it was pointed out that the same statesman who had so sincerely and vehemently protested in the case of William Forster and Mr Balfour against the revival of 'obsolete' statutes, and the suppression of public meetings, had himself been obliged to put obsolete statutes in operation sixteen times, and to prohibit twenty-six public meetings. These however are the whirligigs of politics, and no politician escapes them.

In my eyes Lord Morley's crowning achievement in literature is his biography of Mr Gladstone. How easy it would have been to smother even Mr Gladstone in stale politics! — and how stale politics may become, in that intermediate stage before they pass finally into history! English political literature is full of biography of this kind. The three notable exceptions of recent years which occur to me are Mr Churchill's Life of his father, the Disraeli biography still in progress, and the 'Gladstone'. But it would be difficult indeed to 'stale' the story of either Lord Randolph or Dizzy. A biographer would have to set about it of malice prepense. In the case however of Mr Gladstone, the danger was more real. Anglican orthodoxy, eminent virtue, unfailing decorum; a comparatively weak sense of humour, and literary gift much inferior to his oratorical gift, so that the most famous of his speeches are but cold reading now; interminable sentences, and an unfailing relish for detail all important in its day, but long since dead and buried; — the kind of biography that, with this material, half a dozen of Mr Gladstones's colleagues might have written of him, for all his greatness, rises formidably on the inward eye. The younger generation, waiting for the historian to come — except in the case of those whose professional duty as politicians it would have been to read it — might quite well have yawned and passed by.

But Mr Morley's literary instinct, which is the artistic instinct, solved the problem. The most interesting half of the book will always, I think, be the later half. In the great matters of his hero's earlier career — Free Trade, the Crimean War, the early budgets, the slow development of the Liberal leader from the Church and State Conservative of 1832, down to the franchise battle of the sixties, and the 'great Ministry', as Mr Morley calls it, of 1868, the story is told, indeed, perhaps here and there at too great length, yet with unfailing ease and lucidity. The teller, however, is one who, till the late seventies, was only a spectator, and, on the whole, from a distance, of what he is describing, who was indeed most of the time pursuing his own special aims — i.e. the hewing down of orthodoxy and tradition, together with the preaching of a frank and uncompromising agnosticism, in the *Fortnightly Review*; aims which were of all others most opposed to Mr Gladstone's. But with the eighties everything changes. Mr Morley becomes a great part of what he tells. During the intermediate stage — marked by his editorship of the *Pall Mall Gazette* — the tone of the biography grows sensibly warmer and more vivid, as the writer draws nearer and nearer to the central scene; and with Mr Morley's election to Newcastle and his acceptance of the Chief Secretaryship in 1885, the book becomes the fascinating record of not one man but two, and that without any intrusion whatever on the rights of the main figure. The dreariness of the Irish struggle is lightened by touch after touch that only Mr Morley could have given. Take that picture of the sombre, discontented Parnell, coming, late in the evening to Mr Morley's room in the House of Commons, to complain of the finance of the Home Rule Bill; Mr Gladstone's entrance at 10.30 p.m. after an exhausting day; and how then the man of seventy-seven sat patiently down to work between the Chief Secretary and the Irish leader, till at last with a sigh of weariness, at nearly 1 a.m. the tired Prime Minister pleaded to go to bed! Or the dramatic story, later on, of Committee Room No. 15, where Mr Morley becomes the reporter to Mr Gladstone of that moral and political tragedy, the fall of Parnell; or a hundred other sharp lights upon the inner and human truth of things, as it lay behind the political spectacle. All through the later chapters too, the happy use of conversations between the two men on literary and philosophical matters, relieves what might have been the tedium of the end. For these vivid notes of free talk not only bring the living Gladstone before you in the most varied relation to his time; they keep up a perpetually interesting comparison in the reader's mind between the hero and his biographer. One is as eager to know what Mr Morley is going to say as one is to listen to Mr Gladstone. The two men — with their radical differences and their passionate sympathies — throw light on each other, and the agreeable pages achieve a double end, without ever affecting the real unity of the book. Thus handled, biography, so often the drudge of literature, rises in to its high places, and becomes a delight, instead of an edifying or informing necessity.

I will add one other recollection of this early time — i.e. that in 1881 the reviewing of Mr Morley's 'Cobden' in *The Times* fell to my husband, and as those were the days of many-column reviews, and as the time given for the review was *exceedingly* short, it could only be done at all by a division of labour. We divided the sheets of the book, and we just finished in the time to let my husband rush off to the Printing House Square and correct the proofs as they went through the press, for the morning's issue. In those days, as is well known, *The Times* went to press much later than now, and a leader-writer rarely got home before 4 — and sometimes 5 am.

.   .   .   .

I find it extremely difficult as I look back to put any order into the crowding memories of those early years in London. They were extraordinarily stimulating to us both, and years of great happiness. At home our children were growing up; our own lives were branching out into new activities, and bringing us always new friends, and a more interesting share in that 'great mundane movement,' which Mr Bottles believed would perish without him. Our connection with *The Times* and with the Forsters, and the many new acquaintances and friends we made at this time in that happy meeting-ground of men and causes — Mrs Jeune's drawing-room — opened to us the world of politicians; while my husband's four volumes on 'The English Poets', published just as we left Oxford, volumes to which all the most prominent writers of the day had contributed, together with the ever-delightful fact that Matthew Arnold was my uncle, brought us the welcome of those of our own métier and way of life; and when in '84 my husband became art-critic of the paper, a function which he filled for more than five and twenty years, fresh doors opened on the already crowded scene, and fresh figures stepped in.

The setting of it was twofold — in the first place, our old house in Russell Square, and, in the next, the farm on Rodborough Common, four miles from Godalming, where, amid a beauty of gorse and heather that filled every sense on a summer day with the mere joy of breathing and looking, our children and we spent the holiday hours of seven goodly years. The Russell Square house has been, so to speak, twice demolished, and twice buried, since we lived in it. Some of its stones must still lie deep under the big hotel which now towers on its site. That it does not still exist somewhere, I can hardly believe. The westerly sun seems to me still to be pouring into the beautiful little hall, built and decorated about 1750, with its panels of free scroll-work in blue and white, and to be still glancing through the drawing-rooms to the little powder-closet at the end my tiny workroom, where I first sketched the plan of 'Robert Elsmere' for my sister Julia Huxley, and where after three years I wrote the last words. If I open the door of the back drawing-room, there, to the right, is the children's schoolroom. I see them at their lessons, and the fine plane trees that look in at the window. And upstairs there are the pleasant bedrooms and the nurseries. It was born, the old house, in the year of the Young Pretender, and after serving six generations, perhaps, as faithfully as it served us, it 'fell on sleep'. There should be a special Elysium surely for the houses where the fates have been kind, and where people have been happy; and a special Tartarus for those — of Œdipus or Atreus — in which 'old unhappy far-off things' seem to be always poisoning the present.

As to Borough Farm — now the Headquarters of the vast camp which stretches to Hindhead — it stood then in an unspoilt wilderness of common and wood, approached only by what we called' 'the sandy track' from the main Portsmouth Road, with no neighbours for miles but a few scattered cottages. Its fate has been harder than that of 61 Russell Square. The old London house has gone clean out of sight, translated, whole and fair, into a world of memory. But Borough and the common are still here — as war has made them. Only — may I never see them again!

It was in 1882, the year of Tel-el-Kebir, when we took Peperharrow Rectory (the Murewell Vicarage of 'Robert Elsmere') for the summer, that we first came across Borough Farm. We left it in 1889. I did a great deal of work, there and in London, in those seven years. The *Macmillan* papers I have already spoken of. They were on many subjects — Tennyson's 'Becket', Mr Pater's 'Marius', 'The Literature of Introspection', Jane Austen, Keats, Gustavo Becquer, and various others. I still kept my Spanish to some extent, and I twice examined — in 1882 and 1888 — for the Taylorian scholarship in Spanish at Oxford; our old friend, Dr Kitchin, afterwards Dean of Durham, writing to me with glee that I should be 'making history', as 'the first woman examiner of men at either University.' My colleague on the first occasion was the old Spanish scholar, Don Pascual de Gayangos, to whom the calendaring of the Spanish MSS, in the British Museum had been largely entrusted; and the second time, Mr York Powell of Christ Church — I suppose one of the most admirable Romance scholars of the time — was associated with me. But if I remember right, I set the papers almost entirely, and wrote the report on both occasions. It gave me a feeling of safety in 1888, when my knowledge, such as it was, had grown very rusty, that Mr York Powell overlooked the papers, seeing that to set Scholarship questions for post-graduate candidates is not easy for one who has never been through any proper 'mill'! But they passed his scrutiny satisfactorily, and in 1888 we appointed as Taylorian Scholar a man to whom for years I confidently looked for *the* history of Spain — combining both the Spanish and Arabic sources — so admirable had his work been in the examination. But alack! That great book has still to be written. For Mr Butler Clarke died prematurely in 1904, and the hope died with him.

For *The Times* I wrote a good many long, separate articles before 1884, on 'Spanish Novels', 'American Novels', and so forth; the 'leader' on the death of Anthony Trollope; and various elaborate reviews of books on Christian origins, a subject on which I was perpetually reading, always with the same vision before me, growing in clearness as the years passed.

But my first steps towards its realisation were to begin with the short story of 'Miss Bretherton', published in 1884, and then the translation of Amiel's 'Journal Intime,' which appeared in 1885. 'Miss Bretherton' was suggested to me by the brilliant success in 1883 of Mary Anderson, and by the controversy with regard to her acting — as distinct from her delightful beauty, and her attractive personality — which arose between the fastidious few and the enchanted many. I maintained then, and am quite sure now, that Isabel Bretherton was in no sense a portrait of Miss Anderson. She was to me a being so distinct from the living actress that I offered her to the world with an entire good faith, which seems to myself now, perhaps, thirty years later, hardly less surprising than it did to the readers of the time. For undoubtedly the situation in the novel was developed out of the current dramatic debate. But it became to me just *a* situation — *a* problem. It was really not far removed from Diderot's problem in the 'Paradoxe sur le Comédien'. What is the relation of the actor to the part represented? One actress is plain — Rachel; another actress is beautiful, and more than beautiful, delightful — Miss Anderson. But all the time, is there or is there not a region in which all these considerations count for nothing in comparison with certain others? Is there a dramatic *art* — exacting, difficult, supreme — or is there not? The choice of the subject, at that time, was — it may be confessed — a piece of naïveté, and the book itself was young and naïve throughout. But something in it has kept it in circulation all this while; and for me it marks with a white stone the year in which it appeared. For it brought me my first critical letter from Henry James; it was the first landmark in our long friendship.

Beloved Henry James! It seems to me that my original meeting with him was at the Andrew Langs in 1882. He was then forty-two, in the prime of his working life, and young enough to be still 'Henry James, Junior,', to many. I cannot remember anything else of the 'Langs' dinner-party except that we were also invited to meet the author of 'Vice Versa,', 'which Mr Lang thinks' — as I wrote to my mother —'the best thing of its kind since Dickens'. But shortly after that Mr James came to see us in Russell Square, and a little incident happened which stamped itself for good on a still plastic memory. It was a very hot day; the western sun was beating on the drawing-room windows, through the room within was comparatively dark and cool. The children were languid with the heat, and the youngest, Janet, then five, stole into the drawing-room, and stood looking at Mr James. He put out a half-conscious hand to her; she came nearer, while we talked on. Presently she climbed on his knee. I suppose I made a maternal protest. He took no notice, and folded his arm round her. We talked on; and presently the abnormal stillness of Janet recalled her to me and made me look closely through the dark of the room. She was fast asleep, her pale little face on the young man's shoulder, her long hair streaming over his arm. Now Janet was a most independent and critical mortal, no indiscriminate 'climber up of knees'; far from it. Nor was Mr James an indiscriminate lover of children; he was not normally much at home with them, though *always* good to them. But the childish instinct had in fact divined the profound tenderness and chivalry which were the very root of his nature; and he was touched and pleased, as one is pleased when a robin perches on one's hand.

From that time, as the precious bundle of his letters shows, he became the friend of all of us — myself, my husband, and the children; through with an increased intimacy from the nineties onwards. In a subsequent chapter I will try and summarise the general mark left on me by his fruitful and stainless life. His letter to me about 'Miss Bretherton' is dated December 9, 1884. He had already come to see me about it, and there was never any critical discussion like his, for its suggestion of a hundred points of view, its flashing of unexpected lights, its witness to the depth and richness of his own artistic knowledge.

> The whole thing is delicate and distinguished (he wrote me) and the reader has the pleasure and security of feeling that he is with a woman (distinctly a woman!) who knows how (rare bird!) to write. I think your idea, your situation interesting in a high degree — But — (and then come a series of convincing 'buts'! He objects strongly to the happy ending). — I wish that your actress had been carried away from Kendal (her critical lover, who worships herself, but despises her art) altogether, carried away by the current of her artistic life, the sudden growth of her power, and the excitement, the ferocity and egotism (those of the artist realising success, I mean; I allude merely to the normal dose of those elements) which the effort to create, to 'arrive' (once she had had a glimpse of her possible successes) would have brought with it. (Excuse that abominable sentence.) Isabel, the Isabel you describe, has too much to spare for Kendal — Kendal being what he is; and one doesn't feel her, enough, as the pushing actress, the *cabotine*! She lapses towards him as if she were a failure, whereas you make her out a great success. No! — she wouldn't have thought so much of him at such a time as that — though very possibly she would have come back to him later.

The whole letter indeed is full of admirable criticism, sprung from a knowledge of life, which seemed to me, his junior by twelve years, unapproachably rich and full. But how grateful I was to him for the criticism! — how gracious and chivalrous was his whole attitude towards the writer and the book! Indeed as I look over the bundle of letters which concern this first novel of mine, I am struck by the good fortune which brought me such mingled chastening and praise, in such long letters, from judges so generous and competent. Henry James, Walter Pater, John Morley, 'Mr Creighton' (then Emmanuel Professor at Cambridge), Cotter Morrison, Sir Henry Taylor, Edmond Scherer — they are all there. Besides the renewal of the old throb of pleasure as one reads them, one feels a sort of belated remorse that so much trouble was taken for so slight a cause! Are there similar friends nowadays to help the first steps of a writer? Or is there no leisure left in this choked life of ours?

The decisive criticism perhaps, of all, is that of Mr Creighton: 'I find myself carried away by the delicate feeling with which the development of character is trace.' But — 'You wrote this book as a critic not as a creator. It is a sketch of the possible worth of criticism in an unregenerate world. This was worth doing once; but if you are going with novels you must throw criticism overboard, and let yourself go, as a partner of common joys, common sorrows, and common perplexities. There — I have told you what I think, just as I think it.'

. . . .

'Miss Bretherton' was a trial trip, and it taught me a good deal. When it came out I had nearly finished the translation of Amiel, which appeared in 1885, and in March of that year some old friends drove me up the remote Westmorland valley of Long Sleddale, at a moment when the blackthorn made lines of white along the lanes; and from that day onward the early chapters of 'Robert Elsmere' began to shape themselves in my mind. All the main ideas of the novel were already there. Elsmere was to be the exponent of a freer faith; Catherine had been suggested by an old friend of my youth; while Langham was the fruit of my long communing with the philosophic charm and the tragic impotence of Amiel. I began the book in the early summer of 1885, and thenceforward it absorbed me until its appearance in 1888.

1885, indeed, was a year of expanding horizons, of many new friends, quickened pulses generally. The vastness of London and its myriad interests seemed to be invading our life more and more. I can recall one summer afternoon, in particular, when as I was in a hansom driving idly westward towards Hyde Park Gate, thinking of a hundred things at once, this consciousness of *intensification*, of a heightened meaning in everything — the broad street, the crowd of moving figures and carriages, the houses looking down upon it — seized upon me with a rush. 'Yes, it is good — the mere living!' Joy in the infinite variety of the great city as compared with the 'cloistered virtue' of Oxford; the sheer pleasure of novelty, of the kind new faces, and the social discoveries one felt opening on many sides; the delight of new perceptions, new powers in oneself; — all this seemed to flower for me in those few minutes of reverie — if one can apply such a word to an experience so vivid. And meanwhile, the same intensity of pleasure from nature that I had always been capable of, flowed in upon me from new scenes; above all from solitary moments at Borough Farm, in the heart of the Surrey commons, when the September heather blazed about me; or the first signs of spring were on the gorse and the budding trees; or beside some lonely pool; and always heightened now by the company of my children. It was a stage — in normal life. But I might have missed it so easily! The Fates were kind to us in those days.

As to the social scene, let me gather from it first a recollection of pure romance. One night at a London dinner-party I found myself sent down with a very stout gentleman, an American Colonel, who proclaimed himself an 'esoteric Buddhist', and provoked in me a rapid and vehement dislike. I turned my back upon him, and examined the table. Suddenly, I became aware of a figure opposite to me, the figure of a young girl who seemed to me one of the most ravishing creatures I had ever seen. She was very small, and exquisitely made. Her beautiful head, with its mass of light-brown hair, the small features, and delicate neck, the clear pale skin, the lovely eyes, with rather heavy lids, which gave a slight look of melancholy to the face; the grace and fire of every movement when she talked, the dreamy silence into which she sometimes fell, without a trace of awkwardness or shyness. But how vain is any mere catalogue to convey the charm of Laura Tennant — the first Mrs Alfred Lyttelton — to those who never saw her!

I asked to be introduced to her as soon as we left the dining-room, and we spent the evening in a corner together.

I fell in love with her there and then. The rare glimpses of her that her busy life and mine allowed, made one of my chief joys thenceforward, and her early death was to me — as to so many, many others! — a grief never forgotten.

In the recent biography of Alfred Lyttelton, War Minister in Mr Balfour's latest Cabinet, and himself one of the best-loved men of our generation, his second wife has beautifully conveyed to the public of thirty years later some idea of Laura's charm. And I greatly hope that it may be followed some day by a collection of her letters, for there are many in existence, and young as she was, they would, I believe, throw much light upon a crowded moment in our national life. Laura was the fourth daughter of Sir Charles Tennant, a rich Glasgow manufacturer, and the elder sister of Mrs Asquith. She and her sisters came upon the scene in the early eighties; and without any other extrinsic advantage but that of wealth, which in this particular case would not have taken them very far, they made a conquest — the two younger, Laura and Margot, in particular — of a group of men and women who formed a kind of intellectual and social *élite*; who were all of them accomplished; possessed, almost all of them, of conspicuous good looks, or of the charm that counts as much; and among whom there happened to be a remarkable proportion of men who have since made their mark on English history. My generation knew them as 'The Souls'. 'The Souls' were envied, mocked at, caricatured, by those who were not of them. They had their follies — why not? They were young, and it was their golden day. Their dislike of convention and routine had effect on many — and those not fools — of making convention and routine seem particularly desirable. But there was not, I think, a young man or woman admitted to their inner ranks who did not possess in some measure, a certain quality very difficult to isolate and define. Perhaps, to call it 'disinterestedness' comes nearest. For they were certainly no seekers after wealth, or courtiers of the great. It might be said, of course, that they had no occasion; they had as much birth and wealth as anyone need want, among themselves. But that does not explain it. For push and greed are among the commonest faults of an aristocracy. The immortal pages of Saint Simon are there to show it. 'Where your treasure is, there will your heart be also,' says the Gospel. Now the 'treasure' among The Souls was, ultimately — or at least, tended to be — something spiritual. The typical expression of it, at its best, is to be found in those exquisite last words left by Laura Lyttelton for her husband, which the second Mrs Alfred Lyttelton has, as I think, so rightly published. That unique 'will', which for thirty years before it appeared in print was known to a wide circle of persons, many of whom had never seen the living Laura, was the supreme expression of a quality which, in greater or lesser degree, The Souls seemed to demand of each other, and of those who wished to join their band. Yet, combined with this passion, this poetry, this religious feeling, was first the maddest delight in simple things — in open air and physical exercise; then, a headlong joy in literature, art music, acting; a perpetual spring of fun; and a hatred of all the solemn pretences that too often make English society a weariness.

No doubt there is something — perhaps much — to be said on the other side. But I do not intend to say it. I was never a Soul, nor could have been. I came from too different a world. But there were a certain number of persons — of whom I was one — who were their 'harbourers' and spectators. I found delight in watching them. They were quite a new experience to me; and I saw them dramatically, like a scene in a play, full of fresh implications and suggestions. I find in an old letter to my mother an account of an evening at 40 Grosvenor Square, where the Tennants lived.

> It was not an evening party — we joined a dinner party there, after somewhere else. So that the rooms were empty enough to let one see the pretty creatures gathered in it, to perfection. In the large drawing-room, which is really a ballroom with a polished floor, people were dancing, or thought-reading, or making music as it pleased them.

Mr Balfour was there, with whom we had made friends, as fellow-guests, on a weekend visit to Oxford, not long before; Alfred Lyttelton, then in the zenith of his magnificent youth; Lord Curzon, then plain Mr Curzon, and in the Foreign Office; Mr Harry Cust; Mr Rennell Rodd, now the British Ambassador in Rome, and many others — a goodly company of young men in their prime. And among the women there was a very high proportion of beauty — but especially of grace. 'The half-lit room, the dresses and the beauty', says my letter, 'reminded one of some *festa* painted by Watteau or Lancret'. But with what a difference! For after all, it was English, through and through.

A little after this evening, Laura Tennant came down to spend a day at Borough Farm with the children and me. Another setting! Our principal drawing-room there in summer was sand-pit, shaded by an old ash tree, and haunted by innumerable sand-martins. It was Ascension Day, and the commons were in their spring loveliness. Our guest, I find, was to have come down 'with Mr Balfour and Mr Burne-Jones'. But in the end she came down alone; and we talked all day, sitting under hawthorns white with bloom, wandering through rushy fields ablaze with marsh marigold and orchids. She wrote to me the same evening after her return to London: —

I sit with my eyes resting on the mediæval purple of the sweet breathing orchids you gave me, and my thoughts feasting on the wonderful beauty of the snowy blossom against the blue . . . . .

This has been a real Ascension Day.

Later in the year — in November — she wrote to me from Scotland she was then twenty-one: —

I am still in Scotland, but don't pity me, for I love it more than anything else in the wide world. If you could only hear the wind throwing his arm against my window, and sobbing down the glen. I think I shall never have a Lover I am so fond of as the wind. None ever serenaded me so divinely. And when I open my window wide and ask him what he wants, and tell him I am quite ready to elope with him now — this moment — he only moans and sighs thro' my outblown hair — and gives me neuralgia . . . . I read all day, except when I am out with my Lover, or playing with my little nephew and niece, both of whom I adore — for they are little poets. We have had a house full ever since August, so I am delighted to get a little calm. It is so dreadful never, never to be alone — and really the housemaid would do just as well! And yet, whenever I go to my sanctum I am routed out as if I was of as much use as plums to plum pudding, and either made to play lawn tennis or hide-and-seek, or to talk to a young man whose only idea of the Infinite is the Looking-glass. All these are the trials that attend the 'young lady' of the house. Poor devil! Forgive strong language — but really my sympathy is deep.

I have however some really nice friends here, and am not entirely discontented. Mr Gerald Balfour left the other day. He is very clever — and quite beautiful — like a young god. I wonder if you know him. I know you know Arthur. . . . Lionel Tennyson who was also here with Gerald Balfour has a splendid humour — witty and 'fin' which is rare in England. Lord Houghton, Alfred Lyttelton, Godfrey Webb, George Curzon, the Chesterfields, the Hayters, Mary Gladstone, and a lot more have been here. I went north too to the land of Thule and was savagely happy. I wore no hat — no gloves — I bathed, fished, boated, climbed, and kissed the earth and danced round a cairn. It was opposite Skye at a Heaven called Loch Ailsa . . . . Such beauty — such weather — such a fortnight will not come again. Perhaps it would be unjust to the crying world for one human being to have more of the Spirit of Delight but one is glad to have tasted of the cup, and while it was in my hands I drank deeply.

I have read very little. I am hungering for a month or two's silence.

But there was another lover than the West Wind waiting for this most lovable of mortals. A few days afterwards she wrote to me from a house in Hampshire, where many of her particular friends were gathered, amongst them Alfred Lyttelton.

The conversation is pyrotechnic — and it is all quite delightful. A beautiful place — paradoxical arguments — ideals raised and shattered — temples torn and battered — temptations given way to — newspapers unread — acting — rhyming — laughing — *ad infinitum*. I wish you were here!

Six weeks afterwards she was engaged to Mr Lyttelton. She was to be married in May, and in Easter week of that year we met her in Paris, where she was buying her trousseau, enjoying it like a child, making friends with all her dressmakers, and bubbling over with fun about it. 'It isn't "dressing,"' she said — 'unless you apply main force to them. What they *want* is always — "*Presque pas de corsage et pas du tout de manches!*"'

One day she and Mr Lyttelton, and Mr Balfour, and one or two others came to tea with us at the Hotel Chatham to meet Victor Cherbuliez. The veteran French novelist fell in love with her, of course, and their talk — Laura's French was as spontaneous and apparently as facile as her English — kept the rest of us happy. Then she married in May, with half London to see, and Mr Gladstone — then Prime Minister — mounted on the chair, to make the wedding speech. For by her marriage Laura became the great man's niece, since Alfred Lyttelton's mother was a sister of Mrs Gladstone.

Then in the autumn came the hope of a child — to her who loved children so passionately. But all through the waiting time she was overshadowed by a strangely strong presentiment of death. I went to see her sometimes towards the end of it, when she was resting on her sofa in the late evening, and used to leave her listening for her husband's step, on his return from his work, her little weary face already lit up with expectation. The weeks passed, and those who loved her began to be anxious. I went down to Borough Farm in May, and there, just two years after she had sat with us under the hawthorn, I heard the news of her little son's birth, and then days later the news of her death.

With that death, a ray of pure joy was quenched on earth. But Laura Lyttelton was not only youth and delight — she was also embodied love. I have watched her in a crowded room where everybody wanted her, quietly seek out the neglected person there, the stranger, the shy secretary or governess, and make them happy — bring them in — with an art that few noticed, because in her it was nature. When she died, she left an enduring mark in the minds of many who have since governed or guided England; but she was mourned also by scores of humble folk, and by disagreeable folk whom only she befriended. Mrs Lyttelton quotes a letter written by the young wife to her husband:

> Tell me you love me and always will. Tell me, so that when I dream I may dream of Love, and when I sleep dreamless Love may be holding me in his wings and I wake Love may be the spirit in my feet, and when I die Love may be the Angel that takes me home.

And in the room of death, when the last silence fell on those gathered there, her sister Margot — by Laura's wish, expressed some time before — read aloud the 'will', in which she spoke her inmost heart.

'She was a flame, beautiful, dancing, ardent,' — writes the second Mrs Lyttelton. — 'The wind of life was too fierce for such a spirit, she could not live in it.'

I make no apology for dwelling on the life and early death of this young creature who was only known to a band — though a large band — of friends during her short years. Throughout social and literary history there have been a few apparitions like hers, which touch with peculiar force, in the hearts of men and women, the old, deep, human notes which 'make us men'. Youth, beauty, charm, death — they are the great themes with which all art, plastic or literary, tries to conjure. It is given to very few to handle them simply, yet sufficiently; with power, yet without sentimentality. Breathed into Laura's short life, they affected those who knew her like the finest things in poetry.

CHAPTER XI

London Friends

It was in 1874, as I have already mentioned, that on an introduction from Matthew Arnold we first made friends with M. Edmond Scherer, the French writer and Senator, who more than any other person — unless perhaps one divides the claim between him and M. Faguet — stepped into the critical chair of Sainte Beuve, after that great man's death. For M. Scherer's weekly reviews in the *Temps* (1863-78) were looked for by many people over about fifteen years, as persons of similar tastes had looked for the famous 'Lundis', in the *Constitutionnel* of an earlier generation.

We went out to call upon the Scherers at Versailles, coupling with it, if I remember right, a visit to the French National Assembly then sitting in the Chateau. The road from the station to the palace was deep in snow, and we walked up behind two men in ardent conversation, one of them gesticulating freely. My husband asked a man beside us, bound also, it seemed, for the Assembly, who they were. 'M. Gambetta and M. Jules Favre,' was the answer. So there we had in front of us the intrepid organiser of the Government of National Defence, whose services to France, France will never forget, and the unfortunate statesman to whom it fell, under the tyrannic and triumphant force of Germany (which was to prove, as we now know, in the womb and process of time, more fatal to herself than to France!) to sign away Alsace-Lorraine. And we had only just settled ourselves in our seats when Gambetta was in the tribune making a short but impassioned speech. I but vaguely remember what the speech was about, but the attitude of the lion head thrown back, and the tones of the famous voice remain with me — as it rang out in the recurrent phrase — '*Je proteste! — Messieurs, je proteste!*' It was the attitude of the statue in the Place du Carrousel, and of the *méridional*, Numa Roumestan, in Daudet's well-known novel. Every word said by the speaker seemed to enrage the benches of the Right, and the tumult was so great at times that we were still a little dazed by it when we reached the quiet of the Scherer's drawing-room.

M. Scherer rose to greet us, and to introduce us to his wife and daughters. A tall, thin man, already white-haired, with something in his aspect which suggested his Genevese origin — something at once ascetic, and delicately sensitive. He was then in his sixtieth year, deputy for the Seine et Oise, and an important member of the Left Centre. The year after we saw him he became a Senator, and remained so through his life, becoming more Conservative as the years went on. But his real importance was as a man of Letters; one of the recognised chiefs of French Literature and thought, equally at war with the forces of Catholic reaction, then just beginning to find a leader in M. Bourget, and with the scientific materialism of M. Taine. He was — when we first knew — a Protestant who had ceased to believe in any historical religion; a Liberal who, like another friend of ours, Mr Goschen, about the same time, was drifting into Conservatism; and also, a man of strong subtle character to whom questions of ethics were at all times as important as questions of pure literature. Above all, he was a scholar, specially conversant with England and English letters. He was, for instance, the 'French critic on Milton', on whom Matthew Arnold wrote one of his most attractive essays; and he was fond of maintaining — and proving — that when French people did make a serious study of England and English books, which he admitted was rare, they were apt to make fewer mistakes about us than English writers make about France.

Dear Monsieur Scherer! — I see him first in the little suite of carpetless rooms, empty save for books and the most necessary tables and chairs, where he lived and worked at Versailles; amid a library 'read, marked, learned and inwardly digested' like that of Lord Acton, his English junior. And then — in a winter walk along the Champs Elysées, a year or two later, discussing the prospects of Catholicism in France. 'They haven't a man — a speaker — a book! It is a real drawback to us Liberals that they are so weak, no negligible. We have nothing to hold us together!' At the moment, Scherer was perfectly right. But the following years were to see the flowing back of Catholicism into literature, the Universities, the École Normale. Twenty years later I quoted this remark of Scherer's to a young French philosopher, 'True, for its date,' he said 'There was then scarcely a single Catholic in the École Normale (i.e. at the head-waters of French education). There are now a great many. *But they are all Modernists!*' Since then, again, we have seen the growing strength of Catholicism in the French literature of imagination, in French poetry and fiction. Whether in the end it will emerge the stronger for the vast stirring of the waters caused by the present war is one of the most interesting questions of the present day.

But I was soon to know Edmond Scherer more intimately. I imagine that it was he who in 1884 sent me a copy of the 'Journal Intime' of Henri Frederic Amiel, edited by himself. The book laid its spell upon me at once; and I felt a strong wish to translate it. M. Scherer consented and I plunged into it. It was a delightful but exacting task. At the end of it, I knew a good deal more French than I did at the beginning! For the book abounded in passages that put one on one's mettle, and seemed to challenge every faculty one possessed. M. Scherer came over with his daughter Jeanne — a 'schöne Seele', if ever there was one — and we spent hours in the Russell Square drawing-room, turning and twisting the most crucial sentences this way and that.

But at last the translation and my Introduction were finished and the English book appeared. It certainly obtained a warm welcome both here and in America. There is something in Amiel's mystical and melancholy charm which is really more attractive to the Anglo-Saxon than the French temper. At any rate in the English-speaking countries the book spread widely, and has maintained its place till now.

The Journal is very interesting to me (wrote the Master of Balliol). It catches and detains many thoughts that have passed over the minds of others, which they rarely express, because they must take a sentimental form, from which most thinkers recoil. It is all about 'self', yet it never leaves an egotistical or affected impression. It is a curious combination of scepticism and religious feeling, like Pascal, but its elements are compounded in different proportions and the range of thought is far wider and more comprehensive. On the other hand Pascal is more forcible, and looks down upon human things from a higher point of view.

Why was he unhappy? ... But after all commentaries on the lives of distinguished men are of very doubtful value. There is the life; — take it and read it who can.

Amiel was a great genius as is shown by his power of style.

.... His Journal is a book in which the thoughts of many hearts are revealed .... There are strange forms of mysticism, which the poetical intellect takes. I suppose we must not try to explain them. Amiel was a Neo-Platonist and a sceptic in one.

For myself (wrote Walter Pater), I shall probably think on finishing the book that there was still something Amiel might have added to those elements of natural religion, which he was able to accept at times with full belief and always with the sort of hope which is a great factor in life. To my mind, the beliefs and the function in the world of the historic church form just one of those obscure but all-important possibilities which the human mind is powerless effectively to dismiss from itself, and might wisely accept, in the first place, as a workable hypothesis. The supposed facts on which Christianity rests, utterly incapable as they have become of any ordinary test, seem to me matters of very much the same sort of assent we give to any assumptions, in the strict and ultimate sense, moral. The question whether those facts are real will, I think, always continue to be what I should call one of the *natural* questions of the human mind.

A passage, it seems to me, of considerable interest as throwing light upon the inner mind of one of the most perfect writers, and most important influences of the nineteenth century. Certainly there is no sign in it on Mr Pater's part of 'dropping Christianity'; —very much the contrary.

.   .   .   .

But all this time, while literary and meditative folk went on writing and thinking, how fast the political world was rushing! Those were the years, after the defeat of the first Home Rule Bill, and the dismissal of Mr. Gladstone, of Lord Salisbury's Government and Mr Balfour's Chief Secretaryship. As I look back upon them — those five dramatic years culminating first in the Parnell Commission, and then in Parnell's tragic downfall and death, I see everything grouped round Mr Balfour. From the moment when, in succession to Sir Michael Hicks Beach, Mr Balfour took over the Chief Secretaryship, his sudden and swift development seemed to me the most interesting thing in politics. We had first met him, as I have said, on a weekend visit to the Talbots at Oxford. It was then a question whether his health would stand the rough and tumble of politics. I recollect he came down late and looked far from robust. We travelled up to London with him, and he was reading Mr Green's 'Prolegomena to Ethics', which, if I remember right, he was to review for *Mind*.

He was then a member of the Fourth Party, and engaged — though in a rather detached fashion — in those endless raids and excursions against the 'Goats', i.e. the bearded veterans of his own party, Sir Stafford Northcote in particular, of which Lord Randolph was the leader. But compared to Lord Randolph he had made no parliamentary mark. One thought of him as the metaphysician, the lover of music, the delightful companion, always, I feel now, in looking back, with a prevailing consciousness of something reserved and potential in him, which gave a peculiar importance and value to his judgements of men and things. He was a leading figure among 'The 'Souls', and I remember some delightful evenings in his company before '86, when the conversation was entirely literary or musical.

Then, with the Chief Secretaryship there appeared a new Arthur Balfour. The courage, the resource, the never-failing wit and mastery with which he fought the Irish members in Parliament, put down outrage in Ireland, and at the same time laid the foundation in a hundred directions of that social and agrarian redemption of Ireland, on which a new political structure will some day be reared — is perhaps even now about to rise: — these things make one of the most brilliant, one of the most dramatic chapters in our modern history.

It was in 1888, two years after Mr Forster's death, that we found ourselves for a Sunday at Whittinghame. It was, I think, not long before the opening of the Special Commission which was to enquire into the charges brought by *The Times* against the Parnellites and the Land League. Nothing struck me more in Mr Balfour than the absence in him of any sort of excitement or agitation, in dealing with the current charges against the Irishmen. It seemed to me that he had quietly accepted the fact that he was fighting a revolution, and while perfectly clear as to his own course of action, wasted no nervous force on moral reprobation of the persons concerned. His business was to protect the helpless, to punish crime, and to expose the authors of it, whether high or low. But he took it as a job to be done — difficult — unpleasant — but all in the way of business. The tragic or pathetic emotion that so many people were ready to spend upon it, he steadily kept at a distance. His nerve struck me as astonishing, and the absence of any disabling worry about things past. 'One can only do one's best at the moment,' he said to me once, *àpropos* of some action of the Irish government which had turned out badly — 'if it doesn't succeed, better luck next time! Nothing to be gained by going back upon things.' After this visit to Whittinghame, I wrote to my father: —

> I came away more impressed and attracted by Arthur Balfour than ever. If intelligence and heart, and pure intentions can do anything for Ireland, he at least has got them all. Physically he seems to have broadened and heightened since he took office, and his manner, which was always full of charm, is even brighter and kindlier than it was — or I fancied it. He spoke most warmly of Uncle Forster.

And the interesting and remarkable thing was the contrast between an attitude so composed and stoical and his delicate physique, his sensitive sympathetic character. All the time, of course, he was in constant personal danger. Detectives, much to his annoyance, lay in wait for us as we walked through his own park, and went with him in London wherever he dined. Like my uncle, he was impatient of being followed and guarded, and only submitted to it for the sake of other people. Once, at a dinner-party at our house, he met an old friend of ours, one of the most original thinkers of our day, Mr Philip Wicksteed, economist, Dante scholar, and Unitarian minister. He and Mr Balfour were evidently attracted to each other, and when the time for departure came, the two, deep in conversation, instead of taking cabs, walked off together in the direction of Mr Balfour's house in Carlton Gardens. The detectives below-stairs remained for some time blissfully unconscious of what had happened. Then word reached them; and my husband, standing at the door to see a guest off, was the amused spectator of the rush in pursuit of two splendid long-legged fellows, who had however no chance whatever of catching up the Chief Secretary.

Thirty years ago, almost! And during that time the name and fame of Arthur Balfour have become an abiding part of English history. Nor is there any British statesman of our day who has been so much loved by his friends, so little hated by his opponents, so widely trusted by the nation.

. . . .

As to the Special Commission and the excitement produced by *The Times'* attack on the Irish Members, including the publication of the forged Parnell letter in 1887, our connection with *The Times* brought us of course into the full blast of it. Night after night, I would sit up half asleep to listen to the different phases of the story when in the early hours of the morning my husband came back from *The Times*, brimful of news, which he was as eager to tell as I to hear. My husband, however, was only occasionally asked to write upon Ireland, and was not in the inner counsels of the paper on that subject. We were both very anxious about the facsimiled letter, and when, after long preliminaries, the Commission came to *The Times* witnesses, I well remember the dismay with which I heard the first day of Mr Macdonald's examination. Was that *all*? I came out of the Court behind Mr Labouchere's and Sir George Lewis, and in Mr Labouchere's exultation one read the coming catastrophe. I was on the Riviera when Pigott's confession, flight and suicide held the stage; yet even at that distance the shock was great. *The Times'* attack was fatally discredited, and the influence of the great paper temporarily crippled. Yet how much of that attack was sound, how much of it was abundantly justified! After all, the report of the Commission — apart altogether from the forged letter or letters — certainly gave Mr Balfour in Ireland later on the reasoned support of English opinion, in his hand-to-hand struggle with the Land League methods, as the Commission had both revealed and judged them. After thirty years one may well admit that the Irish land system had to go, and that the Land League was 'a sordid revolution,', with both the crimes and the excuses of a revolution. But at the time, British statesmean had to organise reform with one hand, and stop boycotting and murder with the other; and the light thrown by the Commission on the methods of Irish disaffection was invaluable to those who were actually grappling day by day with the problems of Irish government.

It was probably at Mrs Jeune's that I first saw Mr Goschen, and we rapidly made friends. His was a great position at that time. Independent of both parties, yet trusted by both; at once disinterested and sympathetic; a strong Liberal in some respects, an equally strong Conservative in others, he never spoke without being listened to, and his support was eagerly courted both by Mr Gladstone, from whom he had refused office in 1880, without however breaking with the Liberal party, and by the Conservatives, who instinctively felt him their property, but were not yet quite clear as to how they were to finally capture him. That was decided in 1886 when Mr Goshen voted in the majority that killed the Home Rule Bill, and more definitely in the following year when Randolph Churchill resigned the Exchequer in a fit of pique, thinking himself indispensable, and not at all expecting Lord Salisbury to accept his resignation. But in his own historic phrase, he 'forgot Goschen', and Mr Goschen stepped easily into his shoes and remained there.

I find from an old diary that the Goschens dined with us in Russell Square two nights before the historic division on the Home Rule Bill, and I remember how the talk raged and ranged. Mr Goschen was an extremely agreeable talker, and I seem still to hear his husky voice with the curious deep notes in it, and to be looking into the large but short-sighted and spectacled eyes — he refused the Speakership mainly on the grounds of his sight — of which veiled look often made what he said the more racy and unexpected. A letter he wrote me in '86 after his defeat at Liverpool, I kept for many years as the best short analysis I had ever read of the Liberal Unionist position, and the probable future of the Liberal party.

Mrs Goschen was as devoted a wife as Mrs Gladstone, or Mrs Disraeli, and the story of the marriage was a romance enormously to Mr Goschen's credit. Mr Goschen must have been a most faithful lover, and he certainly was a delighted friend. We stayed with them at Seacox, their home in Kent, and I remember one rainy afternoon there, the greater part of which I spent listening to his talk with John Morley, and — I think — Sir Alfred Lyall. It would have been difficult to find a trio of men better worth an audience.

Mrs Goschen, through full of kindness and goodness, was not literary, and the house was somewhat devoid of books, except in

Mr Goschen's study. I remember J.R.G.'s laughing fling when Mrs Goschen complained that she could not get 'Pride and Prejudice', which he had recommended to her, 'from the library'. 'But you could have bought it for sixpence at the railway bookstall,' said J.R.G. Mr Goschen himself however was a man of wide cultivation, as befitted the grandson of the intelligent German bourgeois who had been the publisher of both Schiller and Goethe. His biography of his grandfather in those happy days before the present life and death struggle between England and Germany has now a kind of symbolic value. It is a study by a man of German descent who had become one of the most trusted of English statesman, of that earlier German life — with its measure, its kindness, its idealism — on which Germany has turned its back. The writing of this book was the pleasure of his later years, amid the heavy work which was imposed upon him as a Free-Trader, in spite of his personal friendship for Mr Chamberlain, by the Tariff Reform campaign of 1903 onwards; and the copy which he gave me reminds me of many happy talks with him, and of my own true affection for him. I am thankful that he did not live to see 1914.

Lord Goschen reminds me of Lord Acton another new friend of the eighties. Yet Lord Acton had been my father's friend and editor, in the *Home and Foreign Review*, long before he and I knew each other. Was there ever a more interesting or a more enigmatic personality than Lord Acton's! His letters to Mrs Drew, addresseds evidently in many cases to Mr Gladstone, through his daughter, have always seemed to me one of the most interesting documents of our time. Yet I felt sharply, in reading them, that the real man was only partially there; and in the new series of letters just published (October 1917) much and welcome light is shed upon the problem of Lord Acton's mind and character. The perpetual attraction for me, as for many others, lay in the contrast between Lord Acton's Catholicism, and the universalism of his learning; and, again, between what his death revealed of the fervour and simplicity of his Catholic faith, and the passion of his Liberal creed. Oppression — tyranny — persecution — those were the things that stirred his blood. He was a Catholic, yet he fought Ultramontanism and the Papal Curia to the end; he never lost his full communion with the Church of Rome, yet he could never forgive the Papacy for the things it had done, and suffered to be done; and he would have nothing to do with the excuse that the moral standards of one age are different from those of another, and therefore the crimes of a Borgia weigh more lightly and claim more indulgence than similar acts done in the nineteenth century.

> There is one moral standard for all Christians — there has never been more than one (he would say inexorably). The Commandments and the Sermon on the Mount have been always there. It was the wickedness of men that ignored them in the fifteenth century — it is the wickedness of men that ignores them now. Tolerate them in the past, and you will come to tolerate them in the present and future.

It was in 1885 that Mr — then recently made Professor — Creighton showed me at Cambridge an extraordinarily interesting summary, in Lord Acton's handwriting, of what should be the principles — the ethical principles — of the modern historian in dealing with the past. They were, I think, afterwards embodied in an introduction to a new edition of Machiavelli. The gist of them however is given in a letter written to Bishop Creighton in 1887, and printed in the biography of the Bishop. Here we find a devout Catholic attacking an Anglican writer for applying the epithets 'tolerant and enlightened' to the later mediæval Papacy.

> 'These men' (i.e. the Popes of the thirteenth and fourteenth centuries), he says, 'instituted a system of persecution. . . . . The person who authorises the act shares the guilt of the person who commits it . . . . Now the Liberals think persecution a crime of a worse order than adultery, and the acts done by Ximenes' (through the agency of the Spanish Inquisition) 'considerably worse than the entertainment of Roman courtesans by Alexander VIth.'

These lines of course point to the Acton who was the lifelong friend of Döllinger and fought, side by side with the Bravarian scholar, the promulgation of the dogma of Papal Infallibility, at the Vatican Council of 1870. But while Döllinger broke with the church, Lord Acton never did. That was what made the extraordinary interest of conversation with him. Here was a man whose denunciation of the crimes and corruption of Papal Rome — of the historic church indeed and the clergy in general — was far more unsparing than that of the average educated Anglican. Yet he died a devout member of the Roman Church in which he was born; after his death it was revealed that he had never felt a serious doubt either of Catholic doctrine, or of the supernatural mission of the Catholic Church; and it was to a dearly-loved daughter on her deathbed that he said with calm and tender faith — 'My child, you will soon be with Jesus Christ.' All his friends, except the very few who knew him most intimately, must I think have been perpetually puzzled by this apparent paradox in his life and thought. Take the subject of Biblical criticism. I had many talks with him while I was writing 'Robert Elsmere', and was always amazed at his knowledge of what Liddon would have called 'German infidel' books. He had read them all, he possessed them all; he knew a great deal about the lives of the men who have written them; and he never spoke of them, both the books and the writers without complete and, as it seemed to me, sympathetic tolerance. I remember after the publication of the dialogue on 'The New Reformation', in which I tried to answer Mr Gladstone's review of 'Robert Elsmere', by giving an outline of the history of religious enquiry and Biblical criticism from Lessing to Harnack that I met Lord Acton one evening on the platform of Bletchley station, while we were both waiting for a train. He came up to me with a word of congratulation on the article. 'I only wish,' I said, 'I had been able to consult you more about it.' 'No, no,' he said — '*Votre siège est faite!* But I think you should have given more weight to so-and-so, and you have omitted so-and-so.' Whereupon we walked up and down in the dusk, and he poured out that learning of his, in that way he had — so courteous, modest, thought-provoking — which made one both wonder at and love him.

As to his generosity and kindness towards younger students, it was endless. I asked him once when I was writing for *Macmillan*, to give me some suggestions for an article on Chateaubriand. The letter I received from him the following morning is a marvel of knowledge, bibliography, and kindness. And not only did he give me such a 'scheme' of reading as would have taken any ordinary person months to get through, but he arrived the following day in a hansom, with a number of the books he had named, and for a long time they lived on my shelves. Alack, I never wrote the article, but when I came to the writing of 'Eleanor', for which certain material was drawn from the life of Chateaubriand, his advice helped me. And I don't think he would have thought it thrown away. He never despised novels!

Once on a visit to us at Stocks, there were nine books of different sorts in his room which I had chosen and placed there. By Monday morning he had read them all. His library, when he died, contained about 60,000 volumes — all read; and it will be remembered that Lord Morley, to whom Mr Carnegie gave it, has handed it to the University of Cambridge.

In '84 when I first knew him, however, Lord Acton was every bit as keen a politician as he was a scholar. As is well known, he was a poor speaker, and never made any success in Parliament; and this was always, it seemed to me, the drop of gall in his otherwise happy and distinguished lot. But if he was never in an English Cabinet, his influence over Mr Gladstone through the whole of the Home Rule struggle gave him very real political power. He and Mr Morley were the constant friends and associates to whom Mr Gladstone turned through all that critical time. But the great split was rushing on, and it was also in '84 that, at Admiral Maxse's one night at dinner, I first saw Mr Chamberlain, who was to play so great a part in the following years. It was a memorable evening to me, for the other guest in a small party was M. Clemenceau.

M. Clemenceau was then at the height of his power as the marker and unmaker of French Ministries. It was he more than any other single man who had checkmated the Royalist reaction of 1877, and driven MacMahon from power; and in the year after we first met him, he was to bring Jules Ferry to grief over 'L'affaire de Tongkin'. He was then in the prime of life, and he is still (1917), thirty-three years later,[1] one of the most vigorous of French political influences. Mr Chamberlain, in 1884, was forty-eight, five years older than the French politician, and was at that time, of course, the leader of the Radicals, as distinguished from the old Liberals, both in the House of Commons and Mr Gladstone's Cabinet.

---

[1] These lines were written shortly before, on the overthrow of M. Painlevé, M. Clemenceau, at the age of seventy-seven, became Prime Minister of France, at what may well be the deciding moment of French destiny (January 1918).

How many great events, in which those two men were to be concerned, were still in the 'abysm of time', as we sat listening to them at Admiral Maxse's dinner-table! — Clemenceau, the younger, and the more fiery and fluent; Chamberlain, with no graces of conversation, and much less ready than the man he was talking with, but producing already the impression of a power, certain to leave its mark, if the man lived, on English history. In a letter to my father after the dinner-party, I described the interest we had both felt in M. Clemenceau. 'Yet he seems to me a light weight to ride such a horse as the French democracy!'

In the following year, 1885, I remember a long conversation on the Gordon catastrophe with Mr Chamberlain at Lady Jeune's. It was evident, I thought, that his mind was greatly exercised by the whole story of that disastrous event. He went through it from step to step, ending up deliberately, but with a sigh — 'I have never been able to see, from day to day, and I do not see now, how the Ministry could have taken any other course than that they did take.'

Yet the recently published biography of Sir Charles Dilke shows clearly how very critical Mr Chamberlain had already become of his great leader, Mr Gladstone, and how many causes were already preparing the rupture of 1886.

. . . .

I first met Mr Browning in '84 or '85, if I remember right, at a Kensington dinner-party, where he took me down. A man who talked loud and much was discoursing on the other side of the table; and a spirit of opposition had clearly entered into Mr Browning. À *propos* of some recent acting in London we began to talk of Molière, and presently, as though to shut out the stream of words opposite, which was damping conversation, the old poet — how the splendid brow, and the white hair come back to me! — fell to quoting from the famous sonnet scene in 'Le Misanthrope': — first of all Alceste's rage with Phillinte's flattery of the wretched verses declaimed by Oronte — 'Morbleu, vil complaisant, vous louez des sottises' — then the admirable fencing between Oronte and Alceste, where Alceste at first tries to convey his contempt for Oronte's sonnet indirectly, and then bursts out —

> Ce n'est que jeu de mots, qu'affectation pure,
> Et ce n'est point ainsi que parle la nature!

— breaking immediately into the 'vieille chanson', one line of which is worth all the affected stuff that Célimène and her circle admire.

Browning repeated the French in an undertone, kindling as he went, I urging him on, our two heads close together. Every now and then he would look up to see if the plague outside was done, and finding it still went on, would plunge again into the seclusion of our *tâte-à-tâte*; till the 'chanson' itself — 'Si le roi m'avoit donné — Paris, sa grand' ville' — had been said, to his delight and mine.

The recitation lasted through several courses, and our hostess once or twice threw uneasy glances towards us, for Browning was the 'lion' of the evening. But once launched he was not to be stopped; and as for me, I shall always remember that I heard Browning — spontaneously, without a moment's pause to remember or prepare — recite the whole, or almost the whole, of one of the immortal things in literature.

He was then seventy-two or seventy-three. He came to see us once or twice in Russell Square, but alack! We arrived too late in the London world to know him well. His health began to fail just about the time when we first met, and early in 1889 he died in the Palazzo Rezzonico.

He did not like 'Robert Elsmere', which appeared the year before his death; and I was told a striking story by a common friend of his and mine, who was present at a discussion of the book at a literary house. Browning, said my friend, was of the party. The discussion turned on the divinity of Christ. After listening a while, Browning expressed his entire disagreement with the main argument of the book, repeating with dramatic force the anecdote of Charles Lamb, in conversation with Leigh Hunt on the subject of 'Persons one would wish to have seen'; when, after ranging through literature and philosophy, Lamb added, 'There is one other Person — If Shakespeare was to come into the room, we should all rise up to meet him; but if that Person was to come into it, we should fall down and try to kiss the hem of his garment!'

Some fourteen years after his death I seemed to be brought very near in spirit to this great man, and — so far as a large portion of his work is concerned — great poet. We were in Venice. I was writing the 'Marriage of William Ashe', and being in want of a Venetian setting for some of the scenes, I asked Mr Pen Browning, who was, I think, at Asolo, if he would allow me access to the Palazzo Rezzoncico, which was then uninhabited. He kindly gave me free leave to wander about it as I liked; and I went most days to sit and write in one of the rooms of the *mezzanin*. But when all chance of a tourist had gone, and the palace was shut, I used to walk all about it in the rich May light, finding it a little creepy! — but endlessly attractive and interesting. There was a bust of Mr Browning, with an inscription, in one of the rooms, and the place was haunted for me by his great ghost. It was there he had come to die, in the palace which he had given to his only son, whom he adored. The *concierge* pointed out to me what he believed to be the room in which he passed away. There was very little furniture in it. Everything was chill and deserted. I did not want to think of him there. I liked to imagine him strolling in the stately hall of the palace with its vast chandelier, its pillared sides and Tiepolo ceiling, breathing in the Italian spirit which through such long years had passed into his, and delighting, as a poet delights — not vulgarly, but with something of a child's adventurous pleasure — in the mellow magnificence of the beautiful old place.

. . . .

Mr Lowell is another memory of these early London days. My first sight of him was at Mr and Mrs Westlake's house — in a temper! For someone had imprudently talked of 'Yankeeisms', perhaps with some 'superior' intonation. And Mr Lowell — the Lowell of 'A Certain Condenscension in Foreigners' had flashed out: 'It's you English who don't know your own language and your own literary history. Otherwise you would realise that most of what you call "Yankeeisms" are merely good old English, which you have thrown away.'

Afterwards, I find records of talks with him at Russell Square, then of Mrs Lowell's death in 1885, and finally of dining with him in the spring of 1887, just before his return to America. At that dinner was also the German Ambassador, Count Hatzfeldt, a handsome man, with a powerful, rather sombre face. I remember some talk with him after dinner on current books and politics. Just thirty years ago! Mr Lowell had then only four years to live. He and all other diplomats had just passed through an anxious spring. The scare of another Franco-German war had been playing on the nerves of Europe; started in the main by the military party in Germany, in order to ensure the passing of the famous Army law of that year — the first landmark in that huge military expansion, of which we see the natural fruit in the present Armageddon.

A week or two before this dinner the German elections had given the Conservatives an enormous victory. Germany indeed was in the full passion of economic and military development — all her people growing rich — intoxicated besides, with vague dreams of coming power. Yet I have still before me the absent indecipherable look of her Ambassador — a man clearly of high intelligence — at Mr Lowell's table. Thirty years! — and at the end of them America was to be at grips with Germany, sending armies across the Atlantic to fight in Europe. It would have been as impossible for any of us, on that May evening in Lowndes Square, even to imagine such a future, as it was for Macbeth to credit the absurdity that Birnam wood would ever come to Dunsinane!

A year later Mr Lowell came back to London for a time in a private capacity, and I got to know him better and to like him much. Here is a characteristic touch in a note I find among the old letters:

> I am glad you found something to like in my book and much obliged to you for saying so. Nobody but Wordsworth ever got beyond need of sympathy, and he started there!

CHAPTER XII

The Publication of 'Robert Elsmere'

It was in 1885, after the completion of the Amiel translation, that I began 'Robert Elsmere', drawing the opening scenes from that expedition to Long Sleddale in the spring of that year which I have already mentioned. The book took me three years — nearly — to write. Again and again I found myself dreaming that the end was near, and publication only a month or two away; only to sink back on the dismal conviction that the second, or the first, or the third volume — or some portion of each — must be rewritten, if I was to satisfy myself at all. I actually wrote the last words of the last chapter in March 1887, and came out afterwards, from my tiny writing-room at the end of the drawing-room, shaken with tears, and wondering as I sat alone on the floor, by the fire, in the front room, what life would be like now that the book was done! But it was nearly a year after that before it came out, a year of incessant hard work, of endless re-writing, and much nervous exhaustion. For all the work was saddened and made difficult by the fact that my mother's long illness was nearing its end, and that I was torn incessantly between the claim of the book, and the desire to be with her whenever I could possibly be spared from my home and children. Whenever there was a temporary improvement in her state. I would go down to Borough alone to work feverishly at revision, only to be drawn back to her side before long by worse news. And all the time London life went on as usual, and the strain at times was great.

The difficulty of finishing the book arose first of all from its length. I well remember the depressed countenance of Mr George Smith — who was to be to me through fourteen years afterwards the kindest of publishers and friends — when I called one day in Waterloo Place, bearing a basketful of typewritten sheets. 'I am afraid you have brought us a perfectly unmanageable book!' he said; and I could only mournfully agree that so it was. It was far too long, and my heart sank at the thought of all there was still to do. But how patient Mr Smith was over it! — and how generous in the matter of unlimited fresh proofs and endless corrections. I am certain that he had no belief in the book's success; and yet on the ground of his interest in 'Miss Bretherton' he had made liberal terms with me, and all through the long incubation he was always indulgent and sympathetic.

The root difficulty was of course the dealing with such a subject in a novel at all. Yet I was determined to deal with it so, in order to reach the public. There were great precedents — Froude's 'Nemesis of Faith', Newman's 'Loss and Gain', Kingsley's 'Alton Locke', — for the novel of religious or social propaganda. And it seemed to me that the novel was capable of holding and shaping real experience of any kind, as it affects the lives of men and women. It is the most elastic, the most adaptable of forms. No one has a right to set limits to its range. There is only one final test. Does it interest? — Does it appeal? — Personally, I should add another. Does it make in the long run for *beauty*? Beauty taken in the largest and most generous sense, and especially as including discord, the harsh and jangled notes which enrich the rest — but still Beauty — as Tolstoy was a master of it.

But at any rate, no one will deny that *interest* is the crucial matter.

> There are five and twenty ways
> Of constructing tribal lays —
> And every single one of them is right!

— always supposing that the way chosen quickens the breath and stirs the heart of those who listen. But when the subject chosen has two aspects, the one intellectual and logical, the other poetic and emotional, the difficulty of holding the balance between them so that neither overpowers the other, and interest is maintained, is admittedly great.

I wanted to show how a man of sensitive and noble character, born for religion, comes to throw off the orthodoxies of his day and moment, and to go out into the wilderness where all is experiment, and spiritual life begins again. And with him I wished to contrast a type no less fine of the traditional and guided mind — and to imagine the clash of two such tendencies of thought, as it might affect all practical life, and especially the life of two people who loved each other.

Here then — to begin with — were Robert and Catherine. Yes — but Robert must be made intellectually intelligible. Closely looked at, all novel-writing is a sort of shorthand. Even the most simple and broadly human situation cannot really be told in full. Each reader in following it unconsciously supplies a vast amount himself. A great deal of the effect is owing to things quite out of the picture given — things in the reader's own mind, first and foremost. The writer is playing on common experience; and mere suggestion is often far more effective than analysis. Take the paragraph in Turguénieff's 'Lisa' — it was pointed out to me by Henry James — where Lavretsky on the point of marriage, after much suffering, with the innocent and noble girl whom he adores, suddenly hears that his intolerable first wife whom he had long believed dead is alive. Turguénieff, instead of setting out the situation in detail, throws himself on the reader. 'It was dark. Lavretsky went into the garden, and walked up and down there till dawn.'

That is all. And it is enough. The reader who is not capable of sharing that night walk with Lavretsky, and entering into his thoughts, has read the novel to no purpose. He would not understand, though Lavretsky or his creator were to spend pages on explaining.

But in my case, what provoked the human and emotional crisis — what produced the *story* — was an intellectual process. Now the difficulty here in using suggestion — which is the master tool of the novelist — is much greater than in the case of ordinary experience. For the conscious use of the intellect on the accumulated data of life — through history and philosophy — is not ordinary experience. In its more advanced forms, it only applies to a small minority of the human race.

Still, in every generation, while a minority is making or taking part in the intellectual process itself, there is an atmosphere, a diffusion, produced around them, which affects many, many thousands who have but little share — but little *conscious* share, at any rate — in the actual process.

Here then is the opening for suggestion — in connection with the various forms of imagination which enter into Literature; with poetry, and fiction, which, as Goethe saw, is really a form of poetry. And a quite legitimate opening. For to use it is to quicken the intellectual process itself, and to induce a larger number of minds to take part in it.

The problem then, in intellectual poetry or fiction, is so to suggest the argument, that both the expert and the popular consciousness may feel its force. And to do this without overstepping the bounds of poetry or fiction; without turning either into mere ratiocination, and so losing the 'simple, sensuous, passionate' element which is their true life.

It was this problem which made 'Robert Elsmere' take three years to write instead of one. Mr Gladstone complained in his famous review of it that a majestic system which had taken centuries to elaborate, and gathered into itself the wisest brains of the ages had gone down in a few weeks or months before the onslaught of the Squire's arguments; and that if the Squire's arguments were few the orthodox arguments were fewer! The answer to the first part of the charge is that the well-taught schoolboy of today is necessarily wiser in a hundred respects than Sophocles or Plato, since he represents not himself, but the brainwork of a hundred generations since those great men lived. And as to the second, if Mr Gladstone had seen the first redactions of the book — only if he had, I fear he would never have read it! — he would hardly have complained of lack of argument on either side, whatever he might have thought of its quality. Again and again I went on writing for hours, satisfying the logical sense in one's self, trying to put the arguments on both sides as fairly as possible, only to feel despairingly at the end that it must all come out. It might be decent controversy; but life, feeling, charm, *humanity* had gone out of it; it had ceased therefore to be 'making', to be literature.

So that in the long run there was no other method possible than suggestion — and of course *selection*! — as with all the rest of one's material. That being understood, what one had to aim at was so to use suggestion as to touch the two zones of thought — that of the scholar, and that of what one may call the educated populace; who without being scholars, were yet aware, more or less clearly, of what the scholars were doing. It is from these last that 'atmosphere' and 'diffusion' come; the atmosphere and diffusion which alone make wide penetration for a book illustrating an intellectual motive possible. I had to learn that, having read a great deal, I must as far as possible wipe out the traces of reading. All that could be done was to leave a few signposts as firmly planted as one could, so as to recall the real journey to those who already knew it, and for the rest, to trust to the floating interest and passion surrounding a great controversy — the *second* religious battle of the nineteenth century — with which it had seemed to me both in Oxford and in London that the intellectual air was charged.

I grew very weary in the course of the long effort, and often very despairing. But there were omens of hope now and then; first, a letter from my dear eldest brother, the late W.T. Arnold, who died in 1904, leaving a record as journalist and scholar which has been admirably told by his intimate friend and colleague, Mr — now Captain — C.E. Montague. He and I had shared many intellectual interests connected with the history of the Empire. His monograph on 'Roman Provincial Administration', first written as an Arnold Essay, still holds the field; and in the realm of pure literature, his one volume edition of Keats is there to show his eagerness for beauty and his love of English verse. I sent him the first volume in proof, about a year before the book came out, and awaited his verdict with much anxiety. It came one May day in 1889. I happened to be very tired and depressed at the moment, and I remember sitting alone for a little while with the letter in my hand, without courage to open it. Then at last I opened it.

Warm congratulation — Admirable! — Full of character and colour . . . . 'Miss Bretherton' was an intellectual exercise. This is quite a different affair, and has interested and touched me deeply, as I feel sure it will all the world. The biggest thing that — with a few other things of the same kind — has been done for years.

Well! — that was enough to go on with, to carry me through the last wrestle with proofs and revision. But by the following November, nervous fatigue made me put work aside for a few weeks, and we went abroad for rest, only to be abruptly summoned home by my mother's state.

Thenceforward I lived a double life — the one overshadowed by my mother's approaching death, the other amid the agitation of the book's appearance, and all the incidents of its rapid success.

I have already told the story in the Introduction to the Library Edition of 'Robert Elsmere', and I will only run through it here, as rapidly as possible, with a few fresh incidents and quotations. There was never any doubt at all of the book's fate, and I may repeat again that before Mr Gladstone's review of it the three volumes were already in a third edition, the rush at all the libraries was in full course, and Matthew Arnold — so gay and kind, in those March weeks before his own sudden death! — had clearly foreseen the rising boom. 'I shall take it with me to Bristol next week and get through it there, I hope (but he didn't achieve it!) It is one of my regrets not to have known the Green of your dedication.' And a week or two later he wrote an amusing letter to his sister describing a country-house party at beautiful Wilton, Lord Pembroke's home near Salisbury, and the various stages in the book reached by the members of the party, including Mr Goschen, who were all reading it, and all talking of it. I never, however, had any criticism of it from him, except of the first volume, which he liked. I doubt very much whether the second and third volumes would have appealed to him. My uncle was a Modernist long before the time. In 'Literature and Dogma', he threw out in detail much of the argument suggested in 'Robert Elsmere', but to the end of his life he was a contented member of the Anglican Church, so far as attendances at her services was concerned, and belief in her mission of 'edification' to the English people. He had little sympathy with people who 'went out'. Like Mr Jowett, he would have liked to see the Church slowly reformed and 'modernised' from within. So that with the main theme of my book — that a priest who doubts must depart — he could never have had full sympathy. And in the course of years — as I showed in a later novel written twenty-four years after ' Robert Elsmere' — I feel that I have very much come to agree with him! These great national structures that we call churches are too precious for iconoclast handling, if any other method is possible. The strong assertion of individual liberty within them, as opposed to the attempt to break them down from without; — that seems to me now the hopeful course. A few more heresy trials like those which sprang out of 'Essays and Reviews', or the persecution of Bishop Colenso, would let in fresh life and healing nowadays, as did those old stirrings of the waters. The first Modernist bishop who stays in his place, forms a Modernist chapter and diocese around him, and fights the fight where he stands, will do more for liberty and faith in the Church, I now sadly believe, than those scores of brave 'forgotten dead' who have gone out of her conscience' sake, all these years.

But to return to the book. All through March the tide of success was rapidly rising; and when I was able to think of it, I was naturally carried away by the excitement and astonishment of it. But with the later days of March a veil dropped between me and the book. My mother's suffering and storm-beaten life was coming rapidly to its close, and I could think of nothing else. In an interval of slight improvement, indeed, when it seemed as though she might rally for a time, I heard Mr Gladstone's name quoted for the first time in connection with the book. It will be remembered that he was then out of office, having been overthrown on the Home Rule Question in '86, and he happened to be staying for an Easter visit with the Warden of Keble, and Mrs Talbot, who was his niece by marriage. I was with my mother about a mile away, and Mrs Talbot, who came to ask for news of her, reported to me that Mr Gladstone was deep in the book. He was reading it pencil in hand, marking all the passages he disliked or quarrelled with, with the Italian '*Ma!*' — and those he approved of with mysterious signs which she who followed him through the volumes could not always decipher. Mr Knowles, she reported, the busy editor of the *Nineteenth Century*, was trying to persuade the great man to review it. But 'Mr G.' had not made up his mind.

Then all was shut out again. Through many days my mother asked constantly for news of the book, and smiled with a flicker of her old brightness, when anything pleased her in a letter or review. But finally there came long hours when to think or speak of it seemed sacrilege. And on April 7 she died.

.   .   .   .

The day after her death, I saw Mr Gladstone at Keble. We talked for a couple of hours and then when I rose to go, he asked if I would come again on the following morning before he went back to town. I had been deeply interested and touched, and I went again for another long visit. My account, written down at the time, of the first day's talk, has been printed as an appendix to the Library Edition of the book. Of the second conversation, which was the more interesting of the two since we came to much closer quarters in it, my only record is the following letter to my husband:

> I have certainly had a wonderful experience last night and this morning! Last night two hours' talk with Gladstone, this morning, again, an hour and a half's strenuous argument; during which the great man got quite white sometimes and tremulous with interest and excitement . . . . The talk this morning was a battle royal over the book and Christian evidences. He was *very* charming personally, through at times he looked stern and angry and white to a degree, so that I wondered sometimes how I had the courage to go on — the drawn brows were so formidable! There was one moment when he talked of 'trumpery objections,', in his most House of Commons manner. It was as I thought. The new lines of criticism are not familiar to him, and they really press him hard. He meets them out of Bishop Butler, and things analogous. But there is a sense, I think, that question and answer don't fit, and with it ever increasing interest and — sometimes — irritation. His own autobiographical reminiscences were wonderfully interesting, and his repetition of the 42nd psalm — 'Like as the hart desireth the water-brooks' — *grand*!
>
> He said that he had never read any book on the hostile side written in such spirit of 'generous appreciation' of the Christian side.

Yes — those were hours to which I shall always look back with gratitude and emotion. Wonderful old man! I see him still standing, as I took leave of him, one hand leaning on the table beside him, his lined, pallid face and eagle eyes, framed in his noble white hair, shining amid the dusk of the room. 'There are still two things left for me to do!' he said, finally, in answer to some remark of mine. — 'One is to carry Home Rule — the other is to prove the intimate connection between the Hebrew and Olympian revelations!'

Could any remark have been more characteristic of that double life of his — the life of the politician, and the life of the student — which kept him fresh and eager to the end of his days? Characteristic too of the amateurish element in all his historical and literary thinking. In dealing 'with early Greek mythology, genealogy and religion,' says his old friend

175

Lord Bryce, Mr Gladstone's theories 'have been condemned by the unanimous voice of scholars as fantastic.' Like his great contemporary, Newman — on whom a good deal of our conversation turned — he had no critical sense of evidence; and when he was writing on 'The Impregnable Rock of Scripture' Lord Acton, who was staying at Hawarden at the time, ran after him in vain, with Welhausen or Kuenen under his arm, if haply he might persuade his host to read them.

But it was not for that he was born; and those who look back to the mighty work he did for his country in the forty years preceding the Home Rule split, can only thank the Powers 'that hold the broad Heaven' for the part which the passion of his Christian faith, the eagerness of this love for letters — for the Homer and the Dante he knew by heart — played in refreshing and sustaining so great a soul. I remember returning shaken and uplifted, through the April air, to the house where my mother lay in death; and among my old papers lies a torn fragment of a letter thirty years old, which I began to write to Mr Gladstone a few days later, and was too shy to send.

> This morning (says the letter, written from Fox How, on the day of my mother's funeral) we laid my dear Mother to rest in her grave among the mountains, and this afternoon I am free to think a little over what has befallen me personally and separately during this past week. It is not that I wish to continue our argument — quite the contrary. As I walked home from Keble on Monday morning, I felt it a hard fate that I should have been arguing, rather than listening . . . . Argument perhaps was inevitable, but none the less I felt afterwards as though there were something incongruous and unfitting in it. In a serious discussion it seemed to me right to say plainly what I felt and believed; but if in doing so, I have given pain, or expressed myself on any point with a too great trenchancy and confidence, please believe that I regret it very sincerely. I shall always remember our talks. If consciousness lasts 'beyond these voices' — my inmost hope as well as yours — we shall know of all these things. Till then I cherish the belief that we are not so far apart as we seem.

But there the letter abruptly ended, and was never sent. I probably shrank from the added emotion of sending it, and I found it again the other day in a packet that had not been looked at for many years. I print it now as evidence of the effect that Mr Gladstone's personality could produce on one forty years younger than himself, and in sharp rebellion at that time against his opinions and influence in two main fields — religion and politics.

.   .   .   .

Four days later, Monday, April 16, my husband came into my room with the face of one bringing ill tidings. 'Matthew Arnold is dead!' My uncle, as many will remember, had fallen suddenly in a Liverpool street while walking with his wife to meet his daughter expected that day from America, and without a sound or movement had passed away. The heart disease which killed so many of his family was his fate also. A merciful one it always seemed to me, which took him thus suddenly and without pain from the life in which he had played so fruitful and blameless a part. That word 'blameless' has always seemed to me particularly to fit him. And the quality to which it points, was what made his humour so sharp-tipped and so harmless. He had no hidden interest to serve — no malice — not a touch, not a trace of cruelty — so that men allowed him to jest about their most sacred idols and superstitions and bore him no grudge.

To me his death at that moment was an irreparable personal loss. For it was only since our migration to London that we had been near enough to him to see much of him. My husband and he had become fast friends, and his visits to Russell Square, and our expeditions to Cobham where he lived, in the pretty cottage beside the Mole, are marked in memory with a very white stone. The only drawback to the Cobham visits were the 'dear, dear boys'! — i.e. the dachshunds, Max and Geist, who, however adorable in themselves, had no taste for visitors and no intention of letting such intruding creatures interfere with their possession of their master. One would go down to Cobham, eager to talk to 'Uncle Matt' about a book or an article — covetous at any rate of *some* talk with him undisturbed. And it would all end in a breathless chase after Max, through field after field where the little wretch was harrying either sheep or cows, with the dear poet, hoarse with shouting, at his heels. The dogs were always *in the party*, talked to, caressed, or scolded exactly like spoilt children; and the cat of the house was almost equally dear. Once, at Harrow, the then ruling cat — a tom — broke his leg, and the house was in lamentation. The vet. was called in, and hurt him horribly. Then Uncle Matt ran up to town, met Professor Huxley at the Atheneaum, and anxiously consulted him. 'I'll go down with you,' said Huxley. The two travelled back instanter to Harrow, and while Uncle Matt held the cat, Huxley — who had begun life, let it be remembered, as Surgeon to the *Rattlesnake*! — examined him, the two black heads together. There is a rumour that Charles Kingsley was included in the consultation. Finally the limb was put in splints, and left to nature. All went well.

Nobody who knew the modest Cobham cottage while its master lived, will ever forget it; the garden beside the Mole, where every bush and flowerbed had its history; and that little study-dressing-room where some of the best work in nineteenth century letters was done. Not a great multitude of books, but all cherished, all read, each one the friend of its owner. No untidiness anywhere; the ordinary; the ordinary litter of an author's room was quite absent. For long after his death, the room remained just as he had left it, his coat hanging behind the door, his slippers beside his chair, the last letters he had received, and all the small and simple equipment of his writing-table ready to his hand, waiting for the master who would never know 'a day of return'. In that room — during fifteen years — he wrote 'God and the Bible', the many suggestive and fruitful Essays, including the American addresses, of his later years — seeds, almost all of them, dropped into the mind of his generation for a future harvesting; a certain number of poems, including the noble elegiac poem on Arthur Stanley's death, 'Geist's Grave' and 'Poor Matthias'; a mass of writing on education which is only now — helped by the war — beginning to tell on the English mind; and the endlessly kind and gracious letters to all sorts and conditions of men — and women — the literary beginner, the young teacher wanting advice, even the stranger greedy for an autograph. Every little playful note to friends or kinsfolk he ever wrote was dear to those who received it; but he — the most fastidious of men — would have much disliked to see them all printed at length in Mr. Russell's indiscriminate volumes. He talked to me once of his wish to make a small volume — 'such a little one!' — of George Sand's best letters. And that is just what he would have wished for himself.

Among the letters that reached me on my uncle's death was one from Mr. Andrew Lang denouncing almost all the obituary notices of him. 'Nobody seems to know that he *was a poet*! cries Mr Lang. But his poetic blossoming was really over with the sixties, and in the hubbub that arose round his critical and religious work — his attempts to drive 'ideas' into the English mind, in the sixties and seventies — the main fact that he, with Browning and Tennyson, *stood for English poetry*, in the mid nineteenth century, was often obscured, and only slowly recognised. But it was recognised; and he himself had never any real doubt of it, from the moment when he sent the 'Strayed Reveller' to my father in New Zealand in 1849, to those later times when his growing fame was in all men's ears. He writes to his sister in 1878: —

> It is curious how the public is beginning to take my poems to its bosom after long years of comparative neglect. The wave of thought and change has rolled on until people begin to find a significance and an attraction in what had none for them formerly.

But he had put it himself in poetry long before — this slow emergence above the tumult and the shouting of the stars that are to shine upon the next generation. Mr Garnett in the careful and learned notice of my uncle's life and work in the 'Dictionary of National Biography' says of his poetry that 'most of it' — is 'immortal'. This indeed is the great, the mystic word that rings in every poet's ear from the beginning. And there is scarcely any true poet who is not certain that sooner or later his work will 'put on immortality'. Matthew Arnold expressed, I think, his own secret faith, in the beautiful lines of his early poem, 'The Bacchanalia — or the New Age.'

> The epoch ends, the world is still
> The age has talk'd and work'd its fill —
>
> . . . .
>
> And in the after-silence sweet
> Now strife is hush'd, our ears doth meet,
> Ascending pure, the bell-like fame
> Of this or that down-trodden name,
> Delicate spirits, push'd away

>In the hot press of the noon-day.
>And o'er the plain, where the dead age
>Did its now silent warfare wage —
>O'er that wide plain, now wrapt in gloom,
>Where many a splendour finds its tomb,
>Many spent fames and fallen nights —
>The one or two immortal lights
>Rise slowly up into the sky
>To shine there everlastingly,
>Like stars over the bounding hill.
>The epoch ends, the world is still.

. . . .

It was on the way home from Laleham after my uncle's burial there, that Mr George Smith gave me fresh and astonishing news of 'Robert Elsmere's' success. The circulating libraries were being fretted to death for copies, and the whirlwind of talk was constantly rising. A little later in the same month of April, if I remember right, I was going from Waterloo to Godalming and Borough Farm, when, just as the train was starting, a lady rushed along the platform waving a book aloft and signalling to another lady who was evidently waiting to see her off. 'I've got it — I've got it!' she said triumphantly. 'Get in, Ma'am — get in!' said the porter, bundling her into the compartment where I sat alone. Then she hung out of the window breathlessly talking. 'They told me no chance for weeks — not the slightest! Then — just as I was standing at the counter, who should come up, but somebody bringing back the first volume. Of course it was promised to somebody else — but as I was *there*, I laid hands on it, and here it is!' The train went off, my companion plunged into her book, and I watched her as she turned the pages of the familiar green volume. We were quite alone. I had half a mind to say something revealing; but on the whole it was more amusing to sit still!

And meanwhile letters poured in.

'I try to write upon you,' wrote Mr Gladstone, — 'wholly despair of satisfying myself — cannot quite tell whether to persevere or desist.' Mr Pater let me know that he was writing on it for *The Guardian*. 'It is a *chef d'œuvre* after its kind, and justifies the care you have devoted to it.' 'I see,' said Andrew Lang on April 30, 'that R.E. is running into as many editions as "The Rights of Man" by Tom Paine . . . . You know he is not *my* sort (at least unless you have a ghost, a murder, a duel and some savages).' Burne-Jones wrote with the fun and sweetness that made his letters a delight: —

> Not one least bitter word in it! — threading your way through intricacies of parsons so finely and justly . . . . As each new one came on the scene, I wondered if you would fall upon him and rend him — but you never do . . . . . Certainly I never thought I should devour a book about parsons — my desires lying towards — 'time upon once there was a dreadful pirate' — but I am back again five and thirty years and feeling softened and subdued with memories you have wakened up so piercingly — and I wanted to tell you this.

And in the same packet lie letters from the honoured and beloved Edward Talbot, now Bishop of Winchester, Stopford Brooke — the Master of Balliol — Lord Justice Bowen — Professor Huxley — and so many, many more. Best of all, Henry James! His two long letters I have already printed, naturally with his full leave and blessing, in the Library Edition of the novel. Not his the grudging and fault-finding temper that besets the lesser man when he comes to write of his contemporaries! Full of generous honour for what he thought good and honest work, however faulty, his praise kindled, — and his blame no less. He appreciated so fully *your* way of doing it; and his suggestion, alongside, of what would have been *his* way of doing it, was so stimulating — touched one with so light a Socratic sting, and set a hundred thoughts on the alert. Of this delightful critical art of his letters to myself over many years are one long illustration.

And now — 'There is none like him — none!' The honied lips are silent, and the helping hand at rest.

With May appeared Mr Gladstone's review — 'the refined criticism of Robert Elsmere' — 'typical of his strong points,' as Lord Bryce describes it: — certainly one of the best things he ever wrote. I had no sooner read it than, after admiring it, I felt it must be answered. But it was desirable to take time to think how best to do it. At the moment my one desire was for rest and escape. At the beginning of June we took our two eldest children, aged eleven and thirteen, to Switzerland for the first time. Oh! The delight of Glion! — with its hayfields thick with miraculous spring flowers, the 'peak of Jaman delicately tall', and that gorgeous pile of the Dent du Midi, bearing up the June heaven, to the east! — the joy of seeing the children's pleasure, and the relief of the mere physical rebound in the Swiss air, after the long months of strain and sorrow. My son — a slip of a person in knickerbockers — walked over the Simplon as though Alps were only made to be climbed by boys of eleven; and the Defile of Gondo, Domo d'Ossola, and beautiful Maggiore: — they were all new and heavenly to each member of the party. Every year now there was growing on me the spell of Italy, the historic, the Saturnian land; and short as this wandering was, I remember, after it was over, and we turned homeward across the St Gotthard, leaving Italy behind us, a new sense as of a hidden treasure in life — of something sweet and inexhaustible always waiting for one's return; like a child's cake in a cupboard, or the gold and silver hoard of Odysseus, that Athene helped him to hide in the Ithacan cave.

. . . .

Then one day towards the end of June or the beginning of July, my husband put down beside me a great brown paper package which the post had just brought. 'There's America beginning!' he said, and we turned over the contents of the parcel in bewilderment. A kind American friend had made a collection for me of the reviews, sermons and pamphlets that had been published so far about the book in the States, the correspondences, the odds and ends of all kinds, grave and gay. Every mail, moreover, began to bring me American letters from all parts of the States. 'No book since "Uncle Tom's Cabin" has had so sudden and wide a diffusion among all classes of readers,' — wrote an American man of Letters — 'and I believe that no other book of equal seriousness ever had so quick a hearing. I have seen it in the hands of nursery-maids and of shop-girls behind the counters; of frivolous young women who read every novel that is talked about; of business men, professors, and students. . . . The proprietors of those large shops where anything — from a pin to a piano — can be bought, vie with each other in selling the cheapest edition. One pirate put his price even so low as four cents — two pence!' (Those, it will be remembered, were the days before Anglo-American copyright.)

Oliver Wendell Holmes, to whom I was personally a stranger, wrote to me just such a letter as one might have dreamed of from the 'Autocrat': — 'One of my elderly friends of long ago, called a story of mine you may possibly have heard of — "Elsie Venner" — "a medicated novel", and such she said she was not in the habit of reading. I liked her expression; it titillated more than it tingled. "Robert Elsmere" I suppose we should all agree is" a medicated novel". But it is, I think, beyond question, the most effective and popular novel we have had since "Uncle Tom's Cabin".'

A man of science, apparently an agnostic, wrote severely — 'I regret the popularity of "Robert Elsmere" in this country. Our western people are like sheep in such matters. They will not see that the book was written for a people with a State Church on its hands, so that a gross exaggeration of the importance of religion was necessary. It will revive interest in theology and retard the progress of rationalism.'

Another student and thinker from one of the Universities of the West, after a brilliant criticism of the novel, written about a year after its publication, winds up — 'The book, here, has entered into the evolution of a nation.'

Goldwin Smith — my father's and uncle's early friend — wrote me from Canada: —

The Grange, Toronto, Oct. 31, 1888.

My Dear Mrs Ward, — You may be amused by seeing what a stir you are making even in this sequestered nook of the theological world, and by learning that the antidote to you is 'Ben Hur'. I am afraid, if it were so, I should prefer the poison to the antidote.

The state of opinion on this Continent is, I fancy, pretty much that to which Robert Elsmere would bring us — Theism, with Christ as a model of character, but without real belief in the miraculous part of Christianity. Churches are still being everywhere built, money is freely subscribed, young men are pressing into the clerical profession, and religion shows every sign of vitality. I cannot help suspecting however that a change is not far off. If it comes, it will come with a vengeance; for over the intellectual dead level of this democracy opinion courses like the tide running in over a flat.

As the end of life draws near I feel like the Scotchman who, being on his deathbed when the trial of O'Connell was going on, desired his Minister to pray for him that he might just live to see what came of O'Connell. A wonderful period of transition in all things however has begun, and I should like very much to see the result. However it is too likely that very rough times may be coming and that one will be just as well out of the way.

Yours most truly,

Goldwin Smith.

Exactly twenty years from the date of this letter, I was in Toronto for the first time, and paid my homage to the veteran fighter, who, living as he did amid a younger generation hotly resenting his separatist and anti-Imperial views, and his contempt for their own ideal of an equal and permanent union of free states under the British flag, was yet generously honoured throughout the Dominion for his services to literature and education. He had been my father's friend at Oxford — where he succeeded to Arthur Stanley's tutorship at University College — and in Dublin. And when I first began to live in Oxford he was still Regius Professor, inhabiting a house very near that of my parents, which was well known to me afterwards through many years as the house of the Max Millers. I can remember the catastrophe it seemed to all his Oxford friends, when he deserted England for America, despairing of the republic, as my father also, for a while in his youth, had despaired, and sick of what seemed to him the forces of reaction in English life. I was eighteen when 'Endymion' came out, with Dizzy's absurd attack on the 'sedentary' professor who was also a 'social parasite'. It would be difficult to find two words in the English language more wholly and ludicrously inappropriate to Goldwin Smith; and the furious letter to *The Times* in which he denounced 'the stingless insults of a coward' might well have been left unwritten. But I was living then among Oxford Liberals, and under the shadow of Goldwin Smith's great reputation as historian and pamphleteer, and I can see myself listening with an angry and sympathetic thrill to my father as he read the letter aloud. Then came the intervening years, in which one learnt to look on Goldwin Smith as par excellence the great man 'gone wrong', on that vital question, above all, of a sane Imperialism. It was difficult after a time to keep patience with the Englishman whose most passionate desire seemed to be to break up the Empire, to incorporate Canada in the United States, to relieve us of India, that 'splendid curse', to detach from us Australia and South Africa, and thereby to wreck for ever that vision of a banded commonwealth of free nations which for innumerable minds at home was fast becoming the romance of English politics.

So it was that I went with some shrinking, yet still under the glamour of the old Oxford loyalty, to pay my visit at the Grange in 1908, walking thither from the house of one of the staunchest Imperialists in Canada where I had been lunching. 'You are going to see Mr Goldwin Smith?' my host had said. 'I have not crossed his threshold for twenty years. I abhor his political views. All the same we are proud of him in Canada!' When I entered the drawing-room, which was rather dark through it was a late May afternoon, there rose slowly from its chair beside a bright fire, a figure I shall never forget. I had a fairly clear remembrance of Goldwin Smith in his earlier days. This was like his phantom, or, if one may say so, without disrespect — his mummy. Shrivelled and spare, yet erect as ever, the iron-grey hair, closely-shaven beard, dark complexion, and black eyes still formidably alive, made on me an impression at once of extreme age, and unabated will. A prophet! — still delivering his message, but well aware that it found but few listeners in a degenerate world. He began immediately to talk politics, denouncing English Imperialism whether of the Tory or the Liberal type. Canadian loyalty to the Empire was a mere delusion. A few years, he said, would see the Dominion merged in the United States; and it was far best it should be so. He spoke with a bitter, almost a fierce energy, as though perfectly conscious that, although I did not contradict him, did not agree with him; and presently to my great relief he allowed the talk to slip back to old Oxford days.

Two years later he died, still confident of the future as he dreamt it. The 'very rough times' that he foresaw have indeed come upon the world. But, as to the rest, I wish he could have stood with me, eight years after this conversation, on the Scherpenberg Hill, then held by a Canadian division, the approach to its summit guarded by Canadian sentries, and have looked out over that plain where Canadian and British graves, lying in their thousands side by side, have for ever sealed in blood the union of the elder and the younger nations.

As to the circulation of 'Robert Elsmere', I have never been able to ascertain the exact figures in America, but it is probable from the data I have that about half a million copies were sold in the States within a year of the book's publication. In England, an edition of 5000 copies a fortnight was the rule for many months after the one-volume edition appeared; hundreds of thousands have been circulated in the sixpenny and sevenpenny editions; it has been translated into most foreign tongues; and it is still, after thirty years, a living book. Fifteen years after its publication, M. Brunetière, the well-known editor of the *Revue des deux Mondes*, and leader — in some sort — of the Catholic reaction in France, began a negotiation with me for the appearance of a French translation of the whole or part of the book in his *Revue*. 'But how' — I asked him (we were sitting in his editor's sanctum, in the old house of the Rue de l'Université) — 'could it possibly suit you, or the *Revue*, to do anything of the kind? And *now* — after fifteen years?'

But according to him, the case was simple. When the book first appeared, the public of the *Revue* could not have felt any interest in it. France is a logical country — a country of clear-cut solutions. And at that time either one was a Catholic — or a free thinker. And if one was a Catholic, one accepted from the Church — say, the date of the book of Daniel, as well as everything else. Renan indeed left the Church thirty years earlier because he came to see with certainty that the book of Daniel was written under Antiochus Epiphanes, and not when his teachers at St Sulpice said it was written. But while the secular world listened and applauded, the literary argument against dogma made very little impression on the general Catholic world for many years.

'But now,' said M. Bruentière, 'everything is different. Modernism has arisen. It is penetrating the Seminaries. People begin to talk of it in the streets. And 'Robert Elsmere' is a study in Modernism — or at any rate it has so many affinities with Modernism, that *now* — the French public would be interested.'

The length of the book, however, could not be got over, and the plan fell through. But I came away from my talk with a remarkable man, not a little stirred. For it had seemed to show that with all its many faults — and who knew them better than I? — my book had yet possessed a certain representative and pioneering force; and that, to some extent at least, the generation in which it appeared had spoken through it.

CHAPTER XIII

First Visits to Italy

I have already mentioned in these pages that I was one of the examiners for the Spanish Taylorian scholarship at Oxford in 1883, and again in 1888. But perhaps before I go further in these Recollections, I may put down here — somewhat out of its place — a reminiscence connected with the first of these examinations, which seems to me worth recording. My Spanish colleague in 1883 was, as I have said, Don Pascual Gayangos, well known among students for his 'History of Mohammedan Dynasties in Spain', for his edition of the Correspondence of Cardinal Cisneros, and other historical work. *À propos* of the examination, he came to see me in Russell Square, and his talk about Spain revived in me, for the time, a fading passion. Señor Gayangos was born in 1809, so that in 1883 he was already an old man, though full of vigour and work. He told me the following story. Unfortunately I took no contemporary note. I give it now, as I remember it, and if anyone who knew Don Pascual, or any student of Shakespearean lore, can correct and amplify it, no one will be better pleased than I. He said that as quite a young man, somewhere in the thirties of the last century, he was travelling through Spain to England, where if I remember right, he had relations with Sir Thomas Phillipps, the ardent book and MSS collector, so many of whose treasures are now in the great libraries of Europe. Sir Thomas employed him in the search for Spanish MSS and rare Spanish books. I gathered that at the time to which the story refers Gayangos himself was not much acquainted with English or English literature. On his journey north from Madrid to Burgos, which was of course in the days before railways, he stopped at Valladolid for the night, and went to see an acquaintance of his, the newly appointed librarian of an aristocratic family having a 'palace' in Valladolid. He found his friend in the old library of the old house, engaged in a work of destruction. On the floor of the long room was a large *brasero* in which the new librarian was burning up a quantity of what he described as useless and miscellaneous books, with a view to the rearrangement of the library. The old sheepskin or vellum bindings had been stripped off, while the printed matter was burning steadily, and the room was full of smoke. There was a pile of old books whose turn had not yet come lying on the floor. Gayangos picked one up. It was a volume containing the plays of Mr William Shakespeare, and published in 1623. In other words, it was a copy of the First Folio, and, as he declared to me, in excellent preservation. At that time he knew nothing about Shakespeare bibliography. He was struck however by the name of Shakespeare, and also by the fact that, according to an inscription inside it, the book had belonged to Count Gondomar, who had himself lived in Valladolid, and collected a large library there. But his friend the librarian attached no importance to the book, and it was to go into the common holocaust with the rest. Gayangos noticed particularly, as he turned it over, that its margins were covered with notes in a seventeenth-century hand.

He continued his journey to England, and presently mentioned the incident to Sir Thomas Phillipps, and Sir Thomas's future son-in-law, Mr Halliwell — afterwards Halliwell-Phillipps. The excitement of both knew no bounds. A First Folio — which had belonged to Count Gondomar, Spanish Ambassador to England up to 1622 — and covered with contemporary marginal notes! No doubt a copy which had been sent out to Gondomar from England; for he was well acquainted with English life and letters, and had collected much of his library in London. The very thought of such a treasure perishing barbarously in a bonfire of wastepaper was enough to drive a bibliophile out of his wits. Gayangos was sent back to Spain post haste. But alack, he found a library swept and garnished, no trace of the volume he had once held there in his hand, and on the face of his friend the librarian only a frank and peevish wonder that anybody should tease him with questions about such a trifle.

But just dream a little! Who sent the volume? Who wrote the thick marginal notes? An English correspondent of Gondomar's? Or

Gondomar himself, who arrived in England three years before Shakespeare's death, was himself a man of letters, and had probably seen most of the plays?

In the few years which intervened between his withdrawal from England, and his own death (1626) did he annotate the copy, storing there what he could remember of the English stage, and of 'pleasant Willy' himself perhaps, during his two sojourns in London? And was the book overlooked as English and of no importance in the transfer of Gondomar's own library, a hundred and sixty years after his death, to Charles III of Spain? — and had it been sold — perhaps — for an old song — and with other remnants of Gondomar's books, just for their local interest, to some Valladolid grandee?

Above all, did those marginal notes which Gayangos had once idly looked through contain, perhaps, though the First Folio, of course, does not include the Poems, some faint key to the perennial Shakespeare mysteries — to Mr W.H., and the 'dark lady', and all the impenetrable story of the Sonnets?

If so, the gods themselves took care that the veil should not be rent. The secret remains.

> Others abide our question — Thou art free.
> We ask and ask. Thou standest and art still,
> Out-topping knowledge.

. . . .

One other recollection of the 'Robert Elsmere' year may fitly end my story of it. In September we spent an interesting afternoon at Hawarden — the only time I ever saw 'Mr G.' at leisure, amid his own books and trees. We drove over with Sir Robert and Lady Cunliffe, Mr Gladstone's neighbours on the Welsh border with whom we were staying. Sir Robert, formerly an ardent Liberal, had parted from Mr Gladstone in the Home Rule crisis of '86, and it was the first time they had called at Hawarden since the split. But nothing could have been kinder than the Gladstones' reception of them and of us. 'Mr G.' and I let theology alone! — and he was at his best and brightest, talking books and poetry, showing us the octagonal room he had built out for his 60,000 selected letters — among them 'hundreds from the Queen' — his library, the park, and the old keep. As I wrote to my father, his amazing intellectual and physical vigour, and the alertness with which, leading the way, he 'skipped up the ruins of the keep', were enough 'to make a Liberal Unionist thoughtful'. Ulysses was for the time in exile, but the 'day of return' was not far off.

Especially do I remember the animation with which he dwelt on the horrible story of Damiens, executed with every conceivable torture for the attempted assassination of Louis Quinze. He ran through the catalogue of torments so that we all shivered, winding up with a contemptuous — 'And all that, for just pricking the skin of that scoundrel Louis XV.'

I was already thinking of some reply both to Mr Gladstone's article, and to the attack on 'Robert Elsmere' in the *Quarterly*; but it took me longer than I expected; and it was not till March in the following year (1889) that I published 'The New Reformation', a Dialogue, in the *Nineteenth Century*. Into that dialogue I was able to throw the reading and the argument which had been of necessity excluded from the novel. Mr Jowett was nervous about it, and came up on purpose from Oxford to persuade me, if he could, not to write it. His view — and that of Mr Stopford Brooke — was that a work of art moves on one plane, and historical or critical controversy on another, and that a novel cannot be justified by an essay. But my defence was not an essay; I put it in the form of a conversation, and made it as living and varied as I could. By using this particular form, I was able to give the traditional as well as the critical case with some fullness, and I took great pains with both. From a recently published letter, I see that Lord Acton wrote to Mr Gladstone that the rôle played by the orthodox anti-rational and wholly fanatical Newcome in the novel belonged 'to the infancy of art', so little could he be taken as representing the orthodox case. I wonder! I had very good reasons for Newcome. There are plenty of Newcomes in the theological literature of the last century. To have provided a more rational and plausible representative of orthodoxy would, I think, have slackened the pace and chilled the atmosphere of the novel. After all, what really supplied ' the other side', was the whole system of things in which the readers of the book lived and moved — the ideas in which they had been brought up, the books they read, the churches in which they worshipped, the sermons to which they listened every week. The novel challenged this system of things; but it was always there to make reply. It was the eternal *sous-entendu* of the story, and really gave the story all its force.

But, in the dialogue, I could put the underlying conflict of thought into articulate and logical form, and build up, in outline at least, the history of 'a new learning'. When it was published, the dear Master, with a sigh of relief, confessed that it had 'done no harm', and 'showed a considerable knowledge of critical theology'. I too felt that it had done no harm — rather that it had vindicated my right to speak — not as an expert and scholar — to that I never pretended for a moment — but as the interpreter of experts and scholars who had something to say to the English world, and of whom the English world was far too little aware. In the preface to one of the latest editions of his Bampton Lectures, Canon Liddon wrote an elaborate answer to it, which I think, implies that it was felt to have weight; and if Lord Acton had waited for its appearance he might not, perhaps, have been so ready to condemn the character of Newcome as belonging 'to the infancy of art'. That Newcome's type might have been infinitely better presented is indeed most true. But in the scheme of the book, it is *right*. For the ultimate answer to the critical intellect, or, as Newman called it, the 'wild living intellect of man', when it is dealing with Christianity and miracle, is that reason is *not* the final judge — is indeed, in the last resort, the enemy, and must at some point go down, defeated and trampled on. 'Ideal Ward', or Archdeacon Denison, or Mr Spurgeon — and not Dr Figgis, or Dr Creighton — are the apologists who in the end hold the fort.

But with this analysis of what may be called the intellectual presuppositions of 'Robert Elsmere', my mind began to turn to what I believed to be the other side of the Greenian or Modernist message — i.e. that life itself, the ordinary human life and experience of every day as it has been slowly evolved through history, is the true source of religion, if man will but listen to the message in his own soul, to the voice of the Eternal Friend, speaking through Conscience, through Society, through Nature. Hence 'David Grieve', which was already in my mind within a few months of the publication of 'Robert Elsmere'. We were at Borough Farm when the vision of it first came upon me. It was a summer evening of extraordinary beauty, and I had been wandering through the heather and the pinewoods. 'The country' — to quote an account written some years ago — 'was drenched in sunset; white towering thunder-clouds descending upon and mingling with the crimson of the heath, the green stretches of bracken, the brown pools upon the common, everywhere a rosy suffusion, a majesty of light interweaving heaven and earth, and transfiguring all dear familiar things — the old farmhouse, the sandpit where the children played and the sand-martins nested, the woodpile by the farm-door, the phloxes in the tumbledown farmyard, the cottage down the lane. After months of rest, the fount of mental energy which had been exhausted in me the year before, had filled again. I was eager to be at work, and this time on something 'more hopeful, positive, and consoling' than the subject of the earlier book.

A visit to Derbyshire in the autumn gave me some of the setting for the story. Then I took the first chapters abroad during the winter to Valescure, and worked at them in that fragrant, sunny spot, making acquaintance the while with a new and delightful friend, Emily Lawless, the author of 'Hurrish' and 'Grania', and of some few poems that deserve, I think, a long life in English anthologies. She and her most racy, most entertaining mother, old Lady Cloncurry, were spending the winter at Valescure, and my young daughter and I found them a great resource. Lady Cloncurry, who was a member of an old Galway family, the Kirwans of Castle Hackett, seemed to me a typical specimen of those Anglo-Irish gentry who have been harshly called the 'English garrison' in Ireland, but who were really in the last century the most natural and kindly link between the two countries. So far as I knew them, they loved both, with a strong preference for Ireland. All that English people instinctively resent in Irish character, — its dreamy or laughing indifference towards the ordinary business virtues — thrift, prudence, tidiness, accuracy — they had been accustomed to, even where they had not been infected with it, from their childhood. They were not Catholics, most of them, and, so far as they were landlords, the part played by the priests in the Land League agitation tried them sore. But Miss Lawless's 'Grania' is there to show how delicate and profound might be their sympathy with the lovely things in Irish Catholicism, and her best poems — 'The Dirge of the Munster Forest', or 'After Aughrim' — give a voice to Irish suffering and Irish patriotism which it would be hard to parallel in the Nationalist or rebel literature of recent years. The fact that they had both nations in their blood, both patriotisms in their hearts, infused a peculiar pathos often into their lives.

Pathos, however, was not a word that seemed, at first sight at any rate, to have much to do with Lady Cloncurry. She was the most energetic and sprightly *grande dame*, as I remember her, small, with vivid black eyes and hair, her head always swathed in a becoming black lace coif, her hands in black mittens. She and her daughter Emily amused each other perennially, and were endless good company besides for other people. Lady Cloncurry's clothes varied very little. She had an Irish contempt for too much pains about your appearance, and a great dislike for *grande tenue*. When she arrived at an Irish country-house, of which the hostess told me the story, she said to the mistress of the house, on being taken to her room — 'My dear, you don't want me to come down smart? I'm sure you don't! Of course I've brought some smart gowns. *They* (meaning her daughters) make me buy them. But they'll just do for my maid to show your maid!' And there on the wardrobe shelves they lay throughout her visit.

At Valescure we were within easy reach of Cannes, where the Actons were settled at the Villa Madeleine. The awkwardness of the trains prevented us from seeing as much of them as we had hoped; but I remember some pleasant walks and talks with Lord Acton, and especially the vehement advice he gave us, when my husband joined us, and we started on a short, a very short, flight to Italy — for my husband had only a meagre holiday from *The Times* — 'Go to *Rome!* Never mind the journeys. Go! You will have three days there, you say? Well, to have walked through Rome, to have spent an hour in the Forum, another on the Palatine; to have seen the Vatican, the Sistine Chapel, and St Peter's; to have climbed the Janiculum and looked out over the Alban hills and the Campagna — and you can do all that in three days — well! — life is not the same afterwards. If you only had an afternoon in Rome, it would be well worth while. But *three days*!'

We laughed, took him at his word, and rushed on for Rome. And on the way we saw Perugia and Assisi for the first time, dipping into spring as soon as we got south of the Apennines, and tasting that intoxication of Italian sun in winter which turns northern heads. Of our week in Rome, I remember only the first overwhelming impression — as of something infinitely old and *pagan*, through which Christianity moved about like a *parvenu* amid an elder generation of phantom presences, already grey with time long before Calvary: — that, and the making of a few new friends. Of these friends, one, who was to hold a lasting place in my admiration and love through after years, shall be mentioned here — Contessa Maria Pasolini.

Contessa Maria for some thirty years has played a great rôle in the social and intellectual history of Italy. She is the daughter of one of the leading business families of Milan, sister to the Marchese Ponti, who was for long Sindaco of that great city, and intimately concerned in its stormy industrial history. She married Count Pasolini, the head of an old aristocratic family with large estates in the Romagna, whose father was President of the first Senate of United Italy. It was in the neighbourhood of the Pasolini estates that Garibaldi took refuge after '48; and one may pass through them to reach the lonely hut in which Anita Garibaldi died.

Count Pasolini's father was also one of Pio Nono's Liberal Ministers, and the family, at the time at any rate of which I am speaking, combined Liberalism and sympathies for England with an enlightened and ardent Catholicism. I first made friends with Contessa Maria when we found her, on a cold February day, receiving in an apartment in the Piazza dei Santi Apostoli — rather gloomy rooms, to which her dark head and eyes, her extraordinary expressiveness and grace, and the vivacity of her talk, seemed to lend a positive brilliance and charm. In her I first came to know, with some intimacy, a cultivated Italian woman, and to realise what a strong kindred exists between the English and the Italian educated mind. Especially, I think, in the case of the educated *women* of both nations. I have often felt, in talking to an Italian woman friend, a similarity of standards, of traditions and instincts, which would take some explaining, if one came to think it out. Especially on the practical side of life, the side of what one may call the minor morals and judgements; which are often more important to friendship and understanding than the greater matters of the law. How an Italian lady manages her servants, and brings up her children, her general attitude towards marriage, politics, books, social or economic questions: — in all these fields she is, in some mysterious way, much nearer to the Englishwoman than the Frenchwoman is. Of course, these remarks do not apply to the small circle of 'black' families in Italy, particularly in Rome, who still hold aloof from the Italian kingdom and its institutions. But the Liberal Catholic, man or woman, who is both patriotically Italian and sincerely religious, will discuss anything or anybody in heaven or earth, and just as tolerantly as would Lord Acton himself. They are cosmopolitans, and yet deep rooted in the Italian soil. Contessa Maria, for instance, was in 1889 still near the beginnings of what was to prove for twenty-five years the most interesting salon in Rome. Everybody met there: grandees of all nations, ambassadors, ecclesiastics, men of literature, science, archćology, art, politicians, and diplomats — Contessa Pasolini was equal to them all, and her talk, rapid, fearless, picturesque, full of knowledge, yet without a hint of pedantry, gave a note of unity to a scene that could hardly have been more varied or, in less skilful hands, more full of jarring possibilities. But later on, when I knew her better, I saw her also with peasant folk, with the country people of the Campagna and the Alban hills. And here one realised the same ease, the same sympathy, the same instinctive and unerring *success*, as one might watch with delight on one of her 'evenings' in the Palazzo Sciarra. When she was talking to a peasant woman on the Alban ridge, something broad and big and primitive seemed to come out in her, something of the 'Magna parens', the Saturnian land; but something too that our English women, who live in the country and care for their own people, also possess.

But I was to see much more of Contessa Maria and Roman society in later years, especially when we were at the Villa Barberini, and I was writing 'Eleanor' in 1899. Now, I will only recall a little saying of the Contessa's at our first meeting, which lodged itself in memory. She did not then talk English fluently, as she afterwards came to do; but she was learning English, with her two boys, from a delightful English tutor, and evidently pondering English character and ways — 'Ah, you English!' — I can see the white arm and land, with its cigarette, waving in the darkness of the old Roman apartment — the broad brow, the smiling eyes, and glint of white teeth — 'You English! Why don't you *talk?* — why *won't* you talk? If French people come here, there is no trouble. If I just tear up an envelope and throw down the pieces — they will talk about it a whole evening — and so *well*! But you English! — you begin — and then you stop — one must always start again — always wind you up!'

Terribly true! But in her company, even we halting English learnt to talk, in our bad French, or whatever came along.

The summer of '89 was filled with an adventure to which I still look back with unalloyed delight, which provided me moreover with the setting and one of the main themes of 'Marcella'. We were at that time half way through the building of a house at Haslemere, which was to supersede Borough Farm. We had grown out of Borough, and were for the moment houseless, so far as summer quarters were concerned. And for my work's sake, I felt that eagerness for new scenes and suggestions which is generally present, I think, in the storyteller of all shades. Suddenly, in a house-agent's catalogue, we came across an astonishing advertisement. Hampden House, on the Chiltern Hills the ancestral home of John Hampden, of Ship-Money fame, was to let for the summer, and for a rent not beyond our powers. The new Lord Buckinghamshire, who had inherited it, was not then able to live in it. It had indeed, as we knew, been let for a while, some years earlier, to our old friends, Sir Mountstuart and Lady Grant Duff, before his departure for the Governorship of Madras. The agents reported that it was scantily furnished, but quite habitable; and without more ado, we took it! I have now before me the letter in which I reported our arrival, in mid-July, to my husband, detained in town by his *Times* work.

Hampden is enchanting! — more delightful than even I thought it would be, and quite comfortable enough. Of course we want a multitude of things — (baths, wineglasses, tumblers, cans, etc.!) but those I can hire from Wycombe. Our great deficiency is lamps! Last night we crept about in this vast house, with hardly any light. . . . As to the ghost, Mrs Duval (the housekeeper) scoffs at it! The ghost room is the tapestry room, from which there is a staircase down to the breakfast room. A good deal of the tapestry is loose, and when there is any wind it flaps and flaps. Hence all the tales . . . The servants are rather bewildered by the size of everything, and — like me — were almost too excited to sleep. . . . . . The children are wandering blissfully about, exploring everything.

And what a place to wander in! After we left it, Hampden was restored, beautiful and re-furnished. It is now, I have no doubt, a charming and comfortable country-house. But when we lived in it for three months — in its half-furnished and tatterdemalion condition — it was Romance pure and simple. The old galleried hall, the bare rooms, the neglected pictures — among them the 'Queen Elizabeth', presented to the owner of Hampden by The Queen herself after a visit — the grey walls of King John's garden, and just beyond it the little church where Hampden lies buried; the deserted library on the top floor, running along the beautiful garden front, with books in it that might have belonged to the patriot himself, and a stately full-length portrait — painted about 1600 — which stood up, torn and frameless, among lumber of various kinds, the portrait of a beautiful lady in a flowered dress, walking in an Elizabethan garden; the locked room, opened to us occasionally by the agent of the property, which contained some of the ancestral treasures of the house — the family bible among them, with the births of John Hampden and his cousin, Oliver Cromwell, recorded on the same flyleaf; the black cedars outside, and the great glade in front of the house, stretching downwards for half a mile towards the ruined lodges just visible from the windows: — all this mingling of nature and history with the slightest gentlest touch of pathos and decay, seen too under the golden light of a perfect summer sank deep into mind and sense.

Whoever cares to turn to the first chapters of 'Marcella' will find as much of Hampden as could be transferred to paper — Hampden as it was then — in the description of Mellor.

Our old and dear friend, Mrs J. R. Green, the widow of the historian, and herself the most distinguished woman-historian of our time, joined us in the venture. But she and I both went to Hampden to work. I set up in one half-dismantled room, and she in another, with the eighteenth-century drawing-room between us. Here our books and papers soon made home. I was working at 'David Grieve': she, if I remember right, at the brilliant book on 'English Town Life' she brought out in 1891. My husband came down to us for long weekends, and as soon as we had provided ourselves with the absolute necessaries of life, visitors began to arrive. Professor and Mrs Huxley, Sir Alfred Lyall, M. Jusserand, then

'Conseiller d'Ambassade' under M. Waddington, now the French Ambassador to Washington, Mr and Mrs Lyulph Stanley (now Lord and Lady Sheffield), my first cousin H. O. Arnold Forster, afterwards War Minister in Mr Balfour's Cabinet, and his wife, Mrs Graham Smith, Laura Lyttelton's sister, and many kinsfolk. In those days Hampden was six miles from the nearest railway station; the great Central Railway which now passes through the valley below it was not built, and all round us stretched beechwoods and commons and lanes, untouched since the days of Roundhead and Cavalier where the occasional sound of woodcutters in the beech solitudes, was often, through a long walk, the only hint of human life. What good walks and talks we had in those summer days! My sister had married Professor Huxley's eldest son, so that with him and his wife we were on terms always of the closest intimacy and affection. 'Pater' and 'Moo', as all their kith and kin and many of their friends called them, were the most racy of guests. He had been that year pursuing an animated controversy in the *Nineteenth Century* with Dr Wace, now Dean of Canterbury, who had also — about a year before — belaboured the author of 'Robert Elsmere' in the *Quarterly Review*. The Professor and I naturally enjoyed dancing a little on our opponents — when there was none to make reply! — as we strolled about Hampden; but there was never a touch of bitterness in Huxley's nature, and there couldn't have been much in mine at that moment — life was so interesting, and its horizon so full of light and colour. Of his wife — 'Moo' — who outlived him many years, how much one might say! In this very year, 1889, Huxley wrote to her from the Canaries whither he had gone alone for his health:

> Catch me going out of reach of letters again. I have been horridly anxious. Nobody — children or anyone else — can be to me what you are. Ulysses preferred his old woman to immortality, and this absence has led me to see that he was as wise in that as in other things.

They were indeed lovers to the end. He had waited and served for her eight years in his youth, and her sunny, affectionate nature, with its veins both of humour and stoicism, gave her man of genius exactly what he wanted. She survived him for many years, living her own life at

Eastbourne, climbing Beachy Head in all weathers, interested in everything, and writing poems of little or no technical merit, but raised occasionally by sheer intensity of feeling — about her husband — into something very near the real thing. I quote these verses from a privately printed volume she gave me:

> If you were here, — and I were where you lie,
> Would you, beloved, give your little span
> Of life remaining unto tear and sigh?
> No! — setting every tender memory
> Within your breast, as faded roses kept
> For giver's sake, of giver when bereft,
> Still to the last the lamp of work you'd burn
> For purpose high, nor any moment spurn.
> So, as you would have done, I fain would do
> In poorer fashion. Ah, how oft I try,
> Try to fulfil your wishes, till at length
> The scent of those dead roses steals my strength.

As to our other guests, to what company would not Sir Alfred Lyall have added that touch of something provocative and challenging which draws men and women after it, like an Orpheus-music? I can see him sitting silent, his legs crossed, his white head bent, the corners of his mouth drooping, his eyes downcast, like some one spent and wearied, from whom all virtue had gone out. Then someone, a man he liked — but still oftener a woman — would approach him, and the whole figure would wake to life — a gentle, whimsical, melancholy life; yet possessed of a strange spell and pungency. Brooding, sad and deep, seemed to me to hold his inmost mind. The fatalism and dream of those Oriental religions to which he had given so much of his scholar's mind, had touched him profoundly. His poems express it in mystical and sombre verse, and his volumes of 'Asiatic Studies' contain the intellectual analysis of that background of thought from which the poems spring.

Yet no one was shrewder, more acute than Sir Alfred in dealing with the men and politics of the moment. He swore to no man's words, and one felt in him not only the first-rate administrator, as shown by his Indian career, but also the thinker's scorn for the mere party point of view. He was an excellent gossip, of a refined and subtle sort; he was the soul of honour; and there was that in his fragile and delicate personality which earned the warm affection of many friends. So gentle, so absent-minded, so tired he often seemed; and yet I could imagine those grey-blue eyes of Sir Alfred's answering inexorably to any public or patriotic call. He was a disillusioned spectator of the 'great mundane movement', yet eternally interested in it; and the man who loves this poor human life or ours, without ever being fooled by it, at least after youth is past, has a rare place among us. We forgive his insight, because there is nothing in it pharisaical. And the irony he uses on us, we know well that he has long since sharpened on himself.

When I think of M. Jusserand playing tennis on the big lawn at Hampden, and determined to master it, like all else that was English, memory leands one back behind that pleasant scene to earlier days still. We first knew the future Ambassador as an official of the French Foreign Office, who spent much of his scanty holidays in a scholarly pursuit of English literature. In Russell Square we were close to the British Museum, where M. Jusserand, during his visits to London, was deep in Chaucerian and other problems, gathering the learning which he presently began to throw into a series of books on the English centuries from Chaucer to Shakespeare. Who introduced him to us I cannot remember, but during his work at the Museum he would drop in sometimes for luncheon or tea; so that we soon began to know him well. Then, later, he came to London as 'Conseiller d'Ambassade' under M. Waddington, an office which he filled till he became French Minister to Denmark in 1900. Finally, in 1904, he was sent as French Ambassador to the United States, and there we found him in 1908, when we stayed for a delightful few days at the British Embassy with Mr and Mrs Bryce.

It has always been a question with me, which of two French friends is the more wonderful English scholar — M. Jusserand, or M. André Chevrillon, Taine's nephew and literary executor, and himself one of the leaders of French letters; with whom, as with M. Jusserand, I may reckon now some thirty years of friendship. No one could say that M. Jusserand speaks our tongue exactly like an Englishman. He does much better. He uses it — always of course with perfect correctness and fluency — to express French ideas, and French wits, in a way as nearly French as the foreign language will permit. The result is extraordinarily stimulating to our English wits. The slight differences both in accent and phrase keep the ear attentive and alive. New shades emerge; old clichés are broken up. M. Chevrillon has much less accent, and his talk is more flowingly and convincingly English; for which no doubt a boyhood partly spent in England accounts. While for vivacity and ease, there is little or nothing to choose.

But to these two distinguished and accomplished men, England and America owe a real debt of gratitude. They have not by any means always approved of *our* national behaviour. M. Jusserand during his official career in Egypt was, I believe, a very candid critic of British administration and British methods, and in the days of our early acquaintance with him I can remember many an amusing and caustic sally of his at the expense of our politicians and our foreign policy.

M. Chevrillon took the Boer side in the South African war, and took it with passion. All the same, the friendship of both the diplomat and the man of letters for this country, based upon their knowledge of her, and warmly returned to them by many English friends, has been a real factor in the growth of that broad-based sympathy which we now call the Entente. M. Chevrillon's knowledge of us is really uncanny. He knows more than we know ourselves. And his last book about us — 'L'Angleterre et la Guerre' — is not only photographically close to the facts, but full of a spiritual sympathy which is very moving to an English reader. Men of such high gifts are not easily multiplied in any country. But looking to the future of Europe, the more that France and England — and America — can cultivate in their citizens some degree at any rate of that intimate understanding of a foreign nation, which shines so conspicuously in the work of these two Frenchmen, the safer will that future be.

CHAPTER XIV

Amalfi and Rome.
Hampden and 'Marcella'

It was in November 1891 that I finished 'David Grieve', after a long wrestle of more than three years. I was tired out, and we fled south for rest to Rome, Naples, Amalfi, and Ravello. The Cappucini hotel at Amalfi, Madame Palumbo's inn at Ravello, remain with me as places of pure delight, shone on even in winter by a more than earthly sun.

Madame Palumbo was, as her many guests remember, an Englishwoman, and showed a special zeal in making English folk comfortable. And can one ever forget the sunrise over the Gulf of Salerno from the Ravello windows? It was December when we were there; yet nothing spoke of winter. From the inn perched on a rocky point above the coast one looked straight down for hundreds of feet, through lemon-groves and olive gardens, to the blue water. Flaming over the mountains rose an unclouded sun, shining on the purple coast, with its innumerable rock-towns — '*Tot congesta manu prœruptis oppida saxis*' — and sending broad paths over the 'wine-dark' sea. Never, I think, have I felt the glory and beauty of the world more rapturously, more *painfully* — for there is pain in it! — than when one was standing alone on a December morning, at a window which seemed to make part of the precipitous rock itself, looking over that fairest of scenes.

From Ravello we went back to Rome, and a short spell of its joys. What is it makes the peculiar pleasure of society in Rome? A number of elements, of course, enter in. The setting is incomparable; while the clashing of great world policies, represented by the diplomats, and of the main religious and Liberal forces of Europe, as embodied in the Papacy and modern Italy, — kindles a warmth and animation in the social air which matches the clearness of the Roman day, when the bright spells of the winter weather arrive, and the omnipresent fountains of the Eternal City flash the January or February sun through its streets and piazzas. Ours however, on this occasion, was only a brief stay. Again we saw Contessa Maria, this time in the stately setting of the Palazzo Sciarra; and Count Ugo Balzani, an old friend of ours and of the Creightons since Oxford days, historian and thinker, and besides, one of the kindest and truest of men. But the figure perhaps which chiefly stands out in memory as connected with this short visit is that of Lord Dufferin, then our Ambassador in Rome. Was there ever a greater charmer than Lord Dufferin? In the sketch of the 'Ambassador' in 'Eleanor', there are some points caught from the living Lord Dufferin, so closely indeed that before the book came out, I sent him the proofs, and asked his leave — which he gave at once, in one of the graceful little notes of which he was always master. For the diplomatic life and successes of Lord Dufferin are told in many official documents, and in the biography of him by Sir Alfred Lyall; but the key to it all lay in cradle gifts that are hard to put into print.

In the first place he was — even at sixty-five — wonderfully handsome. He had inherited the beauty, and also the humour and the grace of his Sheridan ancestry. For his mother, as all the world knows, was Helen Sheridan, one of the three famous daughters of Tom Sheridan, the dramatist's only son. Mrs Norton, the innocent heroine of the Melbourne divorce suit, was one of his aunts, and the 'Queen of Beauty' at the Eglinton Tournament — then Lady Seymour, afterwards Duchess of Somerset — was the other. His mother's memory was a living thing to him all his life; he published her letters and poems; and at Clandeboye, his Ulster home — in 'Helen's Tower' — he had formed a collection of memorials of her which he liked to show to those of whom he made friends. 'You must come to Clandeboye, and let me show you Helen's Tower,' he would say eagerly, and one would answer with hopeful vagueness. But for me, the time never came. My personal recollections of him, apart from letters, are all connected with Rome, or Paris, whither he was transferred the year after we saw him at the Roman Embassy, in December 1891.

It was therefore his last winter at Rome, and he had only been Ambassador there a little more than two years — since he ceased to be Viceroy of

India in 1889. But he had already won everybody's affection. The social duties of the British Embassy in Rome — what with the Italian world in all its shades, the more or less permanent English colony, and the rush of English tourists through the winter and spring — seemed to me by no means easy. But Lady Dufferin's dignity and simplicity, and Lord Dufferin's temperament, carried them triumphantly through the tangle. Especially do I remember the informal Christmas dance, to which we took, by the Ambassador's special wish, our young daughter of seventeen, who was not really 'out'. And no sooner was she in the room, shyly hiding behind her elders, than he discovered her. I can see him still, as he made her a smiling bow, — his noble grey head, and kind eyes, the blue ribbon crossing his chest. 'You promised me a dance!' And so for her first waltz, in her first grown-up dance, D. was well provided, nervous as the moment was.

There is a passage in 'Eleanor', which commemorates first this playful sympathy and tact which made Lord Dufferin so delightful to all ages, and next, an amusing conversation with him that I remember a year or two later in Paris. As to the first — Lucy Foster, the young American girl, is lunching at the Embassy: —

'Ah! My dear lady!' said the Ambassador, 'how few things in this world one does to please one's self! This is one of them.'

Lucy flushed with a young and natural pleasure. She was on the Ambassador's left, and he had just laid his wrinkled hand for an instant on hers — with a charming and paternal freedom.

'Have you enjoyed yourself ? — Have you lost your heart to Italy?' said her host stooping to her . . . .

'I have seen in fairyland,' said she shyly, opening her blue eyes upon him. 'Nothing can ever be like it again.'

'No — because one can never be twenty again,' said the old man, sighing. 'Twenty years hence, you will wonder where the magic came from. Never mind — just now, anyway, the world's your oyster.'

Then he looked at her a little more closely. . . . He missed some of that quiver of youth and enjoyment he had felt in her before; and there were some very dark lines under the beautiful eyes. What was wrong? Had she met the man — the appointed one?

He began to talk to her with a kindness that was at once simple and stately.

'We must all have our ups and downs,' he said to her presently. 'Let me just give you a word of advice. It'll carry you through most of them. Remember you are very young, and I shall soon be very old.'

He stopped and surveyed her. His eyes blinked through their blanched lashes. Lucy dropped her fork and looked back at him with smiling expectancy.

'Learn Persian!' said the old man, in an urgent whisper — 'and get the dictionary by heart!'

Lucy still looked — wondering.

'I finished it this morning,' said the ambassador, in her ear. 'Tomorrow I shall begin it again. My daughter hates the sight of the thing. She says I overtire myself, and that when old people have done their work they should take a nap. But I know that if it weren't for my dictionary, I should have given up long ago. When too many tiresome people dine here in the evening — or when they worry me from home — I take a column. But generally half a column's enough — good tough Persian roots, and no nonsense. Oh! Oof course I can read Hafiz and Omar Khayyam, and all that kind of thing. But that's the whipped cream. That don't count. What one wants is something to set one's teeth in. Latin verse will do. Last year I put half Tommy Moore into hendecasyllables. But my youngest boy, who's at Oxford, said he wouldn't be responsible for them — so I had to desist. And I suppose the mathematicians have always something handy. But, one way or another, one must learn one's dictionary. It comes next to cultivating one's garden.'

The pretty bit of kindness to a very young girl, in 1892, which I have described, suggested part of this conversation; and I find the foundation of the rest in a letter written to my father from Paris in 1896.

We had a very pleasant three days in Paris. . . including a most agreeable couple of hours with the Dufferins. Lord Dufferin showed me a number of relics of his Sheridan ancestry, and wound up by taking me into his special little den and telling me Persian stories with excellent grace and point! He is wild about Persian just now, and has just finished learning the whole dictionary by heart. He looks upon this as his chief *délassement* from official work. Lady Dufferin, however, does not approve of it at all! His remarks to Humphry as to the ignorance and inexperience of the innumerable French Foreign Ministers with whom he has to do, were amusing. An interview with Berthelot (the famous French chemist and friend of Renan) was really, he said, a deplorable business. Berthelot (Foreign Minister 1891-92) knew *everything* but what he should have known as French Foreign Minister. And Jusserand's testimony was practically the same! He is now acting head of the French Foreign Office, and has had three Ministers in bewildering succession to instruct in their duties, they being absolutely new to everything. Now however in Hanotaux he has got a strong chief at last.

I recollect that in the course of our exploration of the Embassy, we passed through a room with a large cheval-glass, of the Empire period.

Lord Dufferin paused before it, reminding me that the house had once belonged to Pauline Borghese. 'This was her room — and this glass was hers. I often stand before it — and evoke her. She is there somewhere — if one had eyes to see!'

And I thought, in the darkening room, as one looked into the shadows of the glass, of the beautiful shameless creature as she appears in the Canova statue in the Villa Borghese, or as David has fixed her, immortally young, in the Louvre picture.

But before I leave this second Roman visit of ours, let me recall one more figure in the *entourage* of the Ambassador — a young attaché, fair-haired, with all the good looks and good manners that belong to the post, and how much else of solid wit and capacity the years were then to find out. I had already seen Mr Rennell Rodd in the Tennant circle, where he was everybody's friend. Soon we were to hear of him in Greece, whence he sent me various volumes of poems and an admirable study of Morea, then in Egypt, and afterwards in Sweden; while through all these arduous years of war (I write in 1917) he has been Ambassador in that same Rome where we saw him as second Secretary in 1891.

The appearance of 'David Grieve' in February 1892, four years after 'Robert Elsmere', was to me the occasion of very mixed feelings. The public took warmly to the novel from the beginning; in its English circulation and its length of life it has, I think, very nearly equalled 'Robert Elsmere'; only after twenty-five years has it now fallen behind its predecessor. It has brought me correspondence from all parts and all classes, more intimate and striking perhaps than in the case of any other of my books. But of hostile reviewing at the moment of its appearance, there was certainly no lack! It was violently attacked in *The Scots Observer*, then the organ of a group of Scotch Conservatives and literary men, with W. E. Henley at their head, and received unfriendly notice from Mrs Oliphant in *Blackwood*. The two *Quarterlies* opened fire upon it, and many lesser guns. A letter from Mr Meredith Townsend, the very able, outspoken and wholly independent colleague of Mr Hutton in the editorship of *The Spectator*, gave me some comfort under these onslaughts!

> I have read every word of 'David Grieve'. Owing to the unusual and unaccountable imbecility of the reviewing — (the Athenśum man, for example, does not even comprehend that he is reading a biography!) — it may be three months or so before the public fully takes hold, but I have no doubt of the ultimate verdict . . . . The consistency of the leading characters is wonderful, and there is not one of the twenty-five, except possibly Dora — who is not human enough — that is not the perfection of lifelikeness . . . . Louie is a vivisection. I have the misfortune to know her well . . . . and I am startled page after page by the accuracy of the drawing.

Walter Pater wrote: 'It seems to me to have all the forces of its predecessor at work in it, with perhaps a mellower kind of art.' Henry James reviewed it — so generously! — so subtly! — in the *English Illustrated*. Stopford Brooke, and Bishop Creighton, wrote to me with a warmth and emphasis that soon healed the wounds of *The Scots Observer*; and that the public was with them, and not with my castigators, was quickly visible from the wide success of the book.

Some of the most interesting letters that reached me about it were from men of affairs, who were voracious readers but not makers of books — such as Mr Goschen, who 'could stand an examination on it'; Sir James — afterwards Lord — Hannen, one of the Judges of the Parnell Commission; and Lord Derby, the Minister who seceded, with Lord Carnarvon, from Disraeli's Government in 1878. We had made acquaintance not long before with Lord Derby, through his niece Lady Winifred Byng (now Lady Burghclere), to whom we had all lost our hearts — children and parents — at Lucerne in 1888. There are few things I regret more in relation to London social life than the short time allowed me by fate wherein to see something more of Lord Derby. If I remember right, we first met him at a small dinner-party at Lady Winifred's in 1891, and he died early in 1893. But he made a very great impression upon me, and though he was generally thought to be awkward and shy in general society, in the conversations I remember with him nothing could have been more genial or more attractive than his manner. He had been at Rugby under my grandfather, which was a link to begin with; though he afterwards went to Cambridge, and never showed, that I know of, any signs of the special Rugby influence which stamped men like Dean Stanley and Clough. And yet, of the moral independence and activity which my grandfather prized and cultivated in his boys, there was certainly no lack in Lord Derby's career. For the greater part of his political life he was nominally a Conservative, yet the rank and file of his party only half trusted a mind trained by John Stuart Mill, and perpetually brooding on social reform. As Lord Stanley, his close association and personal friendship with Disraeli during the Ministries and politics of the mid-nineteenth century have been well brought out in Mr Buckle's last volume of the Disraeli 'Life'. But the ultimate parting between himself and Dizzy was probably always inevitable. For his loathing of adventurous policies of all kinds, and of any increase whatever in the vast commitments of England, was sure at some point to bring him into conflict with the imagination or, as we may now call it, the prescience of Disraeli. It was strange to remember, as one watched him at the dinner-table, that had been offered the throne of Greece in 1862.

'If he accepts the charge,' wrote Dizzy to Mrs Bridges-Williams, 'I shall lose a powerful friend and colleague. It is a dazzling adventure for the house of Stanley, but they are not an imaginative race, and I fancy they will prefer Knowsley to the Parthenon, and Lancashire to the Attic plain. It is a privilege to live in this age of rapid and brilliant events. What an error to consider it an utilitarian age! It is one of infinite romance. Thrones tumble down and crowns are offered like a fairy tale.'

Sixteen years later came his famous resignation in 1878, when the Fleet was ordered to the Dardanelles, and Lord Derby, as he had now become, then Foreign Secretary, refused to sanction a step that might lead to war. That, for him, was the end as far as Toryism was concerned. In 1880 he joined Mr Gladstone, but only to separate from him on Home Rule in 1886; and when I first knew him, in 1891, he was leader of the Liberal Unionist peers in the House of Lords. A little later he became President of the great Labour Commission of 1892, and before he could see Gladstone's fresh defeat in 1893, he died.

Speculatively he was as open-minded as a reader and follower of Mill might be expected to be. He had been interested in 'Robert Elsmere', and the discussion of book and persons to which it led him in conversation with me, showed him fully aware of the new forces abroad in literature and history. Especially interested, too, as to what Labour was going to make of Christianity — and well aware — how could he fail to be, as Chairman of that great, that epoch-making Commission of 1892? — of the advancing strength of organised labour on all horizons. He appeared to me too, as a typical North-countrymen — a son of Lancashire, proud of the great Lancashire towns, and thoroughly at home in the life of the Lancashire countryside. He could tell a story in dialect admirably. And I realised that he had thought much — in his balanced, reticent way — on matters in which I was then groping: how to humanise the relations between employer and employed, how to enrich and soften the life of the workman, how, in short, to break down the barrier between modern industrialism and the stored-up treasures — art, science, thought — of man's long history.

So that when 'David Grieve' was finished, I sent it to Lord Derby, not long after our first meeting, in no spirit of empty compliment, and I have always kept his letter in return as a memento of a remarkable personality. Some day I hope there may be a Memoir of him; for none has yet appeared. He had not the charm, the versatility, the easy classical culture of his famous father — 'the Rupert of debate'. But with his great stature — he was six foot two — his square head and strong smooth-shaven face, he was noticeable everywhere. He was a childless widower when I first knew him; and made the impression of a lonely man, for all his busy political life and his vast estates. But he was particularly interesting to me, as representing a type I have once or twice tried to draw — of the aristocrat standing between the old world, before railways and the first Reform Bill, which saw his birth, and the new world and new men of the later half of the century. He was traditionally with the old world; by conviction and conscience, I think, with the new; yet not sorry, probably, that he was to see no more than its threshold!

1892, it will be remembered, was the first year of American copyright; and the great success of 'David Grieve' in America, following on the extraordinary vogue there of 'Robert Elsmere', in its pirated editions, brought me largely increased literary receipts. It seemed that I was not destined after all to 'ruin my publishers', as I had despondently foretold in a letter to my husband before the appearance of 'Robert Elsmere'; but that with regular work, I might look forward to a fairly steady income. We therefore felt justified in seizing an opportunity brought to our notice by an old friend who lived in the neighbourhood, and migrating to a house north of London, in the real heart of Middle England. After leaving Borough Farm, we had built a house on a hill near Haslemere, looking south over the blue and purple Weald; but two years' residence had convinced me that Surrey was almost as populous as London, and that real solitude for literary work was not to be found there — at any rate in that corner of it where we had chosen to build. And also, while we were nursing our newly planted shrubberies of baby pines and rhododendrons, there was always in my mind, as I find from letters of the time, a discontented yearning for 'an old house and old trees'! We found both at Stocks, whither we migrated in the summer of 1892. The little estate had then been recently inherited by Mrs Grey, mother of Sir Edward Grey, now Lord Grey of Falloden. We were at first tenants of the house and grounds, but in 1896 we bought the small property from the Greys, and have now been for more than twenty years its happy possessors. The house lies on a high upland, under one of lof the last easterly spurs of the Chilterns. It was built in 1780 (we rebuilt it in 1908) in succession to a much older house of which a few fragments remain, and the village at its gates had changed hardly at all in the hundred years which preceded our arrival. A few new cottages had been built; more needed to be built; and two residents, intimately connected with the past of the village, had built houses just outside it. But villadom did not exist. The village was rich in old folk, in whom were stored the memories and traditions of its quiet past. The postmaster, 'Johnny Dolt', who was nearing his eighties, was the universal referee on all local questions — rights of way, boundaries, village customs and the like; and of some of the old women of the village, as they were twenty-five years ago, I have drawn as faithful a picture as I could in one or two chapters of 'Marcella'.

But the new novel owed not only much of its scenery and setting, but also its main incident, to the new house. We first entered into negotiation for Stocks in January 1892. In the preceding December two gamekeepers had been murdered on the Stocks property, in a field under a big wood, not three hundred yards from the house; and naturally the little community, as it lay in its rural quiet beneath its wooded hills, was still, when we first entered it, under the shock and excitement of the tragedy. We heard all the story on the spot, and then viewed it from another point of view — the socio-political — when we went down from London to stay at one of the neighbouring country-houses, in February, and found the Home Secretary, Mr Matthews, afterwards Lord Llandaff, among the guests. The trial was over, the verdict given, and the two murderers were under sentence of death. But there was a strong agitation going on in favour of a reprieve; and what made the discussion of it, in this country-house party, particularly piquant was that the case, at that very moment, was a matter of close consultation between the judge and the Home Secretary. It was not easy therefore to talk of it in Mr Matthews presence. Voices dropped and groups dissolved when he appeared. Mr Asquith, who succeeded Mr Matthews that very year as Home Secretary, was also, if I remember right, of the party; and there was a good deal of rather hot discussion of the game-laws, and of English landlordism in general.

With these things in my mind, as soon as we had settled into Stocks, I began to think of 'Marcella'. I wrote the sketch of the book in September '92 and finished it in February '94. Many things went to the making of it: — not only the murdered keepers, and the village talk, not only the remembered beauty of Hampden which gave me the main setting of the story, but a general ferment of mind, connected with much else that had been happening to me.

For the New Brotherhood of 'Robert Elsmere' had become in some sort a realised dream; so far as any dream can ever take to itself the practical garments of this puzzling world. To show that the faith of Green and Martineau and Stopford Brooke was a faith that would wear and work — to provide a home for the new learning of a New Reformation, and a practical outlet for its enthusiasm of humanity — were the chief aims in the minds of those of us who in 1890 founded the University Hall Settlement in London. I look back now with emotion on that astonishing experiment. The scheme had taken shape in my mind during the summer of 1889, and in the following year I was able to persuade Dr Martineau, Mr Stopford Brooke, my old friend, Lord Carlisle, and a group of other religious Liberals, to take part in its realisation. We held a crowded meeting in London, and an adequate subscription list was raised without difficulty. University Hall in Gordon Square was taken as a residence for young men, and was very soon filled. Continuous teaching by the best men available, from all the churches, on the history and philosophy of religion was one half the scheme; the other half busied itself with an attempt to bring about some real contact between brain and manual workers. We took a little dingy hall in Marchmont Street, where the residents of the Hall started clubs and classes, Saturday mornings for children and the like. The foundation of Toynbee Hall — the Universities Settlement — in East London, in memory of Arnold Toynbee, was then a fresh and striking fact in social history. A spirit of fraternisation was in the air, an ardent wish to break down the local and geographical barriers that separated rich from poor, East End from West End. The new venture in which I was interested attached itself therefore to a growing movement. The work in Marchmont Street grew and prospered. Men and women of the working class found in it a real centre of comradeship, and the residents at the Hall in Gordon Square, led by a remarkable man of deeply religious temper and Quaker origin, the late Mr Alfred Robinson, devoted themselves in the evenings to a work marked by a very genuine and practical enthusiasm.

Soon it was evident that larger premises were wanted. It was in the days when Mr Passmore Edwards was giving large sums to institutions of different kinds in London, but especially to the founding of public libraries. He began to haunt the shabby hall in Marchmont Street, and presently offered to build us a new hall there for classes and social gatherings. But the scheme grew and grew, in my mind as in his. And when the question of a site arose, we were fortunate enough to interest the practical and generous mind of the chief ground landlord of Bloomsbury, the Duke of Bedford. With him I explored various sites in the neighbourhood, and finally the Duke offered us a site in Tavistock Place, on most liberal terms, he himself contributing largely to the building, granting us a 999 years' lease, and returning us the ground rent.

And there the Settlement now stands, the most beautiful and commodious Settlement building in London, with a large garden behind it, made by the Duke out of various private gardens, and lent to the Settlement for its various purposes. Mr Passmore Edwards contributed Ł14,000 to its cost, and it bears his name. It was opened in 1898 by Lord Peel and Mr Morley, and for twenty years it has been a centre of social work and endeavour in St Pancras. From it we have sprung the Physically Defective Schools under the Education Authority, now so plentiful in London, and so frequent in our other large towns. The first school of the kind was opened at this Settlement in 1898; and the first school ambulance in London was given to us by Sir Thomas Barlow for our Cripple Children. The first Play Centre in England began there in 1898; and the first Vacation School was held there in 1902.

During those twenty years the Settlement has played a large part in my life. We have had our failures and our successes; and the original idea has been much transformed with time. The Jowett Lectureship, still devoted to a religious or philosophical subject, forms a link with the religious lecturing of the past; but otherwise the Settlement, like the Master himself, stands for the liberal and spiritual life, without definitions or exclusions. Up to 1915, it was, like Toynbee Hall, a Settlement for University and professional men who gave their evenings to the work. Since 1915 it has been a Women's Settlement under a distinguished head — Miss Hilda Oakeley, M.A., formerly Warden of King's College for Women. It is now full of women residents and full of work. There is a Cripple School building belonging to the Settlement, to the East; our cripples still fill the Duke's garden with the shouts of their play; and hundreds of other children crowd into the building every evening in the winter, or sit under the plane trees in summer. The charming hall of the Settlement is well attended every winter week by people to whom the beautiful music that the Settlement gives is a constant joy; the Library dedicated to the memory of T.H. Green, has 400 members; the classes and popular lectures have been steadily held even during this devastating war; the Workers' Educational Association carry on their work under our roof; mothers bring their babies to the Infant Welfare Centre in the afternoon; there are orchestral and choral classes, boys' clubs and girls' clubs. Only one club has closed down — the Men's Club, which occupied the top floor of the Invalid Children's School before the war. Their members are scattered over France, Salonika, Egypt and Mesopotamia, and the Roll of Honour is a long one.

Twenty years! How clearly one sees the mistakes, the lost opportunities of such an enterprise! But so much is certain — that the Settlement has been an element of happiness in many many lives. It has had scores of devoted workers, in the past — men and women to whom the heart of its founder goes out in gratitude. And I cannot imagine a time when the spacious and beautiful house and garden, with all the activities that have a home there, will not be necessary and welcome to St Pancras. I see it, in my dreams at least, half a century hence, when all those who first learnt from it and in it have gone their way, still serving 'the future hour' of an England reborn. To two especially among the early friends of the Settlement let me turn back with grateful remembrance — George Howard, Lord Carlisle, whom I have already mentioned, and Stopford Brooke. Lord Carlisle was one of the most liberal and most modest of men, an artist himself, and the friend of artists. On a Sunday in Russell Square, when the drawing-room door opened to reveal his fine head, and shy, kind eyes, one felt how well worth while it was to stay at home on Sunday afternoons! I find a little note from him in 1891, the year in which we left Russell Square to move westwards, regretting the 'interesting old house', 'with which I associate you in my mind'. He was not an easy talker, but his listening had the quality that makes others talk their best; while the sudden play of humour or sarcasm through the features that were no less strong than refined, and the impression throughout of a singularly upright and humane personality, made him a delightful companion. There were those who would gladly have seen him take a more prominent part in public life. Perhaps a certain natural indolence held him back; perhaps a wonderful fairness of mind which made him slow to judge, and abnormally sensitive to 'the other side'. It is well known that as a landlord he left the administration of his great estates in the north almost wholly to his wife, and that, except in the great matter of temperance, he and she differed in politics, Lady Carlisle — who was a Stanley of Alderley — going with Mr Gladstone at the time of the Home Rule split, while Lord Carlisle joined the Liberal Unionists. Both took a public part, and the political differences of the parents were continued in their children. Only a very rare and selfless nature could have carried through so difficult a situation without lack of either dignity or sweetness. Lord Carlisle, in the late eighties and early nineties, when I knew him best, showed no want of either. The restrictions he laid upon his own life were perhaps made natural by the fact that he was first and foremost an artist by training and temperament, and that the ordinary occupations, rural, social, or political, of the great land-owning noble, had little or no attraction for him. In the years at any rate when I saw him often, I was drawn to him by our common interest in the liberalising of religion, and by a common love of Italy and Italian art. I remember him once in the incomparable setting of Naworth; but more often in London, and Stopford Brooke's company.

For he was an intimate friend and follower of Mr Brooke's, and I came very early under the spell of that same strong and magnetic personality. While we were still at Oxford, through J.R.G. we made acquaintance with Mr Brooke, and with the wife whose early death in 1879 left desolate one of the most affectionate of men. I remember well Mr Brooke's last sermon in the University pulpit, before his secession, on grounds of what we should now call Modernism, from the Church of England. Mrs Brooke, I think, was staying with us, while Mr Brooke was at All Souls, and the strong individuality of both the husband and wife made a deep impression upon one who was then much more responsive and recipient than individual. The sermon was a great success; but it was almost Mr Brooke's latest utterance within the Anglican Church. The following year came the news of Mrs Brooke's mortal illness. During our short meeeting ion 1877 I had been greatly attracted by her, and the news filled me with unbearable pain. But I had not understood from it that the end itself was near, and I went out into our little garden which was a mass of summer roses, and in a bewilderment of feeling gathered all I could find — a glorious medley of bloom — that they might surround her, if only for a day, with the beauty she loved. Next day, or the day after, she died; and that basket of roses, arriving in the house of death — belated, incongruous offering! — has stayed with me as the symbol of so much else that is too late in life, and of our human helplessness and futility in the face of sorrow.

After our move to London, my children and I went for a long time regularly to hear Mr Brooke at Bedford Chapel. At the time, I often felt very critical of the sermons. Looking back I cannot bring myself to say a critical word. If only one could still go and hear him! Where are the same gifts, the same magnetism, the same compelling personality to be found today, among religious leaders? I remember a sermon on Elijah and the priests of Baal, which for colour and range, for modernness, combined with ethical force and power, remains with me as perhaps the best I ever heard. And then, the service. Prayers simplified, repetitions omitted, the Beatitudes instead of the Commandments, a dozen jarring, intolerable things left out: but for the rest no needless break with association. And the relief and consolation of it! The simple Communion service, adapted very slightly from the Anglican rite, and administered by Mr Brooke with a reverence, an ardour, a tenderness one can only think of with emotion, was an example of what *could* be done with our religious traditions, for those who want new bottles for new wine, if only the courage and the imagination were there.

The biography of Mr Brooke, which his son-in-law, Principal Jacks, has just brought out, will, I think, reveal to many what made the spell of Stopford Brooke, to a degree which is not common in biography. For *le papier est bête*! — and the charm of a man who was both poet and artist, without writing poems or painting pictures, is very hard to hand on to those who never knew him. But luckily Stopford Brooke's diaries and letters reflect him with great fullness and freedom. They have his faults, naturally. They are often exuberant or hasty — not, by any means, always fair to men and women of a different temperament from his own. Yet on the whole, there is the same practical, warm-hearted wisdom in them, that many a friend found in the man himself when they went to consult him in his little study at the back of Bedford Chapel; where he wrote his sermons and books, and found quiet, without however barring out the world, if it wanted him. And there breathes from them also the enduring, eager passion for natural and artistic beauty which made the joy of his own life, and which his letters and journals may well kindle in others. His old age was a triumph in the most difficult of arts. He was young to the end, and every day of the last waiting years was happy for himself, and precious to those about him. He knew what to give up and what to keep, and his freshness of feeling never failed. Perhaps his best and most enduring memorial will be the Wordsworth Cottage at Grasmere, which he planned and carried out. And I like to remember that my last sight of him was at a spot only a stone's throw from that cottage on the Keswick Road, his grey hair beaten back by the light breeze coming from the pass, and his cheerful eyes, full often, as it seemed to me, of a mystical content, raised towards the evening glow over Helm Crag and the Easedale fells.

On the threshold also of the Settlement's early history there stands the venerable figure of James Martineau — thinker and saint. For he was a member of the original Council, and his lectures on the Gospel of St Luke, in the old 'Elsmerian' hall, marked the best of what we tried to give in those first days. I knew Harriet Martineau in my childhood at Fox How. Well I remember going to tea with that tremendous woman when I was eight years old; sitting through a silent meal, in such awe of her cap, her strong face, her ear trumpet; and then being taken away to a neighbouring room by a kind niece, that I might not disturb her further. Once or twice, during my growing up I saw her. She lived only a mile from Fox How, and was always on friendly terms with my people. Matthew Arnold had a true admiration for her — sturdy fighter that she was in Liberal causes. So had W.E. Forster; only he suffered a good deal at her hands, as she disapproved of the Education Bill, and contrived so to manage her trumpet when he came to see her, as to take all the argument and give him all the listening! When my eldest child was born, a cot-blanket arrived, knitted by Miss Martineau's own hands — the busy hands (soon then to be at rest) that wrote the 'History of the Peace', 'Feats on the Fiord', the 'Settlers at Home,' and those excellent biographical sketches of the politicians of the Reform and Corn Law days in the *Daily News*, which are still well worth reading.

Between Hariett Martineau and her brother James, as many people will remember, there arose an unhappy difference in middle life which was never mended or healed. I never heard him speak of her. His standards were high and severe, for all the sensitive delicacy of his long distinguished face, and visionary eyes; and neither he nor she were of the stuff that allows kinship to supersede conscience. He published a somewhat vehement criticism of a book in which she was part author, and she never forgave it. And although to me, in the University Hall venture, he was gentleness and courtesy itself, and though his presence seemed to hallow a room directly he entered it, one felt always that he was *formidable*. The prophet and the Puritan lay deep in him. Yet in his two famous volumes of Sermons there are tones of an exquisite tenderness and sweetness, together with harmonies of prose style, that remind me often how he loved music, and how his beautiful white head might be seen at the Monday Popular Concerts, week after week, his thinker's brow thrown back to catch the finest shades of Joachim's playing.

The year after 'David Grieve' appeared, Mr Jowett died. His long letter to me on the book contained some characteristic passages, of which I quote the following:

> I should like to have a good talk with you. I seldom get anyone to talk on religious subjects. It seems to me that the world is growing rather tired of German criticism, having got out of it nearly all that it is capable of giving. To me it appears one of the most hopeful signs of the present day that we are coming back to the old, old doctrine, 'he can't be wrong whose life is in the right'. Yet this has to be taught in a new way, adapted to the wants of the age. We must give up doctrine and teach by the lives of men, beginning with the life of Christ, instead. And the best words of men, beginning with the Gospels and the prophets, will be our Bible.

At the end of the year we spent a weekend with him at Balliol, and that was my last sight of my dear old friend. 1893 was for me a year of illness, and of hard work both in the organisation of the new Settlement and in the writing of 'Marcella'. But that doesn't reconcile me to the recollection of how little I knew of his failing health till, suddenly, in September the news reached me that he was lying dangerously ill in the house of Sir Robert Wright, in Surrey.

'Everyone who waited on him in his illness loved him,' wrote an old friend of his and mine who was with him to the end. What were almost his last words — 'I bless God for my life! — I bless God for my life!' — seemed to bring the noble story of it to a triumphant close; and after death he lay 'with the look of a little child on his face. . . . He will live in the hearts of those who loved him, as well as in his work.'

He lives indeed; and as we recede further from him the originality and greatness of his character will become more and more clear to Oxford and to England. The men whom he trained are now in the full stream of politics and life. His pupils and friends are or have been everywhere, and they have borne, in whatever vocation, the influence of his mind, or the mark of his friendship. Lord Lansdowne, Mr Asquith, Lord Justice Bowen, Lord Coleridge, Lord Milner, Sir Robert Morier, Matthew Arnold, Huxley, Tennyson, Lord Goschen, Miss Nightingale, and a hundred others of the nation's leaders: — amid profoundest difference, the memory of the 'Master' has been for them a common and a felt bond. No other religious personality of the nineteenth century — unless it be that of Newman — has stood for so much. In his very contradictions and inconsistencies of thought, he was the typical man of ata time beset on all sides by new problems to which Jowett knew very well there was no intellectual answer; while through the passion of his faith in a Divine Life, which makes itself known to man, not in miracle or mystery, but through the channels of a common experience, he has been a kindling force in many hearts and minds, and those among the most important to England. Meanwhile, to these great matters, the Jowettan oddities and idiosyncrasies added just that touch of laughter and surprise that makes a man loved by his own time, and arrests the eye and ear of posterity.

CHAPTER XV

'Helbeck of Bannisdale'

The coming out of 'Marcella', in April 1894, will always mark for me perhaps the happiest date in my literary life. The book, for all the hard work that had gone to it, had none the less been a pleasure to write; and the good will that greeted it made the holiday I had earned — which again was largely spent in Rome — a golden time. Not long after we left England, 'Piccadilly,' my sister wrote me, was 'placarded with "Marcella",' the name appearing on the notice-boards of most of the evening papers — a thing which never happened to me before or since; and when we arrived in Rome, the content-bills of the London newspapers, displayed in the Piazza di Spagna, announced her no less flamingly. The proof-sheets of the book had been tried on various friends, as usual, with some amusing results. Bishop Creighton, with only the first two-thirds of the book before him, wrote me denunciations of Marcella.

> I am greatly interested in the book and pine for the *denouement*. So far Marcella, though I know her quite well, does not in the least awaken my sympathy. She is an intolerable girl — but there are many of them. . . . I only hope that she may be made to pay for it. Mr and Mrs Boyce are good and original, so is Wharton. I hope that condign vengeance awaits him. He is the modern politician entirely. . . . . I really hope Marcella may be converted. It would serve her right to marry her to Wharton; he would beat her.

Another old friend, one of the industrial leaders of the north, carried off half the proofs to read on his journey to Yorkshire.

> I so ravened on them that I sat still at Bilsworth instead of getting out! The consequence is that all my plans are disarranged. I shall not get to M —— in time for my meeting, and for all this Marcella is to blame. . . . The station-master assured me he called out 'Change for Northampton', but I was much too deep in the scene between Marcella, Lord Maxwell and Raeburn, to heed anything belonging to the outer world.

Mr Goschen wrote:

I don't know how long it is since I have enjoyed reading anything so much. I can't satisfy myself as to the physical appearance of Wharton. . . . I do know some men of a *character* not quite unlike him, but they haven't the boyish face with curls. Marcella I see before me. Mrs Boyce and Lord Maxwell both interested me very much. . . . Alack, I must turn from Marcella's enthusiasm and aspirations to Sir W. Harcourt's speech — a great transition.

And dear Alfred Lyttelton wrote:

I feel a ridiculous pride in her triumphs which I have had the joy of witnessing on every side. . . . At least permit an expert to tell you that his heart beat over the ferrets (in the poaching scene) and at the intense vividness and truth of the legal episodes.

But there is one letter in this old packet which moves me specially. It was on the 1st of March, 1894, that Mr Gladstone said 'Goodbye' to his Cabinet in the Cabinet room at Downing Street, and a little later in the afternoon walked away for the last time from the House of Commons. No one who has read it will forget the telling of that episode, in Mr Morley's biography, with what concentration, what dignity! — worthy alike of the subject, and of the admirable man of letters — himself an eyewitness — who records it.

While Lord Kimberley and Sir William Harcourt, on behalf of the rest of their colleagues, were bidding their great chief farewell, 'Mr Gladstone sat composed and still as marble, and the emotion of the Cabinet did not gain him for an instant'. When the spokesmen ceased, he made his own little speech of four or five minutes in reply: — 'then hardly above a breath, but every accent heard, he said "God bless you all." He rose slowly and went out of one door, while his colleagues with minds oppressed filed out by other.'

On this moving scene, there followed what Mr Gladstone himself described as the first period of comparative leisure he had ever known, extending to four and a half months. They were marked first by increasing blindness, then by an operation for cataract and finally by a moderate return of sight. In July he notes that 'during the last months of partial incapacity I have not written with my own hand probably so much as one letter a day.' In this faded packet of mine lies one of these rare letters, written with his own hand — a full sheet — from Dollis Hill, on April 27.

When 'Marcella' arrived my thankfulness was alloyed with a feeling that the state of my eyesight made your kindness for the time a waste. But Mr Nettleship has since then by an infusion supplied a temporary stimulus to the organ, such that I have been enabled to begin, and am reading the work with great pleasure and an agreeable sense of congeniality which I do not doubt I shall retain to the close.

Then he describes a book — a novel — dealing with religious controversy, which he had lately been reading, in which every character embodying views opposed to those of the author 'is exhibited as odious'. With this he warmly contrasts the method and spirit of 'David Grieve', and then continues:

Well I have by my resignation passed into a new state of existence. And in that state I shall be very glad when our respective stars may cause our paths to meet. I am full of prospective work; but for the present a tenacious influenza greatly cripples me and prevents my making any definitive arrangement for an expected operation on my eye.

Eighty-five! — greatly crippled by influenza and blindness — yet 'full of prospective work'! The following year, remembering 'Robert Elsmere' days, and apropos of certain passages in his review of that book, I ventured to send him an Introduction I had contributed to my brother-in-law Leonard Huxley's translation of Hausrath's 'New Testament Times'. This time the well-known handwriting is feebler, and the old 'fighter' is not roused. He puts discussion by, and turns instead to kind words about a near relative of my own who had been winning distinctions at Oxford.

It is one of the most legitimate interests of the old to watch with hope and joy these opening lives, and it has the secondary effect of whispering to them that they are not yet wholly frozen up. . . . I am busy as far as my limited powers of exertion allow upon a new edition of Bishop Butler's Works, which costs me a good deal of labour, and leaves me after a few hours upon it, good for very little else. And my perspective, dubious as it is, is filled with other work, in the Homeric region lying beyond. I hope it will be very long before you know anything of compulsory limitations on the exercise of your powers. Believe me always.

Sincerely yours,
W.E. Gladstone.

But it was not till 1897, as he himself records, that the indomitable spirit so far yielded to these limitations as to resign — or rather contemplate resigning — the second great task of which he had spoken to me at Oxford, nine years before. 'I have begun seriously to ask myself whether I shall ever be able to face — "The Olympian Religion".'

It was I think in the winter of 1895 that I saw him for the last time at our neighbours, the Rothschilds, at Tring Park. He was then full of animation and talk, mainly of things political, and indeed not long before he had addressed a meeting at Chester on the Turkish massacres in Armenia, and was still to address a large audience at Liverpool on the same subject, his last public appearance — a year later. When 'George Tressady' appeared he sent me a message through Mrs Drew that he feared George Tressady's Parliamentary conduct 'was inconceivable in a man of honour'; and I was only comforted by the emphatic and laughing dissent of Lord Peel, to whom I repeated the verdict. 'Nothing of the kind! But of course he was thinking of *us* — the Liberal Unionists.'

Then came the last months when, amid a world's sympathy and reverence, the great life, in weariness and pain wore to its end. The 'lying in state' in Westminster Hall seemed to me ill-arranged. But the burying remains with me as one of those perfect things, which only the Anglican Church at its best in combination with the immemorial associations of English history can achieve. After it, I wrote to my son:

I have now seen four great funerals in the Abbey — Darwin, Browning, Tennyson, and the funeral service for Uncle Forster which was very striking too. But no one above forty of those in the Abbey yesterday will ever see the like again. It was as beautiful and noble as the 'lying-in-state' was disappointing and ugly. The music was exquisite, and fitting in every respect; and when the high sentence rang out — 'and their name liveth for evermore', the effect was marvellous. One seemed to hear the voice of the future already pealing through the Abbey — as though the verdict were secured, the judgement given.

We saw it all, admirably, from the Muniment Room which is a sort of lower Triforium above the south Transept. To me perhaps the most thrilling moment was when, bending forward, one saw the white covered coffin disappear amid the black crowd round it, and knew that it had sunk for ever into its deep grave, amid that same primćval clay of Thorny Island on which Edward's Minister was first reared and the Red King built his hall of judgement and Council. The statue of Dizzy looked down on him — 'So you have come at last!' — and all the other statues on either side seemed to welcome and receive him. . . . The sloping seats for Lords and Commons filled the transepts, a great black mass against the jewelled windows, the Lords on one side, the Commons on the other; in front of each black multitude was the glitter of a mace, and in the hollow between, the whiteness of the pall — perhaps you can fancy it so.

But the impetus of memory has carried me on too fast. There are some other figures and scenes to be gathered from these years — '93-'98 — that may still interest this present day. Of the most varied kind! For as I turn over letters and memoranda a jumble of recollections passes through my mind. Baron Ferdinand de Rothschild on one hand, a melancholy kindly man, amid the splendours of Waddesden; a meeting of the Social Democratic Federation in a cellar in Lisson Grove; days of absorbing interest in the Jewish East End, and in sweaters' workshops, while 'George Tressady' was in writing; a first visit to Mentmore while Lady Rosebery was alive; a talk with Lord Rosebery some time after her death, in a corner of a local ball-room, while 'Helbeck' was shaping itself, about the old Catholic families of England, which revealed to me yet another and unsuspected vein of knowledge in one of the best furnished of minds; the Asquith marriage in 1894; new acquaintances and experiences in Lancashire towns, again connected with 'George Tressady', and in which I was helped by that brilliant writer, worker, and fighter, Mr Sidney Webb; a nascent friendship with Sir William Harcourt, one of the most racy of all possible companions; happy evenings in the Tadema and Richmond studios with music and good talk; occasional meetings with and letters from 'Pater,', the dear and famous Professor, who like my uncle fought half the world, and scarcely made an enemy; visits to Oxford and old friends: — such are the scenes and persons that come back to me as I read old letters, while all through it ran the continual strain of hard literary work, mingled with the new social and religious interests which the foundation of the Passmore Edwards Settlement had brought me.

We have been at Margot Tennant's wedding today (I wrote to my son — on May 10, 1894) — a great function, very tiring, but very brilliant and amusing — occasionally dramatic too, as when after the service had begun, the sound of cheering in the street outside drowned the voice of the Bishop of Rochester, and warned us that Mr Gladstone was arriving. Afterwards at the house, we shook hands with three Cabinet Ministers on the doorstep, and there were all the rest of them inside! The bride carried herself beautifully and was as composed and fresh as though it were any ordinary party. From our seat in the church one saw the interior of the vestry and Mr Gladstone's white head against the window as he sat to sign the register; and the greeting between him and Mr Balfour when he had done.

This was written while Lord Rosebury was Prime Minister and Mr Balfour, still free, until the following year, from the trammels of office, was finishing his brilliant 'Foundations of Belief', which came out in 1895. In acknowledging the copy which he sent me, I ventured to write some pages on behalf of certain arguments of the Higher Criticism which seemed to me to deserve a fuller treatment than Mr Balfour had been willing to give them — in defence also of our English idealists, such as Green and Caird, in their relation to orthodoxy. A year or two earlier I find I had been breaking a lance on behalf of the same school of writers with a very different opponent. In the controversy between Professor Huxley and Dr Wace in 1889, which opened with the famous article on 'The Gadarene Swine', the Professor had welcomed me as an ally, because of 'The New Reformation' which appeared much about the same time; and the word of praise in which he compared my reply to Mr Gladstone, to the work 'of a strong housemaid brushing away cobwebs', gave me a fearful joy! I well remember a thrilling moment in the Russell Square drawing-room in '89, when 'Pater' and I were in full talk, he in his raciest and most amusing form, and suddenly the door opened, and 'Dr Wace' was announced — the opponent with whom at that moment he was grappling his hardest in the *Nineteenth Century*. Huxley gave me a merry look — and then how perfectly they both behaved! I really think the meeting was a pleasure to both of them, and when my old chief in the 'Dictionary of Christian Biography' took his departure, Huxley found all kinds of pleasant personal things to say about him.

But the Professor and I were not always at one. Caird and Green — and, for other reasons, Martineau — were to me names 'of great pith and moment', and Christian Theism was a reasonable faith. And Huxley, in controversy, was no more kind to my 'sacra' than to other people's. Once I dared a mild remonstrance — in 1892 — only to provoke one of his most vigorous replies:

My Dear M. — Thanks for your pleasant letter. I do not know whether I like the praise or the scolding better. They, like pastry, need to be done with a light hand — especially praise — and I have swallowed all yours, and feel it thoroughly agrees with me.

As to the scolding I am going to defend myself tooth and nail. In the first place, by all my Gods and No Gods, neither Green, nor Martineau, nor the Cairds were in my mind when I talked of 'Sentimental Deism', but the 'Vicaire Savoyard', and Channing, and such as Voysey. There are two chapters of 'Rousseauism.' I have not touched yet — Rousseauism in Theology, and Rousseauism in Education. When I write the former I shall try to show that the people of whom I speak as 'sentimental deists' are the lineal descendents of the Vicaire Savoyard. I was a great reader of Channing in my boyhood, and was much taken in by his theosophic confectionery. At present I have as much (intellectual) antipathy to him as St John had to the Nicolaitans.

. . . . .Green I know only from his Introduction to Hume — which reminds me of nothing so much as a man with a hammer and chisel knocking out bits of bad stone in the Great Pyramid, with the view of bringing it down. . . . As to Caird's 'Introduction to the Philosophy of Religion', I will get it and study it. But as a rule 'Philosophies of Religion' in my experience turn out to be only 'Religions of Philosophers' — quite another business, as you will admit.

And if you please, Ma'am, I wish to add that I think I am *not* without sympathy for Christian feeling — or rather for what you mean by it. Beneath the cooled logical upper strata of my microcosm, there is a fused mass of prophetism and mysticism, and the Lord knows what might happen to me, in case a moral earthquake cracked the superincumbent deposit, and permitted an eruption of the demonic element below. . . . Luckily I am near 70, and not a G.O.M. — so the danger is slight.

One must stick to one's trade. It is my business to the best of my ability to fight for scientific clearness — that is what the world lacks. Feeling, Christian or other, is superabundant. . . .

Ever yours affectionately,

T. H. Huxley

A few more letters from him — racy, and living as himself — and then in '95, just after his first article on the 'Foundations of Belief', we heard with dismay of the illness which killed him. There was never a man more beloved — more deeply mourned.

The autumn of 1896 brought me a great loss in the death of an intimate friend, Lady Wemyss — as marked a personality in her own circle as was her indomitable husband, the famous Lord Elcho, of the Volunteer movement, on the bigger stage. It was at Balliol, at the Master's table, and in the early Oxford days, that we first made friends with Lord and

Lady Wemyss, who were staying with the Master for the Sunday. I was sitting next to Lord Wemyss, and he presently discovered that I was absent-minded. And I found him so attractive and so human that I soon told him why. I had left a sick child at home, with a high temperature, and was fidgeting to get back to him.

'What is the matter? — Fever? — throat? Aconite of course! You're a homeopath, aren't you? All sensible people are. Look here — I've got a servant with me. I'll send him with some aconite at once. Where do you live? — In the Parks? All right. Give me your address.'

Out came an envelope and a pencil. A message was sent round the dinner table to Lady Wemyss, whose powerful dreaming face beside the Master lit up at once. The aconite was sent; the child's temperature went down; and if I remember right, either one or both of his new medical advisers walked up to the Parks the next day to enquire for him. So began a friendship which for just twenty years, especially from about '85 to '96, meant a great deal to me.

How shall I describe Lady Wemyss? An unfriendly critic has recently allowed me the power of 'interesting fashionable ladies in things of the mind'. Was Lady Wemyss a 'fashionable lady'? She was the wife, certainly, of a man of high rank and great possessions; but I met her first as a friend — a dear and intimate friend, as may be seen from his correspondence — of Mr Jowett's; and Mr Jowett was not very tolerant of 'fashionable ladies'. She was in reality a strong and very simple person, with a natural charm working through a very reserved and often harsh manner, like the charm of mountain places in spring. She was a Conservative, and I suppose an aristocrat, whatever that word may mean. She thought the Harcourt death duties 'terrible', because they broke up old families and old estates, and she had been brought up to think that both were useful. Yet I never knew anybody with a more instinctive passion for equality. This means that she was simply and deeply interested in all sorts of human beings, and all sorts of human lots; also that although she was often self-conscious, it was the self-consciousness one sees in the thoughtful and richly-natured young, whose growth in thought or character has out run their means of expression: — and never mean or egotistical. Her deep voice; her fine, marked features; and the sudden play of humour, silent, self-restrained, yet most infectious to the bystander, that would lighten through them; her stately ways; and yet withal, her child-like love of loving and being loved by the few to whom she gave her deepest affection: — in some such phrases one tries to describe her; but they go a very little way.

I can see her now at the dinner-table at Gosford, sardonically watching a real 'fashionable lady' who had arrived in the afternoon, and was sitting next Lord Wemyss at the further end — with a wonderful frizzled head, an infinitesimal waist sheathed in white muslin and blue ribbons, rouged cheeks, a marvellous concatenation of jewels, and a caressing, gesticulating manner meant, at fifty, to suggest the ways of 'sweet and twenty'. The frizzled head drew nearer and nearer to Lord Wemyss, the fingers flourished and pointed; and suddenly I heard Lady Wemyss's deep voice meditatively amused, beside me —

'Her fingers will be in Frank's eyes soon!'

Or again, I see her, stalled beneath the drawing-room table, on all fours, by her imperious grand-children, patiently playing 'horse' or 'cow', till her scandalised daughter-in-law discovered her, and ran to her release. Or in her last illness, turning her noble head and faint welcoming smile to the few friends that were admitted; and finally, in the splendid rest after death, when those of us who had not known her in youth, could guess what the beauty of her youth had been.

She was an omnivorous and most intelligent reader; and a friend that never failed Matthew Arnold was very fond of her, and she of him; Laura Lyttelton, who was nearly forty years her junior, loved her dearly, and never felt the bar of years; the Master owed much to her affection; and gratefully acknowledged it. The 'Commonplace Book', privately printed after her death, showed the range of interests which had played upon her fresh and energetic mind. It was untrained, I suppose, compared to the woman graduate of today. But it was far less tired; and all its adventures were of its own seeking.

It was in 1896, not long after the appearance of 'George Tressady', that a conversation in a house on the outskirts of the Lakes suggested to me the main plot of 'Helbeck of Bannisdale'. The talk turned on the fortunes of that interesting old place, Sizergh Castle, near Kendal, and of the Catholic family to whom it then still belonged, though mortgages and lack of pence were threatening imminently to submerge an ancient stock that had held it unbrokenly, from father to son, through many generations.

The relation between such a family, pinched and obscure, yet with its own proud record, and inherited consciousness of an unbroken loyalty to a once persecuted faith — and this modern world of ours, struck me as an admirable subject for a novel. I thought about it the next day, all through a long railway journey from Kendal to London, and by the time I reached Euston, the plot of 'Helbeck of Bannisdale' was more or less clear to me.

I confided it to Lord Acton a little while afterwards. We discussed it, and he cordially encouraged me to work it out. Then I consulted my father, my Catholic father, without whose assent I should never have written the book at all; and he raised no difficulty. So I only had to begin.

But I wanted a setting — somewhere in the border country between the Lakes, mountains and Morecambe Bay. And here another piece of good luck befell, almost equal to that which had carried us to Hampden for the summer of 1889. Levens Hall, it appeared, was to be let for the spring — the famous Elizabethan house, five miles from Kendal, and about a mile from Sizergh. I had already seen Levens; and we took the chance at once.

Bannisdale in the novel is a combination, I suppose, of Sizergh and Levens. The two houses, though of much the same date, are really very different, and suggest phases of life quite distinct from each other. Levens compared to Sizergh is — or was then, before the modern restoration of Sizergh — the spoiled beauty beside the shabby ascetic. Levens has always been cared for and lived in by people who had money to spend upon the house and garden they loved, and the result is a wonderful example of Elizabethan and Jacobean decoration, mellowed by time into a perfect whole. Yet, for my purposes, there was always Sizergh, close by, with its austere suggestions of sacrifice and suffering under the penal laws, borne without flinching by a long succession of quiet, simple undistinguished people.

We arrived there in March 1897. The house greeted us on a clear and chilly evening, under the mingled light of a frosty sunset and the blaze of wood fires which had been lit everywhere to warm its new guests.

> At last we arrived — saw the wonderful grey house rising above the river in the evening light, found G — waiting at the open door for us, and plunged into the hall, the sitting-rooms, and all the intricacies of the upper passages and turrets with the delight and curiosity of a pack of children. Wood and peat fires were burning everywhere; the great chimney-pieces in the drawing-room, the arms of Elizabeth over the hall fire, the stucco birds and beasts running round the hall showed dimly in the scanty lamp-light (we shall want about six more lamps!) — and the beauty of the marvellous old place took us all by storm. Then through endless passages and kitchens, bright with long rows of copper pans and moulds, we made our way out into the gardens among the clipped yews and cedars, and had just light enough to see that Levens apparently is like nothing else but itself. . . . The drawback of the house at present is certainly *the cold!*

Thus began a happy and fruitful time. We managed to get warm in spite of a treacherous and tardy spring. Guests came to stay with us: — Henry James above all; the Creightons, he then in the first months of that remarkable London episcopate, which in four short years did so much to raise the name and fame of the Anglican Church in London, at least for the lay mind; the Neville Lytteltons, who had been since '93 our summer neighbours at Stocks; Lord Lytton, then at Cambridge; the Sydney Buxtons; old Oxford friends, and many kinsfolk. The damson blossom along the hedgerows that makes of these northern vales in April a glistening network of white and green, the daffodils and violets, the lilies of the valley in the Brigsteer woods came and went, and 'Helbeck' made steady progress.

But we left Levens in May, and it took me another eight months to finish the book. Except perhaps in the case of 'Bessie Costrell', I was never more possessed by a subject, more shut in by it from the outer world. And though its contemporary success was nothing like so great as that of most of my other books, the response it evoked, as my letters show, in those to whom the book appealed, was deep and passionate.

My first anxiety was as to my father, and after we had left England for abroad, I was seized with misgivings lest certain passages in the talk of Dr Friedland, who, it will perhaps be remembered, is made the spokesman in the book of certain points in the *intellectual* case against Catholicism, should wound or distress him. I therefore no sooner reached Italy than I sent for the proofs again, and worked at them as much as fatigue would let me, softening them, and, I think, improving them too. Then we went on to Florence, and rest, coming home for the book's publication in June.

The joy and emotion of it were great. George Meredith, J. M. Barrie, Paul Bourget, and Henry James — the men who at that time stood at the head of my own art — gave the book a welcome that I can never forget. George Meredith wrote:

> Your Helbeck of Bannisdale held me firmly in the reading and remains with me. . . . If I felt a monotony during the struggle, it came of your being faithful to your theme — rapt — or you would not have had such power over your reader. I know not another book that shows the classic fate so distinctly to view. . . . Yet a word of thanks for Dr Friedland. He is the voice of spring in the book.

J.M. Barrie's generous, enthusiastic note delights and inspires me again as I read it over. Mr Morley, my old editor and critic wrote: — 'I find it intensely interesting and with all the elements of beauty, power, and pathos.' For Leslie Stephen, with whom I had only lately made warm and close friends, I had a copy bound, without the final chapter, that the book might not, by its tragic close, depress one who had known so much sorrow. Sir Alfred Lyall thought — 'the story reaches a higher pitch of vigour and dramatic presentation than is to be found even in your later books'; while Lord Halifax's letter — 'how lovable they both are, each in their way, and how true to the ideal on both sides!' — and others, from Mr Godkin, of the American *Nation*, from Frederic Harrison, Lord Goschen, Lord Dufferin, and many, many more, produced in me that curious mood which for the artist is much nearer dread than boasting — dread that the best is over, and that one will never earn such sympathy again. One letter not written to myself, from Mr George Wyndham to Mr Wilfred Ward, I have asked leave to print as a piece of independent criticism;

> On Sunday I read Helbeck of Bannisdale, and I confess that the book moved me a great deal. It is her best book. It is true tragedy, because the crash is inevitable. This is not so easy to effect in Art as many suppose. There are very few characters and situations which lead to inevitable crashes. It is a thousand to one that a woman who thinks she ought not to marry a man but who loves him passionately, will, in fact, marry him. She will either discover an ingenious way out of her wood, or else, just shut her eyes and 'go it blind' relying on his strength and feeling that it is really right to relinquish to him her sense of responsibility. In choosing a girl with nothing left her in the world but loyalty to a dead father and memory of his attitude towards religion, without knowledge of his arguments for that attitude, I think that Mrs Ward has hit on the only possible 'per-

sona'. Had Laura herself, been a convinced rationalist, or had her Father been still alive, she would have merged herself and her attitude in Helbeck's strength of character. Being a work of art, self-consistent and inevitable, the book becomes symbolic. It is a picture of incompatibility, but, being a true picture, it is a symbolic index to the incompatible which plays so large a part in the experience of man.

For the rest, I remembered vividly the happy holiday of that summer at Stocks; the sense of having come through a great wrestle, and finding everything — my children, the garden, my little Huxley nephews, books and talk, the Settlement where we were just about to open our Cripple School, and all else in life, steeped in a special glamour. It faded soon, no doubt 'into the light of common day'; but if I shut my thoughts and eyes against the troubles of these dark hours of war, I can feel my way back into that 'wind-warm space', and look into the faces that earth knows no more — my father, Leslie Stephen, Alfred Lyall, Mr Goschen, Alfred Lyttelton, H.O. Arnold-Forster, my sister, Julia Huxley, my eldest brother — a vanished company!

And in the following year, to complete the story, I owed to 'Helbeck' a striking and unexpected hour. A message reached me in November, 1898, to the effect that the Empress Frederick who had just arrived at Windsor admired the book and would like to see the writer of it.

A tragic figure at that moment — the Empress Frederick! That splendid Crown Prince, in his White uniform, whom we had seen at Schwalbach in 1872, had finished early in 1890 with his phantom reign and tortured life; and his son reigned in his stead. Bismark, 'the Englishwoman's' implacable enemy, had died some four months before I saw the Empress, after eight years' exclusion from power. The Empress herself was on the verge of the terrible illness which killed her two years later. To me her life and personality — or rather the little I knew of them — had always been very interesting. She had, of course, the reputation of being the ablest of her family, and the bitterness of her sudden and irreparable defeat at the hands of Fate and her son, in 1889-90, had often struck me as one of the grimmest stories in history. One incident in it, not, I think, very generally known, I happened to hear from an eyewitness of the scene, before 1898. It was as follows:

The Empress Fredrick in the midst of the Bismarck crisis of March 1890, when it was evident that the young Emperor William II was bent on getting rid of his Chancellor, and so 'dropping the pilot' of his House, was sitting at home one afternoon, with the companion from whom I heard the story, when a servant, looking a good deal scared, announced that Prince Bismarck had called, and wished to know whether her Majesty would receive him.

'Prince Bismarck!' said the Empress in amazement. She had probably not seen him since the death of her husband, and relations between herself and him had been no more than official for years. Turning to her companion, she said, 'What can he possibly want with me!'

She consented however to receive him, and the old Prince, agitated and hollow-eyed, made his appearance. He had become, as a last hope of placating the new Kaiser, to ask the Empress to use what influence she could on his behalf with her son. The Empress listened in growing astonishment. At the end, there was a short silence. Then she said, with emotion — 'I am sorry! You, yourself, Prince Bismarck, have destroyed all my influence with my son. I can do nothing.'

In a sense, it must have been a moment of triumph. But how tragic are all the implications of the story! It was in my mind as I travelled to Windsor on November 18th, 1898. The following letter was written next day one of my children:

D — and I met at Windsor, and we mounted into the quadrangle, stopped at the third door on the right as Mrs M — had directed us, interviewed various gorgeous footmen, and were soon in Mrs M—'s little sitting-room. Then we found we should have some little time to wait, as the Empress was just going out with the Queen and would see me at a quarter to 1. So we waited, much amused by the talk around us. (It turned, if I remember right, on a certain German Princess, who had arrived a day or two before as the old Queen's guest, and had been taken since her arrival on such a strenuous round of tombs and mausoleums that, hearing on this particular morning that the Queen proposed to take her in the afternoon to see yet another mausoleum, she had stubbornly refused to get up. She had a headache, she said, and would stay in bed. But the ladies in waiting, with fits of laughter, described how the Queen had at once ordered her phenacetin, and how there was really no chance at all for the poor lady. The Queen would get her way, and the departed would be duly honoured — headache or no headache. As indeed it turned out.)

Presently we saw the Queen's little pony-carriage pass along beyond the windows with the Empress Frederick, and the Grand Duke and Duchess Serge walking beside it, and the Indians behind. Then in a little while the Empress Frederick came hurrying back alone, and almost directly came my summons. Countess Perponcher, her lady in waiting, took me up through the Long Corridor, past the entrance to the Queen's rooms on one side, and Gordon's Bible, in its glass case, on the other, till we turned to the left, and I was in a small sitting-room, where a lady, grey-haired and in black, came forward to meet me. . . . We talked for about 50 minutes: — of German books and Universities — Harnack — Renan, for whom she had the greatest admiration — Strauss, of whom she told me various interesting things — German colonies, that she thought were 'all nonsense' — Dreyfus, who in her eyes is certainly innocent — reaction in France — the difference between the Greek Church in Russia, and the Greek Church in Greece, the hopes of Greece, and the freeing of Crete. It is evident that her whole heart is with Greece and her daughter there (the young Queen Sophia, on whose character recently deciphered documents have thrown so strong a light) and she spoke bitterly, as she always does, about the English hanging-back, and the dawdling of the European Concert. Then she described how she read 'George Tressady' aloud to her invalid daughter till the daughter begged her to stop, lest she should cry over it all night — she said charming things of 'Helbeck', talked of Italy, D'Annunzio, quoted 'my dear old friend Minghetti', as to the fundamental paganism in the Italian mind, asked me to write my name in her book, and to come and see her in Berlin — and it was time to go. . . . She is a very attractive, sensitive, impulsive woman, more charming than I had imagined, and, perhaps, less intellectual — altogether the very woman to set up the backs of Bismarck and his like. Never was there a more thorough Englishwoman! I found myself constantly getting her out of focus, by that confusion of mind which made one think of her as German.

And to my father I wrote:

The Empress began by asking after Uncle Matt, and nothing could have been kinder and more sympathetic than her whole manner. But of course Bismarck hated her. She is absolutely English, parliamentary, and anti-despotic. . . . . When I ventured to say in bidding her Goodbye, that I had often felt great admiration and deep sympathy for her, which is true, she threw up her hands with a little sad or bitter gesture — 'Oh! Admiration! — For me!' — as if she knew very well what it was to be conscious of the reverse. A touching, intelligent, impulsive woman, she seemed to me — no doubt often not a wise one — but very attractive.

Nineteen years ago! And two years later, after long suffering, like her husband, the last silence fell on this brave and stormy nature. Let us thank God for it, as we look out upon Europe, and we see what her son has made of it.

CHAPTER XVI

The Villa Barberini. Henry James

It was in the summer of 1898, that some suggestions gathered from the love-story of Chateaubriand and Madame de Beaumont, and jotted down on a sheet of notepaper led to the writing of 'Eleanor'. Madame de Beaumont's melancholy life came to an end in Rome and the Roman setting imposed itself, so to speak, at once. But to write in Rome itself, played upon by all the influences of a place where the currents of life and thought, so far as those currents are political, historical or artistic, seem to be running at double tides, would be, I knew, impossible, and we began to make enquiries for a place outside Rome, yet not too far away, where we might spend the spring. We tried to get an apartment at Frascati, but in vain. Then some friend suggested an apartment in the old Villa Barberini at Castel Gandolfo, well known to many an English and French diplomat, especially to the diplomat's wife and children, flying to the hills to escape the summer heat of Rome. We found by correspondence two kind little ladies living in Rome, who agreed to make all the preparations for us, find servants, and provide against a possibly cold spring to be spent in rooms meant only for *villegiatura* in the summer. We were to go early in March, and fires or stoves must be obtainable, if the weather pinched.

The little ladies did everything, engaged servants, and bargained with the Barberini Steward, but they could not bargain with the weather! On a certain March day when the snow lay thick on the olives and all the furies were wailing round the Alban hills — we arrived. My husband, who had journeyed out with us to settle us in, and was then returning to his London work, was inclined to mocking prophecies that I should soon be back in Rome at a comfortable Hotel. Oh, how cold it was that first night! — how dreary on the great stone staircase, and in the bare comfortless rooms! We looked out over a grey storm-swept Campagna, to distant line of surf-beaten coast; the kitchen was fifty-two steps below the dining room; the Neapolitan cook seemed to us a most formidable gentleman, suggesting stilettos, and we sat down to our first meal, wondering whether we could possibly stay it out.

But with the night (as I wrote some years ago) the snow vanished, and the sun emerged. We ran east to one balcony, and saw the light blazing on the Alban Lake, and had but to cross the apartment to find ourselves, on the other side, with all the Campagna at our feet, sparkling in a thousand colours to the sea. And outside was the garden, with its lemon trees growing in vast jars — like the jars of Knossos — but marked with Barberini bees,' its white and red camellias be-carpeting the soft grass with their fallen petals; its dark and tragic recesses where melancholy trees hung above piled fragments of the great Domitian villa whose ruins lay everywhere beneath our feet; its olive gardens sloping to the west, and open to the sun, open too to white, nibbling goats, and wandering *bambini*; its magical glimpse of St Peter's to the north, through a notch in a group of stone-pines; and, last and best, its marvellous terrace that roofed a cryptoporticus of the old villa, whence the whole vast landscape, from Ostia and the mountains of Viterbo to the Circean promontory, might be discerned, where one might sit and watch the sunsets burn in scarlet and purple down through the wide wet into the shining bosom of the Tyrrhenian sea.

And in one day we had made a home out of what seemed a desert. Books had been unpacked, flowers had been brought in, the stoves were made to burn, the hard chairs and sofas had been twisted and turned into something more human and sociable, and we had began to realise that we were, after all, singularly fortunate mortals, put in possession for three months — at the most moderate of rents! — of as much Italian beauty, antiquity, and romance, as any covetous soul could hope for — with Rome at our gates, and leisurely time for quiet work.

Our earliest guest was Henry James, and never did I see Henry James in a happier light. A new light too. For here, in this Italian country, and in the Eternal City, the man whom I had so far mainly known as a Londoner was far more at home than I; and I realised perhaps more fully than ever before the extraordinary range of his knowledge and sympathies.

Roman history and antiquities, Italian art, Renaissance sculpture, the personalities and events of the Risorgimento, all these solid *connaissances* and many more were to be recognised perpetually as rich elements in the general wealth of Mr James's mind. That he had read immensely, observed immensely, talked immensely, became once more gradually and delightfully clear on this new field. That he spoke French to perfection was of course quickly evident to anyone who had even a slight acquaintance with him. M. Bourget once gave me a wonderful illustration of it. He said that Mr James was staying with himself and Madame Bourget at their villa at Hyāres, not long after the appearance of Kipling's 'Seven Seas'. M. Bourget, who by that time read and spoke English fluently, complained of Mr Kipling's technicalities, and declared that he could not make head or tail of Mc Andrew's Hymn. Whereupon Mr James took up the book, and standing by the fire, fronting his hosts, there and then put Mc Andrew's Hymn into vigorous idiomatic French — an extraordinary feat, as it seemed to M. Bourget. Something similar, it will be remembered, is told of Tennyson. 'One evening,' says F.T. Palgrave of the poet, 'he read out, off-hand, Pindar's great picture of the life of Heaven, in the Second Olympian, into pure modern prose splendidly lucid and musical.' Let who will decide which *tour de force* was the more difficult.

But Mr James was also very much at home in Italian, while in the literature, history and art of both countries he moved with the well-earned sureness of foot of the student. Yet how little one ever thought of him as a student! That was the spell. He wore his learning — and in certain directions he was learned — 'lightly, like a flower'. It was to him not a burden to be carried, not a possession to be proud of, but merely something that made life more thrilling, more full of emotions and sensations; emotions and sensations which he was always eager, without a touch of pedantry, to share with other people. His knowledge was conveyed by suggestion, by the adroitest of hints and indirect approaches. He was politely certain, to begin with, that you knew it all; then to walk *with you* round and round the subject, turning it inside out, playing with it, making mock of it, and catching it again with a sudden grip, or a momentary flash of eloquence, seemed to be for the moment his business in life. How the thing emerged, after a few minutes, from the long involved sentences! — only involved because the impressions of a man of genius are so many, and the resources of speech so limited. This involution, this deliberation in attack, this slowness of approach towards a point which in the end was generally triumphantly rushed, always seemed to me more effective as Mr James used it in speech than as he employed it — some of us would say, to excess — in a few of his latest books. For, in talk, his own living personality — his flashes of fun — of courtesy — of 'chaff' — were always there, to do away with what in the written word, became a difficult strain on attention.

I remember an amusing instance of it, when my daughter D—, who was housekeeping for us at Castel Gandolfo, asked his opinion as to how to deal with the Neapolitan cook, who had been anything but satisfactory, in the case of a luncheon-party of friends from Rome. It was decided to write a letter to the ex-bandit in the kitchen, at the bottom of the fifty-two steps, requesting him to do his best, and pointing out recent short-comings. D—, whose Italian was then rudimentary, brought the letter to Mr James, and he walked up and down the vast *salone* of the Villa striking his forehead, correcting and improvising. 'A really nice pudding' was what we justly desired, since the Neapolitan genius for sweets is well known. Mr James threw out half phrases — pursued them — improved upon them — withdrew them — till finally he rushed upon the magnificent bathos — 'un dolce come si deve!' — which has ever since been the word with us for the tip-top thing.

With the country people he was simplicity and friendship itself. I recollect him in close talk with a brown-frocked bare-footed monk, coming from the monastery of Palazzuola on the farther side of the Alban lake, and how the super-subtle, super-sensitive cosmopolitan found not the smallest difficulty in drawing out the peasant, and getting at something real and vital in the ruder, simpler mind. And again, on a never to be forgotten evening on the Nemi lake, when on descending from Genzano to the strawberry farm that now holds the site of the famous temple of Diana Nemorensis, we found a beautiful youth at the *fattoria*, who for a few pence undertook to show us the fragments that remain. Mr James asked his name. 'Aristodemo,' said the boy, looking as he spoke the Greek name, 'like to a god in form and stature.' Mr James's face lit up; and he walked over the historic ground beside the lad, Aristodemo picking up for him fragments of terracotta from the furrows through which the plough had just passed, bits of the innumerable small *figurines* that used to crowd the temple walls as ex-votos, and are now mingled with the *fragole* in the rich alluvial earth. It was a wonderful evening; with a golden sun on the lake, on the wide stretches where the temple stood, and the niched wall where Lord Savile dug for treasure and found it; on the great ship-timbers also, beside the lake, wreckage from Caligula's galleys, which still lie buried in the deepest depth of the water; on the rock of Nemi, and the fortress-like Orsini villa; on the Alban Mount itself, where it cut the clear sky. I presently came up with Mr James and Aristodemo, who led us on serenely, a young Hermes in the transfiguring light. One almost looked for the winged feet and helmet of the messenger god! Mr James paused — his eyes first on the boy, then on the surrounding scene. 'Aristodemo!' he murmured smiling, and more to himself than me, his voice caressing the word —'what a name! what a place!'

On another occasion I recall him in company with the well-known antiquary, Signor Lanciani, who came over to lunch; amusing us all by the combination of learning with 'le sport' which he affected. Let me quote the account of it given by a girl of the party:

Signor Lanciani is a great man who combines being *the* top authority in his profession, with a kindness and *bonhomie* which makes even an ignoramus feel happy with him — and with the frankest love for *flânerie* and 'sport'. We all fell in love with him. To hear him after lunch in his fluent but lisping English holding forth about the ruins of Domitian's villa — 'what treasures are still to be found in ziz garden if somebody would only *dig*!' — and saying with excitement — 'ziz town, ziz Castello Gandolfo was built upon the site of Alba Longa, not Palazzuola at all. *Here*, Madame, beneath our feet, is Alba Longa' — And then suddenly — a pause, a deep sigh from his ample breast, and a whisper on the summer air —'I vonder — vether — von could make a golf-links around ziz garden!'

And I see still Mr James's figure strolling along the terrace which roofed the crypto-porticus of the Roman villa, beside the professor — the short coat, the summer hat, the smooth-shaven, finely-cut face, now alive with talk and laughter, now shrewdly, one might say coldly observant; the face of a satirist — but so human! — so alive to all that under-world of destiny through which move the weaknesses of men and women. We were sorry indeed when he left us. But there were many other happy meetings to come through the sixteen years that remained; meetings at Stocks and in London; letters and talks that were landmarks in my literary life and in our friendship. Later on I shall quote from his 'Eleanor' letter, the best perhaps of all his critical letters to me, though the 'Robert Elsmere' letters, already published, run it hard. That, too, was followed by many more. But as I do not intend to give more than a general outline of the years that followed on 1900, I will record here the last time but one that I ever saw Henry James — a vision, an impression, which the retina of memory will surely keep to the end. It was at Grosvenor Place in the autumn of 1915, the second year of the war. How doubly close by then he had grown to all our hearts! His passionate sympathy for England and France, his English naturalisation — a *beau geste* indeed, but so sincere, so moving — the pity and wrath that carried him to sit by wounded soldiers, and made him put all literary work aside as something not worth doing, so that he might spend time and thought on helping the American ambulance in France: — one must supply all this as the background of the scene.

It was a Sunday afternoon. Our London house had been let for a time, but we were in it again for a few weeks, drawn into the rushing tide of war-talk and war anxieties. The room was full when Henry James came in. I saw that he was in a stirred, excited mood, and the key to it was soon found. He began to repeat the conversation of an American envoy to Berlin — a well-known man to whom he had just been listening. He described first the envoy's impression of the German leaders, political and military, of Berlin. 'They seemed to him like men waiting in a room from which the air is being slowly exhausted. They *know* they can't win! It is only a question of how long, and how much damage they can do.' The American further reported that after his formal business had been done with the Prussian Foreign Minister, the Prussian — relaxing his whole attitude and offering a cigarette — said —'Now then let me talk to you frankly, as man to man!' — and began a bitter attack on the attitude of President Wilson. Colonel — listened, and when the outburst was done, said — 'Very well! Then I too will speak frankly. I have known President Wilson for many years. He is a very strong man, physically and morally. You can neither frighten him, nor bluff him —'

And then — springing up in his seat — 'And, by Heaven, if you want war with America, you can have it tomorrow!'

Mr James's dramatic repetition of this story, his eyes on fire, his hand striking the arm of his chair, remains with me as my last sight of him in a typical representative moment.

Six months later, on March 6, 1916, my daughter and I were guests at the British Headquarters in France. I was there at the suggestion of Mr Roosevelt and by the wish of our Foreign Office, in order to collect the impressions and information that were afterwards embodied in 'England's Effort'. We came down ready to start for the front, in a military motor, when our kind officer escort handed us some English telegrams which had just come in. One of them announced the death of Henry James; and all through that wonderful day, when we watched a German counter-attack in the Ypres salient from one of the hills south-east of Poperinghe, the ruined tower of Ypres rising from the mists of the horizon, the news was intermittently with me as a dull pain, breaking in upon the excitement and novelty of the great spectacle around us.

'A mortal, a mortal is dead!'

I was looking over ground where every inch was consecrate to the dead sons of England, dead for her; but even through their ghostly voices came the voice of Henry James, who, spiritually, had fought in their fight and suffered in their pain.

One year and a month before the American declaration of war. What he would have given to see it — my dear old friend, whose life and genius will enter for ever into the bonds uniting England and America!

. . . .

Yes ! —

> . . . He was a priest to us all
> Of the wonder and bloom of the world
> Which we saw with his eyes and were glad.

For that was indeed true of Henry James, as of Wordsworth. The 'wonder and bloom', no less than the ugly or heart-breaking things, which like the disfiguring rags of old Laertes, hide them from us — he could weave them all, with an untiring hand, into the many-coloured web of his art. Olive Chancellor, Madame Mauve, Milly, in 'The Wings of a Dove' — the most exquisite in some ways of all his women — Roderick Hudson, St George, the woman doctor in the 'Bostonians', the French family in the 'Reverberation', Brooksmith — and innumerable others: — it was the wealth and facility of it all that was so amazing! There is enough observation of character in a chapter of the 'Bostonians', a story he thought little of, and did not include in his collected edition, to shame a Wells novel of the newer sort, with its floods of clever half-considered journalism in the guise of conversation, hiding an essential poverty of creation. 'Ann Veronica' and the 'New Machiavelli', and several other tales by the same writer, set practically the same scene, and handle the same characters under different names. Of an art so false and confused, Henry James could never have been capable. His people, his situations, have the sharp separateness, and something of the inexhaustibleness — of nature, which does not mix her moulds.

As to method, naturally I often discussed with him some of the difficult problems of presentation. The posthumous sketches of work in progress, published since his death, show how he delighted in these problems, in their very difficulties, in their endless opportunities. As he often said to me, he could never read a novel that interested him without taking it mentally to pieces, and re-writing it in his own way. Some of his letters to me are brilliant examples of this habit of his. Technique — presentation — were then immensely important to him; important as they never could have been to Tolstoy, who probably thought very little consciously about them. Mr James, as we all know, thought a great deal about them, sometimes, I venture to think, too much. In 'The Wings of a Dove', for instance, a subject full of beauty and tragedy is almost spoilt by an artificial technique, which is responsible for a scene on which, as it seems to me, the whole illusion of the book is shattered. The conversation in the Venice apartment where the two *fiancés* — one of whom at least, the man, is commended to our sympathy as a decent and probable human being — make their cynical bargain in the very presence of the dying Milly, for whose money they are plotting, is in some ways a *tour de force* of construction. It is the central point on which many threads converge, and from which many depart. But to my mind, as I have said, it invalidates the story. Mr James is here writing as a *virtuoso*, and not as the great artist we know him to be. And the same, I think, is true of 'The Golden Bowl'. That again is a wonderful exercise in virtuosity; but a score of his slighter sketches seem to me infinitely nearer to the truth and vitality of great art. The book, in which perhaps technique and life are most perfectly blended — at any rate among the later novels — is 'The Ambassador'. There, the skill with which a deeply interesting subject is focussed from many points of view, but always with the fascinating unity given to it, both by the personality of the 'Ambassador', and by the mystery to which every character in the book is related, is kept in its place, the servant, not the master, of the theme. And the climax — which is the river scene, when the 'Ambassador' penetrates at last the long kept secret of the lovers — is as right as it is surprising, and sinks away through admirable modulations to the necessary close. And what beautiful things in the course of the handling! — the old French Academician and his garden, on the *rive gauche*, for example; or the summer afternoon on the upper Seine, with its pleasure-boats, and the red parasol which finally tells all — a picture drawn with the sparkle and truth of a Daubigny, only the better to bring out the unwelcome fact which is its centre. 'Ambassador' is the masterpiece of Mr James's later work and manner, just as 'The Portrait of a Lady' is the masterpiece of the earlier.

And the whole? — his final place? — when the stars of his generation rise into their place above the spent field? I, at least, have no doubt whatever about his security of fame; though very possibly he may be no more generally read in the time to come than are most of the other great masters of literature. Personally, I regret that, from 'What Maisie Knew' onwards, he adopted the method of dictation. A mind so teeming, and an art so flexible, were surely the better for the slight curb imposed by the physical toil of writing. I remember how and when we first discussed the *pros* and *cons* of dictation, on the fell above Cartmel Chapel, when he was with us at Levens in 1887. He was then enchanted by the endless vistas of work and achievement which the new method seemed to open out. And indeed it is plain that he produced more with it than he could have produced without it. Also, that in the use of dictation as in everything else, he showed himself the extraordinary craftsman that he was, to whom all difficulty was a challenge, and the conquest of it a delight. Still, the diffuseness and over-elaboration which were the natural snares of his astonishing gifts were encouraged rather than checked by the new method; and one is jealous of anything whatever that may tend to stand between him and the unstinted pleasure of those to come after.

But when these small cavils are done, one returns in delight and wonder to the accomplished work. To the *wealth* of it above all — the deep draughts from human life that it represents. It is true indeed that there are large tracts of modern existence which Mr James scarcely touches, the peasant life, the industrial life, the small trading life, the political life; though it is clear that he divined them all, enough at least for his purposes. But in his vast, indeterminate range of busy or leisured folk, men and women with breeding and without it, backed with ancestors or merely the active 'sons of their works', young girls and youths and children, he is a master indeed, and there is scarcely anything in human feeling, normal or strange, that he cannot describe or suggest. If he is without passion, as some are ready to declare, so are Stendhal and Turguénieff, and half the great masters of the novel; and if he seems sometimes to evade the tragic or rapturous moments, it is perhaps only that he may make his reader his co-partner, that he may evoke from us that heat of sympathy and intelligence which supplies the necessary atmosphere for the subtler and greater kinds of art.

And all through, the dominating fact is that it is 'Henry James' speaking — Henry James, with whose delicate, ironic mind and most human heart we are in contact. There is much that can be *learnt* in fiction; the resources of mere imitation, which we are pleased to call realism, are endless; we see them in scores of modern books. But at the root of every book is the personality of the man who wrote it. And in the end, that decides.

CHAPTER XVII

Roman Friends. 'Eleanor'

I

The spring of the following year (1900) saw us again in Rome. We spent our April fortnight there, of which I specially remember some amusing hours with Sir William Harcourt. I see myself, for instance, as a rather nervous tourist in his wake and that of the very determined wife of a young diplomat, storming the Vatican library at an hour when a bland *custode* assured us firmly it was *not* open to visitors. But Sir William's great height and bulk, aided by his pretty companion's self-will simply carried us through the gates by their natural momentum. Father Ehrle was sent for and came, and we spent a triumphant and delightful hour. After all one is not an ex-British Cabinet Minister for nothing. Sir William was perfectly civil to everybody, with a blinking smile like that of the Cheshire cat; but nothing stopped him. I laugh still at the remembrance. On the way home it was wet, and he and I shared a *legno*. I remember we talked of Mr Chamberlain, with whom at that moment — May 1899 — Sir William was not in love; and of Lord Hartington. 'Hartington came to me one day when we were both serving under Mr G., and said to me in a temper — "I wish I could get Gladstone to answer letters." "My dear fellow, he always answers letters." "Well I have been trying to do something and I can't get a word out of him." "What have you been trying to do?" "Well to tell the truth, I've been trying to make a bishop." "Have you? Not much in your line I should think. Now if it had been something about a horse — —" "Don't be absurd. He would have made a very good bishop. C — — and S — — (naming two well-known Liberals) told me I must — so I wrote — and not a word! Very uncivil, I call it." "Who was it?" "Oh, I can't remember. Let me think. Oh, yes, it was a man with a double name — Llewellyn-Davies." Sir William, with a shout of laughter — "Why it took me five years to get him made a Canon!"'

The following year I sent him 'Eleanor', as a reminder of our meeting in Rome, and he wrote:

To me the revisiting of Rome is the brightest of the day-dreams of life, and I treasure all its recollections. After the disappointment of the day when we were to have seen Albano and Nemi under your guidance, we managed the expedition, and were entranced with the scene even beyond our hopes, and since that time I have lived through it again in the pages of 'Eleanor', which I read with greediness, waiting each number as it appeared.

Now about Manisty. What a fortunate beggar, to have two such charming women in love with him! It is always so. The less a man deserves it the more they adore him. That is the advantage you women-writers have. You always figure men as they are and women as they ought to be. If I had the composition of the history I should never represent two women behaving so well to one another under the circumstances. Even American girls, according to my observation, do not show so much toleration to their rivals, even though in the end they carry off their man. . . .

Your sincerely attached

W. V. Harcourt

II

Let me detach a few other figures from a gay and crowded time, the ever-delightful and indefatigable Boni — Commendatore Boni — for instance. To hear him talk in the Forum or hold forth at a small gathering of friends on the problems of the earliest Italian races, and the causes that met in the founding and growth of Rome, was to understand how no scholar or archéologist can be quite first-rate who is not also something of a poet. The sleepy blue eyes, so suddenly alive; the apparently languid manner which was the natural defence against the outer world of a man all compact of imagination and sleepless energy; the touch in him of 'the imperishable child', combined with the brooding intensity of the explorer who is always guessing at the next riddle; the fun, simplicity, *bonhomie* he showed with those who knew him well: all these are vividly present to me.

So too are the very different characteristics of Monseigneur Duchesne, the French Lord Acton; like him, a Liberal and a man of vast learning, tarred with the Modernist brush in the eyes of the Vatican, but at heart also, like Lord Acton, by the testimony of all who know, a simple and convinced believer.

When we met Monseigneur Duchesne at the house of Count Ugo Balzani, or in the drawing room of the French Embassy, all that showed, at first, was the witty ecclesiastic of the old school, and *abbé* of the eighteenth century, *fin*, shrewd, well versed in men and affairs, and capable of throwing an infinity of meaning into the inflection of a word, or the lift of an eyebrow. I remember listening to an account by him of certain ceremonies in the catacombs in which he had taken part, in the train of an Ultramontane Cardinal whom he particularly disliked. He himself had preached the sermon. A member of the party said, 'I hear your audience were greatly moved, Monsignore.' Duchesne bowed, with just a touch of irony. Then someone who knew the Cardinal well and the relation between him and Duchesne, said with *malice prepense*, 'Was his Eminence moved, Monsignore?' Duchesne looked up, and shook off the end of his cigarette — '*Non, Monsieur,*' he said drily, 'his Eminence was not moved — oh, not at all!' A ripple of laughter went round the group which had heard the question. For a second, Duchesne's eyes laughed too, and were then as impenetrable as before. My last remembrance of him is as the centre of a small party in one of the famous rooms of the Palazzo Borghese which were painted by the Caracci; this time in a more serious and communicative mood, so that one realised in him more clearly the cosmopolitan and liberal scholar, whose work on the early Papacy, and the origins of Christianity in Rome is admired and used by men of all faiths and none. Shortly afterwards a Roman friend of ours, an Englishman who knew Monseigneur Duchesne well, described to me the impressions of an English Catholic who had gone with him to Egypt on some learned mission, and had been thrown for a time into relations of intimacy with him. My friend reported the touch of astonishment in the Englishman's mind, as he became aware of the religious passion in his companion, the devotion of his daily mass, the rigour and simplicity of his personal life; and we both agreed that as long as Catholicism could produce such types, men at once so daring and so devout, so free, and yet so penetrated with — so steeped in — the immemorial life of Catholicism, the Roman Church was not likely to perish out of Europe.

Let me however contrast with Monseigneur Duchesne another Catholic personality — that of Cardinal Vaughan. I remember being asked to join a small group of people who were to meet Cardinal Vaughan on the steps of St Peter's, and to go with him, and Canon Oakley, an English convert to Catholicism, through the famous crypt and its moments. We stood for some twenty minutes outside St Peter's, while Cardinal Vaughan, in the manner of a cicerone reeling off his task, gave us *in extenso* the legendary stories of St Peter's and St Paul's martyrdoms. Not a touch of criticism, of knowledge, of insight: — a childish tale, told by a man who had never asked himself for a moment whether he really believed it. I stood silently by him, inwardly comparing the performance with certain pages by the Abbé Duchesne, which I had just been reading. Then we descended to the crypt, the Cardinal first kneeling at the statute of St Peter. The crypt, as everyone knows, is full of fragments from Christian antiquity, sarcophagi of early Popes, indications of the structures that preceded the present building, fragments from papal tombs, and so on. But it was quite useless to ask the Cardinal for an explanation or a date. He knew nothing; and he had never cared to know. Again and again, I thought, as we passed some shrine or sarcophagus bearing a name or names that sent a thrill through one's historical sense — 'If only J.R. Green were here! — how these dead bones would live!' But the agnostic historian was in his grave, and the Prince of the Roman Church passed ignorantly and heedlessly by.

A little while before, I had sat beside the Cardinal at a luncheon party, where the case of Dr Schell, the Rector of the Catholic University of Wurzburg, who had published a book condemned by the Congregation of the Index, came up for discussion. Dr Schell's book, 'Catholicismus und Fortschritt', was a plea on behalf of the Catholic Universities of Bavaria against the Jesuit seminaries which threatened to supplant them; and he had shown with striking clearness the disastrous results which the gradual narrowing of Catholic education had had on the Catholic culture of Bavaria. The Jesuit influence at Rome had procured the condemnation of the book. Dr Schell at first submitted; then, just before the luncheon party at which I was present, withdrew his submission.

I saw the news given to the Cardinal. He shrugged his shoulders. 'Oh poor fellow!' he said — 'Poor fellow!' It was not said unkindly, rather with a kind of easy pity; but the recollection came back to me in the crypt of St Peter's, and I seemed to see the man who could not shut his ear to knowledge and history struggling in the grip of men like the Cardinal, who knew no history.

Echoes and reflections from these incidents will be found in 'Eleanor', and it was the case of Dr Schell that suggested Father Benecke.

III

So the full weeks passed on. Half 'Eleanor' had been written, and in June we turned homewards. But before then, one visitor came to the Villa Barberini in our last weeks there, who brought with him, for myself, a special and peculiar joy. My dear father, with his second wife, arrived to spend a week with us. Never before, throughout all his ardent Catholic life, had it been possible for him to tread the streets of Rome, or kneel in St Peter's. At last, the year before his death, he was to climb the Janiculum, and to look out over the city and the plain whence Europe received her civilisation and the vast system of the Catholic Church. He felt as a Catholic; but hardly less as a scholar, one to whom Horace and Virgil had been familiar from his boyhood, the greater portion of them known by heart, to a degree which is not common now. I remember well that one bright May morning at Castel Gandolfo, he vanished from the Villa, and presently after some hours reappeared with shining eyes.

'I have been on the Appian Way — I have walked where Horace walked!'

In his own autobiography he writes: 'In proportion to a man's good sense and soundness of feeling are the love and admiration, increasing with his years, which he bears towards Horace.' An old-world judgement some will say, which to us, immersed in this deluge of war which is changing the face of all things, may sound, perhaps, as a thin and ghostly voice from far away. It comes from the Oxford of Newman and Matthew Arnold, of Jowett, and Clough; and for the moment, amid the thunder and anguish of our time, it is almost strange to our ears. But when the tumult and the shouting die, and 'peace has calmed the world', whatever else may have passed, the poets and the thinkers will be still there, safe in their old shrines, for they are the 'ageless mouths' of all mankind, when men are truly men. The supposed reformers, who thirst for the death of classical education, will not succeed, because man doth not live by bread alone, and certain imperishable needs in him have never been so fully met as by some Greeks and some Latins, writing in a vanished society, which yet, by reason of their thought and genius, is still in some real sense ours. More science? More foreign languages? More technical arts? Yes! All these. But if democracy is to mean the disappearance of the Greek and Latin poets from the minds of the future leaders of our race, the history of three thousand years is there to show what the impoverishment will be.

As to this, a personal experience, even from one who in Greek literature is only a 'proselyte of the gate', may not be without interest. I shall never forget the first time when, in middle life, I read in the Greek, so as to understand and enjoy, the 'Agamemnon' of Aeschylus. The feeling of sheer amazement at the range and power of human thought — and at such a date in history — which a leisurely and careful reading of that play awakened in me, left deep marks behind. It was as though for me, thenceforward, the human intellect had been suddenly related, much more clearly than ever before, to an absolute, ineffable source, 'not itself'. So that, in realising the greatness of the mind of Aeschylus, the creative Mind from which it sprang had in some new and powerful way touched my own; with both new light on the human Past, and mysterious promise for the Future. Now, for many years, the daily reading of Greek and Latin has been not only a pleasure, but the only continuous bit of mental discipline I have been able to keep up.

I do not believe this will seem exaggerated to those on whom Greek poetry and life have really worked. My father, or the Master, or Matthew Arnold, had any amateur spoken in similar fashion to them, would have smiled, but only as those do who are in secure possession of some precious thing, on the eagerness of the novice who has just laid a precarious hold upon it.

At any rate, as I look back upon my father's life of constant labour and many baffled hopes, there are at least two bright lights upon the scene. He had the comfort of religious faith, and the double joy of the scholar and of the enthusiast for letters. He would not have bartered these great things, these seeming phantoms —

> Eternal as the recurrent cloud, as air
> Imperative, refreshful as dawn-dew —

for any of the baser goods that we call real.

A year and a half after his visit to Rome, he died in Dublin, where he had been for years a Fellow and Professor of the Irish University, occupied in lecturing on English literature, and in editing some of the most important English Chronicles for the 'Rolls Series'. His monument, a beautiful medallion by Mr Derwent Wood, which recalls him to the life, hangs on the wall of the University church, in Stephen's Green, which was built in Newman's time, and under his superintendence. The only other monument in the Church is that to the Cardinal himself. So once more, as 1886, they — the preacher and his convert — are together. 'Domine, Deus meus, in Te speravi.' So, on my father's tablet, runs the text below the quiet, sculptured face. It expresses the root fact of his life.

IV

A few weeks before my father's death 'Eleanor' appeared. It had taken me a year and a quarter to write, and I had given it full measure of work. Henry James wrote to me, on receipt of it, that it gave him —

the chance to overflow into my favourite occupation of rewriting as I read, such fiction as — I can read. I took this liberty in an inordinate degree with Eleanor — and I always feel it the highest tribute I can pay. I recomposed and re-constructed her from head to foot — which I give you for the real measure of what I think of her. I think her, less obscurely — a thing of rare beauty, a large and noble performance, rich, complex, comprehensive, deeply interesting and highly distinguished. I congratulate you heartily on having *mené à bonne fin* so intricate and difficult a problem, and on having seen your subject so wrapped in its air and so bristling with its relations. I should say that you had done nothing more homogeneous, nor more hanging and moving together. It has Beauty — the book, the theme, and treatment alike, is magnificently mature, and is really a delightful thing to have been able to do — to have laid at the old golden door of the beloved Italy. You deserve well of her. I can't 'criticise' — though I *could* (that is I *did* — but can't do it again) — re-write. The thing's infinitely delightful and distinguished and that's enough. The success of it, specifically, to my sense is Eleanor, admirably sustained in the 'high-note' way, without a break or a drop. She is a very exquisite and very rendered conception. I won't grossly pretend to you that I think the book hasn't a weakness and rather a grave one, or you will doubt of my intelligence. It *has* one, and in this way, to my troubled sense; that the anti-thesis on which your subject rests isn't a real, valid anti-thesis. It was utterly built, your subject, by your intention, of course, on one; but the one you chose seems to me not efficiently to have operated, so that if the book is so charming and touching even *so*, that is a proof of your affluence. Lucy has in respect to Eleanor — that is the image of Lucy that you have tried to teach yourself to see — has no true, no adequate, no logical antithetic force — and this is not only, I think, because the girl is done a little more *de chic* than you would really have liked to do her, but because the *nearer* you had got to her type the less she would have served that particular condition of your subject. You went too far for her, or going so far, should have brought her back — roughly speaking — stronger. (Irony (and various things!) should at its hour have presided.) But I throw out that more imperfectly, I recognise, than I should wish. It doesn't matter, and not a solitary reader in your millions, or critic in your hundreds, will either have missed, or have made it! And when a book's beautiful, nothing does matter! I hope greatly to see you after the New Year, Good night. It's my usual 1.30 a.m.

Yours, dear Mrs Ward, always

Henry James

I could not but feel indeed that the book had given great pleasure to those I might well wish to please. My old friend, Mr Fredric Harrison, wrote to me: — 'I have read it all through with great attention and delight, and have returned to it again and again. . . . . I am quite sure that it is the most finished and artistic of all your books and one of the most subtle and graceful things in all our modern fiction.' And Charles Eliot Norton's letter from Shady Hill, the letter of one who never praised perfunctorily or insincerely, made me glad: —

'It would be easier to write about the book to anyone else but you. . . . You have added to the treasures of English imaginative literature, and no higher reward than this can any writer hope to gain.' The well-known and much loved editor of the *Century*, Richard Watson Gilder, 'on this the last Sunday of the nineteenth century' so he headed his letter, sat down to give a long hour of precious time to 'Eleanor's' distant author.

How can you reconcile it to your conscience to write a book like 'Eleanor' that keeps a poor fellow reading it to a finish till after three in the morning? Not only that — but that keeps him sobbing and sighing 'like a furnace', that charms him and makes him angry — that hurts and delights him, and will not let him go till all is done! Yes, there are some things I might quarrel with — but ah, how much you give of Italy — of the English, of the American — three nations so well-beloved; and how much of things deeper than peoples or countries.

Imagine me at our New England farm — with the younger part of the family — in my annual 'retreat'. Last year at this time I was here, with the thermometer a dozen degrees below zero; now it is milder but cold, bleak, snowy. Yesterday we were fishing for pickerel through the ice at Hayes's Pond — in a wilderness where fox abound — and where bear and deer make rare appearances — all within a few miles of Lenox and Stockbridge. The farmer's family is at one end of the long farmhouse — I am at the other. It is a great place to read — one reads here with a sort of lonely passion. You know the landscape — it is in 'Eleanor'. Last night (or this morning) I wanted to talk with you about your book — or telegraph — but here I am calmly trying to thank you both for sending us the copy — and, too, for writing it.

Of the 'deeper things' I can really say nothing — except that I feel their truth, and am grateful for them. But may I not applaud (even the Pope is 'applauded', you know) such a perfect touch as — for instance — in Chapter XVI — 'the final softening of that sweet austerity which hid Lucy's heart of gold'; and again 'Italy without the *forestieri*' 'like surprising a bird on its nest'; and the scene beheld of Eleanor — Lucy pressing the terracotta to her lips; — and Italy 'having not enough faith to make a heresy' — (true, too, of France, is it not?) and Chapter XXIII — 'a base and plundering happiness'; then the scene of the confessional; and that sudden phrase of Eleanor's in her talk with Manisty that makes the whole world — and the whole book — right; '*She loves you!*' That is art. . . . But above all, my dear lady, acknowledgements and praise for the hand that created 'Lucy' — that recreated rather — my dear countrywoman! Truly, that is an accomplishment and one that will endear its author to the whole new world.

And again one asks whether the readers of today now write such generous, such encouraging things to the makers of tales, as the readers of twenty years ago! If not, I cannot but think it is a loss. For praise is a great tonic, and helps most people to do their best.

. . . .

It was during our stay on the Alban Hills that I first became conscious in myself, after a good many springs spent in Italy, of a deep and passionate sympathy for the modern Italian State and people; a sympathy widely different from that common temper in the European traveller which regards Italy as the European playground, picture gallery, and curiosity shop, and grudges the smallest encroachment by the needs of the new nation on the picturesque ruin of the past. Italy in 1899 was passing through a period of humiliation and unrest. The defeats of the luckless Erythrean expedition were still hot in Italian memory. The extreme Catholic party at home, the sentimental Catholic tourist from abroad, were equally contemptuous and critical; and I was often indignantly aware of a tone which seemed to me ungenerous and unjust towards the struggling Italian State, on the part of those who had really most cause to be grateful for all that the youngest — and oldest — of European Powers had done in the forty years since 1860 to furnish itself with the necessary equipment, moral, legal and material, of a modern democracy.

This vein of feeling finds expression in 'Eleanor'. Manisty represents the scornful dilettante, the impatient accuser of an Italy he does not attempt to understand; while the American Lucy, on the other side, draws from her New England tradition a glowing sympathy for the Risorgimento and its fruits, for the efforts and sacrifices from which modern Italy arose, that refuses to be chilled by the passing corruptions and scandals of the new *régime*. Her influence prevails and Manisty recants. He spends six solitary weeks wandering through middle Italy, in search of the fugitives, Eleanor and Lucy, who have escaped him, and at the end of it, he sees the old, old country and her people with new eyes, which are Lucy's eyes.

'What rivers — what fertility — what a climate! And the industry of the people! Catch a few English farmers and set them to do what the Italian peasant does, year in and year out, without a murmur! Look at all the coast south of Naples. There is not a yard of it, scarcely, that hasn't been made by human hands. Look at the hill-towns; and think of the human toil that has gone to the making and maintaining of them since the world began. . . *Ecco!* — there they are' — and he pointed down the river to the three of four distant towns, each on its mountain spur, that held the valley between them and Orvieto, pale jewels on the purple robe of rock and wood — 'So Virgil saw them. So the latest sons of time shall see them — the homes of a race that we chatter about without understanding — the most laborious race in the wide world.

.... Anyway, as I have been going up and down their country, ... prating about their poverty, and their taxes, their corruption, the incompetence of their leaders, the mischief of their quarrel with the church; I have been finding myself caught in the grip of older and deeper — incredibly, primevally old! — that still dominate everything, shape everything, shape everything here. There are forces in Italy, forces of land and soil and race — only now fully let loose — that will remake Church no less than State, as the generations go by. Sometimes I have felt as though this country were the youngest in Europe; with a future as fresh and teeming as the future of America. And yet one thinks of it at other times as one vast graveyard; so thick it is with the ashes and the bones of men! The Pope — and Crispi! — waves, both of them, on a sea of life that gave them birth "with equal mind"; and that "with equal mind" will sweep them both to its own goal, not theirs! . . . No — there are plenty of dangers ahead. . . . Socialism is serious; Sicily is serious; the economic difficulties are serious; the House of Savoy will have a rough task, perhaps to ride the seas that may come. — But *Italy* is safe. You can no more undo what has been done than you can replace the child in the womb. The birth is over. The organism is still weak, but it lives. And the forces behind it are, indefinitely, mysteriously stronger than its adversaries think.'

In this mood it was that, when the book came out in the autumn of 1900. I prefixed to it the dedication — 'To Italy, the beloved and beautiful, Instructress of our past, Delight of our present, Comrade of our future, the heart of an Englishwoman offers this book.'

'*Comrade of our future.*' As one looks out today upon the Italian fighting line, where English troops are interwoven with those of Italy and France for the defence of the Lombard and Venetian plain against the attack of Italy's old and bitter enemy, an attack in which are concerned not only the fortunes of Italy, but those also of the British Empire, I wonder what touch of prophecy, what whisper from a far-off day suggested these words written eighteen years ago?

Epilogue

And here, for a time at least, I bring these 'Recollections' to an end with the century in which I was born, and my own fiftieth year. Since 'Eleanor' appeared, and my father died, eighteen years have gone — years for me of constant work, literary and other. On the one hand, increasing interest in and preoccupation with politics, owing to personal links and friendships, and a life spent, as to half the year, in London, have been reflected in my books; and on the other, the English rural scene, with its country houses and villages, its religion, and its elements of change and revolution, has been always at my home gates, as a perpetually interesting subject. Old historic situations, also, have come to life for me again in new surroundings, as in 'Lady Rose's Daughter', 'The Marriage of William Ashe', and 'Fenwick's Career'; in 'Richard Meynell' I attempted the vision of a church of England recreated from within, with a rebel, and not — as in 'Robert Elsmere' — an exile, for a hero; 'Lady Connie' is a picture of Oxford, as I saw her in my youth, as faithful as I can now make it; 'Eltham House' is a return to the method of 'William Ashe', and both 'Lady Connie' and 'Missing' have been written since the war. 'Missing' takes for its subject a fragment from the edge of that vast upheaval which no novel of real life in future will be able to leave out of its ken. In the first two years of the war, the cry both of writers and public — so far as the literature of imagination was concerned — tended to be — 'anything but the war!' There was an eager wish in both, for a time, in the first onrush of the great catastrophe, to escape from it and the newspapers, into the world behind it. That world looks to us now as the Elysian fields looked to Æneas as he approached them from the heights — full not only of souls in a blessed calm, but of those also who had yet to make their way into existence as it terribly *is*, had still to taste reality and pain. We were thankful for a time to go back to that kind, unconscious, unforeseeing world. But it is no longer possible. The war has become our life, and will be so for years after the signing of peace.

As to the three main interests, outside my home life, which, as I look back upon half a century, seem to have held sway over my thoughts — contemporary literature, religious development, and social experiment — one is tempted to say a few last summarising things, though, amid the noise of war, it is hard to say them with any real detachment of mind.

When we came up to London in 1881, George Eliot was just dead (December 1880); Browning and Carlyle passed away in the course of the eighties; Tennyson in 1892. I saw the Tennyson funeral in the Abbey, and remember it vividly. The burying of Mr Gladstone was more stately, this of Tennyson, as befitted a poet, had a more intimate beauty. A great multitude filled the Abbey, and the rendering in Sir Frederick Bridge's setting, of 'Crossing the Bar' by the Abbey Choir sent the 'wild echoes' of the great man's verse flying up on through the great arches overhead with a dramatic effect not to be forgotten. Yet the fame of the poet was waning when he died, and has been hotly disputed since; though, as it seems to me, these later years have seen the partial return of an ebbing tide. What was merely didactic in Tennyson is dead years ago; the difficulties of faith and philosophy, with which his own mind had wrestled, were, long before his death, swallowed up in others far more vital, to which his various optimisms, for all the grace in which he clothed them, had no key, or suggestion of a key, to offer. The Idylls, so popular in their day, and almost all indeed of the narrative and dramatic work, no longer answer to the needs of a generation that has learnt from younger singers and thinkers a more restless method, a more poignant and discontented thought. A literary world fed on Meredith and Henry James, on Ibsen or Bernard Shaw or Anatole France, on Synge or Yeats, rebels against the versified argument, however musical or skilful, built up in 'In Memoriam', and makes mock of what it conceives to be the false history and weak sentiment of the

Idylls. All this, of course, is true, and has been said a thousand times, but — and here again the broad verdict is emerging — it does not touch the lyrical fame of a supreme lyrical poet. It may be that one small volume will ultimately contain all that is really immortal in Tennyson's work. But that volume, it seems to me, will be safe among the golden books of our literature cherished alike by young lovers and the 'drooping old'.

I only remember seeing Tennyson twice: once in a crowded drawing-room, and once on the slopes of Blackdown, in his big cloak. The strong set face under the wide-awake, the energy of undefeated age that breathed from the figure, remains with me, stamped on my memory, like the gentle face of Mrs Wordsworth, or a passing glimpse — a gesture — of George Meredith as we met on the threshold of Mr Cotter Morison's house at Hampstead, one day perhaps in '86 or '87, and he turned his handsome curly head with a smile and a word when Mr Morison introduced us. He was then not yet sixty, already a little lame, but the radiant physical presence scarcely marred. We had some passing talk that day, but — to my infinite regret — that was the only time I ever saw him. Of his work and his genius I began to be aware, when 'Beauchamp's Career' — a much truncated version — was coming out in the *Fortnightly* in 1874. I had heard him and his work discussed in the Lincoln circle, where both the Pattisons were quite alive to Meredith's quality; but I was at the time and for long afterwards under the spell of the French limpidity and clarity, and the Meredithian manner repelled me. About the same time when I was no more than three or four and twenty, I remember a visit to Cambridge, when we spent a weekend at the Bull Inn, and were the guests by day of Frederic Myers, and some of his Trinity and King's friends. Those two days of endless talk in beautiful College rooms with men like Frederic Myers, Edmund Gurney, Mr Gerald Balfour, Mr George Prothero, and others, left a deep mark on me. Cambridge seemed to me then a hearth whereon the flame of thought burnt with far greater daring and freedom than at Oxford. Men were not so afraid of each other; the sharp religious divisions of Oxford were absent; ideas were thrown up like balls in air, sure that some light hand would catch and pass them on.

And among the subjects which rose and fell in that warm electric atmosphere, was the emergence of a new and commanding genius in George Meredith. The place in literature that some of these brilliant men were already giving to 'Richard Fevereal', which had been published some fifteen years earlier, struck me greatly; but if I was honest with myself, my enthusiasm was much more qualified than theirs. It was not till 'Diana of the Crossways' came out, after we had moved to London, that the Meredithian power began to grip me; and to this day the saturation with French books and French ideals that I owed to my uncle's influence during our years at Oxford, stands somewhat between me and a great master. And yet, in this case, as in that of Mr James, there is no doubt that difficulty — even obscurity! —— are part of the spell. The man behind is *great enough*, and rewards the reader's effort to understand him with a sense of heightened power, just as a muscle is strengthened by exercise. In other words, the effort is worth while; we are admitted by it to a world of beauty or romance or humour that without it we should not know; and with the thing gained, goes, as in Alpine climbing, the pleasure of the effort itself

Especially is this the case in poetry, where the artist's thought fashions for itself a manner more intimate and personal, than in prose. George Meredith's poetry is still only the possession of a minority, even among those who form the poetic audience of a generation. There are many of us who have wanted much help, in regard to it, from others — the young and ardent — who are the natural initiates, the 'Mystae' of the poetic world. But once let the strange and poignant magic of it, its music in discord, its sharp sweetness, touch the inward ear: — thenceforward we shall follow its piping.

Let me record another regret for another lost opportunity. In spite of common friends, and worlds that might have met, I never saw Robert Louis Stevenson — the writer who more, perhaps, than any other of his generation touched the feeling and won the affection of his time. And that by a double spell — of the life lived and the books written. Stevenson's hold both upon his contemporaries, and those who since his death have had only the printed word of his letters and tales whereby to approach him, has not been without some points of likeness

— amid great difference — to the hold of the Brontës on their day and ours. The sense of an unsurpassable courage — against great odds — has been the same in both cases; and a great tenderness in the public mind for work so gallant, so defiant of ill fortune, so loyal to its own aims. In Stevenson's case, quite apart from the claims of his work as literature, there was also an added element, which with all their genius, the Brontës did not possess — the element of charm, the *petit carillon*, to which Renan attributed his own success in literature: undefinable, always, this last! — but supreme. There is scarcely a letter of Stevenson's that is without it, it plays about the slender volumes of essays or of travel that we know so well; but it is present not only in the lighter books and tales, not only in the enchanting fairytale, 'Prince Otto', but in his most tragic, or his most intellectual work — in the fragment 'Weir of Hermiston', or in that fine piece of penetrating psychology and admirable narrative, 'The Master of Ballantrae'. It may, I think, be argued whether, in the far future, Stevenson will be more widely and actively remembered — whether he will enter into the daily pleasure of those who love literature — more as a letter-writer, or more as a writer of fiction. Whether, in other words, his own character and personality will not prove the enduring thing, rather than the characters he created. The volumes of letters, with their wonderful range and variety, their humour, their bravery, their *vision* — whether of persons or scenes — already mean to some of us more than his stories, dear to us as these are.

He died in his forty-fifth year, at the height of his power. If he had lived ten — twenty — years longer, he might well have done work that would have set him with Scott in the history of letters. As it is, he remains the most graceful and appealing, the most animated and delightful figure in the literary history of the late nineteenth century. He is sure of his place. 'Myriad-footed Time will discover many other inventions; but mine are mine!' And to that final award his poems no less than his letters will richly contribute — the haunting beauty of the 'Requiem,', the noble lines 'To my Father,', the lovely verses 'In memory of F. A. S.' — surely immortal, so long as mother-hearts endure.

Another great name was steadily finding its place during our first London years. Thomas Hardy had already published some of his best novels in the seventies, and was in full production all through the eighties and nineties. The first of Hardy novels that strongly affected me was the 'Return of the Native', and I did not read it till some time after its publication. Although there had been a devoted, and constantly growing audience for Mr Hardy's books for twenty years before the publication of 'Tess of the Durbervilles', my own recollection is that Tess marked the conversion of the larger public, who then began to read all the earlier books, in that curiously changed mood which sets in when a writer is no longer on trial, but has, so to speak, 'make good'.

And since that date how intimately have the scenes and characters of Mr Hardy's books entered into the mind and memory of his country, compelling many persons, slowly and by degrees — I count myself among this tardy company — to realise their truth, sincerity and humanity, in spite of the pessimism with which so many of them are tinged; their beauty also, not withstanding the clashing discords that a poet, who is also a realist, cannot fail to strike; their permanence in English literature; and the greatness of Mr Hardy's genius! Personally, I would make only one exception. I wish Mr Hardy had not written 'Jude the Obscure'! On the other hand, in the three volumes of 'The Dynasts', he has given us one of the noblest, and possibly one of the most fruitful experiments in recent English letters.

Far more rapid was the success of Mr Kipling, which came a decade later than Mr Hardy's earlier novels. It thrills one's literary pulse now to look back to those early paper-covered treasures, written by a youth, a boy, of genius; which for the first time made India interesting to hundreds of thousands in the Western world; which were the heralds also of a life's work of thirty years, unfailing rich, and still unspent! The debt that two generations owe to Mr Kipling is, I think, past calculating. There is a poem of his specially dear to me — 'To the True Romance'. It contains to my thinking the very essence and spirit of his work. Through all realism, through all technical accomplishment, through all the marvellous and detailed knowledge he has accumulated on this wonderful earth, there rings the lovely Linos-song of the higher imagination, which is the enduring salt of art. Whether it is Mowgli or Kim, or the Brushwood Boy, or McAndrew, or the Centurion of the Roman Wall, or the trawlers and submarines and patrol boats to which he lends actual life and speech, he carries through all the great company the flag of his lady — the flag of the 'True Romance'. It was Meredith's flag, and Stevenson's and Scott's — it comes handed down in an endless chain from the storytellers of old Greece. For a man to have taken undisputed place in that succession is, I think, the best and most that literary man can do. And that it has fallen to our generation to watch and rejoice in Rudyard Kipling's work may be counted among those gifts of the gods which bring no nemesis with them.

Another star — was it the one that danced when Beatrice was born? — was rising about the same time as Rudyard Kipling's. 'The Window in Thrums' appeared in 1889 — a masterpiece to set beside the French masterpiece, drawn likewise from peasant life, of almost the same date, 'Pêcheur d'Islande'. Barrie's gift, also, has been a gift making for the joy of his generation; he too has carried the flag of the True Romance — slight, twinkling, fantastic thing, compared to that of Kipling, but consecrate to the same great service.

And then beside this group of men, who, dealing as they constantly are with the most prosaic and intractable material, are yet poets at heart, there appears that other group who, headed perhaps by Mr Shaw, and kindred in method with Thomas Hardy, are the chief gods of a younger race, as hostile to 'sentimentalism' as George Meredith, but without either the power — or the wish — to replace it by the forces of the poetic imagination. Mr Shaw, whose dramatic work has been the goad, the gadfly of a whole generation, stirring it into thought by the help of a fascinating art, will not, I think, elect to stand upon his novels; through his whole work has deeply affected English novel-writing. But Mr Wells, and Mr Arnold Bennett, have been during the last ten or fifteen years — vitally different as they are — the leaders of the New Novel — of that fiction which at any given moment is chiefly attracting and stimulating the men and women under forty. There is always a New Novel, and a New Poetry, as there was once, and many times, a New Learning. The New Novel may be Romantic, or Realist, or Argumentative.

In our day it appears to be a compound of the last two — at any rate in the novels of Mr Wells.

Mr Wells seems to me a journalist of very great powers, of unequal education, and much crudity of mind, who has inadvertently strayed into the literature of imagination. The earlier books were excellent storytelling, though without any Stevensonian distinction; 'Kipps' was almost a masterpiece; 'Tono-Bungay' a piece of admirable fooling enriched with some real character-creation, a thing extremely rare in Mr Wells's books; while 'Mr Britling sees it through' is perhaps more likely to live than any other of his novels, because the subject with which it deals comes home so closely to so vast an audience. Mr Britling, considered as a character, has neither life nor joints. He, like the many other heroes from other Wells novels, whose names one can never recollect, is Mr Wells himself, talking this time on a supremely interesting topic, and often talking extraordinarily well. There are no more brilliant pages, of their kind, in modern literature than the pages describing Mr Britling's motor drive on the night of the declaration of war. They compare with the description of the Thames in 'Tono-Bungay'. These, and a few others like them, will no doubt appear among the *morceaux choisis* of a coming day.

But who, after a few years more, will ever want to turn the restless, ill-written, undigested pages of 'The New Machiavelli' again — or of half a dozen other volumes, marked often by a curious monotony both of plot and character, and a fatal fluency of clever talk? The only thing which can keep journalism alive — journalism, which is born of the moment, serves the moment, and, as a rule, dies with the moment — is again the Stevensonian secret! — *charm*. Diderot, the prince of journalists, is the great instance of it in literature; the phrase '*sous le charme*' is of his own invention. But Mr Wells has not a particle of charm and the reason of the difference is not far to seek. Diderot wrote for a world of friends — 'C'est pour moi et pour mes amis que je lis, que je réfléchis, que j'écris' — Mr Wells for a world of enemies or fools, whom he wishes to instruct or show up. 'Le Neveu de Rameau' is a masterpiece of satire; yet there is no ill-nature in it. But the snarl is never very long absent from Mr Wells's work: the background of it is disagreeable. Hence its complete lack of magic, of charm. And without some touch of these qualities, the *à peu près* of journalism, of that necessarily hurried and improvised work which is the spendthrift of talent, can never become literature, as it once did — under the golden pen of Denis Diderot.

Sainte Beuve said of Stendhal that he was as *excitateur d'idées*. Mr Wells no doubt deserves the phrase. As an able journalist, a preacher of method, of foresight, and of science, he has much to say that his own time will do well to heed. But the writer among us who has most general affinity with Stendhal, and seems to me more likely to live than Mr Wells, is Mr Arnold Bennett. Mr Bennett's achievement in his three principal books — the 'Old Wives' Tale', 'Clayhanger', and 'Hilda Lessways', has the solidity and relief — the ugliness also! — of Balzac, or of Stendhal; a detachment moreover, and a coolness, which Mr Wells lacks. These qualities may well preserve them, if 'those to come' find their subject-matter sufficiently interesting. But the 'Comédie Humaine' has a breadth and magnificence of general conception which governs all its details, and Stendhal's work is linked to one of the most significant periods of European history, and reflects its teeming ideas. Mr Bennett's work seems to many readers to be choked by detail. But a writer of a certain quality may give us as much detail as he pleases — witness the great Russians. Whenever Mr Bennett succeeds in offering us detail at once so true, and so exquisite as the detail which paints the household of Lissy-Gory in 'War and Peace', or the visit of Dolly to Anna and Wronsky in 'Anna Karénina', or the nursing of the dying Nicolas by Kitty and Levin, he will have justified his method — with all its *longueurs*. Has he justified it yet?

One great writer, however, we possess who can give us any detail he likes without tedium, because of the quality of the intelligence which presents it. Mr Conrad is not an Englishman by race, and he is the master, moreover, of a vast exotic experience of strange lands and foreign seas, where very few of his readers can follow him with any personal knowledge. And yet we instinctively feel that in all his best work he is none the less richly representative of what goes to make the English mind, as compared with the French, or the German, or the Italian mind;

a mind, that is, shaped by sea-power and far-flung responsibilities, by all the customs and traditions, written and unwritten, which are the fruit of our special history, and our long-descended life. It is this which gives value often to Mr Conrad's slightest tales, or intense significance to detail, which, without this background, would be lifeless or dull. In it, of course, he is at one with Mr Kipling. Only the tone and accent are wholly different. Mr Conrad's extraordinary intelligence seems to stand outside his subject, describing what he sees, as though he were crystal-gazing at figures and scenes, at gestures and movements, magically clear and sharp. Mr Kipling, on the other hand, is part of — intimately one with — what he tells us; never for a moment really outside it; through he has at command every detail and every accessory that he needs.

Mr Galsworthy, I hope, when this war is over, on which he has written such vivid, such moving pages (I know! For in some of its scenes — on the Somme battlefields — for instance, I have stood where he has stood), has still the harvest of his literary life before him. Since 'The Country House' it does not seem to me that he has ever found a subject that really suits him — and 'subject is everything'. But he has passion and style, and varied equipment, whether of training or observation; above all, an individuality it is abundantly worth while to know.

Of the religious development of the last thirty years I can find but little that is gladdening, to myself, at any rate, to say. There are ferments going on in the Church of England which have shown themselves in a series of books produced by Oxford and Cambridge men, each of them representing some greater concession to modern critical and historical knowledge than the one before it. The war, no doubt, has gripped the hearts and stirred the minds of men, in relation to the fundamental problems of life and destiny, as nothing else in living experience has ever done. The religious minds among the men who are perpetually fronting death in the battle line, seem to develop on the one hand a new and individual faith of their own, and on the other an instinctive criticism of the faiths hitherto offered them, which in time may lead us far. The complaints meanwhile of 'empty churches' and the failing hold of the Church of England, are perhaps more persistent and more melancholy than of old; and there is a general anxiety as to how the loosening and vivifying action of the war will express itself religiously when normal life begins again. The 'Life and Liberty' movement in the Anglican Church, which has sprung up since the war, is endeavouring to rouse a new Christian enthusiasm, especially among the young; and with the young lies the future. But the war itself has brought us no commanding message, though all the time it may be silently providing the 'pile of grey heather' from which, when the moment comes, the beacon-light may spring.

The greatest figure in the twenty years before the war seems to me to have been George Tyrrell. The two volumes of his biography, with all their absorbing interest, have not, I think, added much to the effect of his books. 'A Much-abused Letter', 'Lex Orandi', 'Scylla and Charybdis', and 'Christianity at the Cross-Roads' have settled nothing. What book of real influence does? They present many contradictions; but are thereby, perhaps, only the more living. For one leading school of thought they go not nearly far enough; for another a good deal too far. But they contain passages drawn straight from a burning, spiritual experience, passages also of a compelling beauty, which can hardly fall to the ground unfruitful. Whether as Father Tyrrell's own, or as assimilated by other minds, they belong, at least, to the free movement of experimental and inductive thought, which, in religion as in science, is ever the victorious movement, however fragmentary and inconclusive it may seem at any given moment to be. Other men — Dr Figgis, for instance — build up shapely and plausible systems, on given material, which, just because they are plausible and shapely, can have very little to do with truth. It is the seekers, the men of difficult, half-inspired speech, like T. H. Green and George Tyrrell, through whose work there flashes at intervals the 'gleam' that lights human thought a little further on its way.

Meanwhile, it must often seem to anyone who ponders these past years, as if what is above all wanting to our religious moment is courage and imagination. If only Bishop Henson had stood his trial for heresy! — there would have been a seed of new life in his lifeless day. If only instead of deserting the churches, the Modernists of today would have the courage *to claim them*! — there again would be a stirring of the waters. Is it not possible that Christianity, which we have thought of as an old faith, is only now, with the falling away of its original sheath-buds, at the beginning of its true and mightier development? A religion of love, rooted in, and verified by the simplest experiences of each common day, possessing in the Life of Christ a symbol and rallying cry of inexhaustible power, and drawing from its own corporate life of service and aspiration, developed through millions of separate lives, the only reasonable hope of immortality, and the only convincing witness to a Divine and Righteous Will at work in the universe; — it is under some such form that one tries to dream the future. The chaos into which religious observance has fallen at the present day is, surely, a real disaster. Religious services in which men and women cannot take part, either honestly, or with any spiritual gain, are better let alone. Yet the ideal of a common worship is an infinitely noble one. Year after year the simplest and most crying reforms in the liturgy of the Church of England are postponed, because nobody can agree upon them. And all the time the starving of 'the hungry sheep' goes on.

But if religious ideals have not greatly profited by the war, it is plain that in the field of social change we are on the eve of transformations — throughout Europe — which may well rank in history with the establishment of the Pax Romana, or the incursion of the northern races upon the Empire; with the Renaissance, or the French Revolution. In our case, the vast struggle, in the course of which millions of British men and women have been forcibly shaken out of all their former ways of life, and submitted to a sterner discipline than anything they have yet known, while, at the same time, they have been roused by mere change of circumstance and scene to a strange new consciousness both of themselves and the world, cannot pass away without permanently affecting the life of the State, and the relation of all its citizens to each other. In the country districts, especially, no one of my years can watch what is going on without a thrilling sense as though, for us who are nearing the last stage of life, the closed door of the future had fallen mysteriously ajar, and one caught a glimpse through it of a coming world which no one could have dreamt of before 1914. Here, for instance, is a clumsy, speechless labourer of thirty-five, called up under the Derby scheme two years ago. He was first in France, and is now in Mesopotamia. On his first leave he reappears in his native village. His family and friends scarcely know him. Always a good fellow, he has risen immeasurably in mental and spiritual stature. For him, as for Cortez, on the 'peak in Darien', the veil has been drawn aside from wonders and secrets of the world that, but for the war, he would have died without even guessing at. He stands erect; his eyes are brighter and larger; his speech is different. Here is another — a boy — a careless and troublesome boy he used to be — who has been wounded, and has had a company officer of whom he speaks, quietly indeed, but as he could never have spoken of anyone in the old days. He has learnt to love a man of another social world, with whom he has gone, unflinching, into a hell of fire and torment. He has seen that other dare and die, leading his men, and has learnt that a 'swell' can reckon *his* life — his humble, insignificant life as it used to be — as worth more than his own.

And there are thousands on whom the mere excitement of the new scenes, the new countries, cities, and men, has acted like flame on invisible ink, bringing out a hundred unexpected aptitudes, developing a mental energy that surprises themselves. 'On my farm,' says a farmer I know, 'I have both men that have been at the front, and are allowed to come back for agricultural purposes, and others that have never left me. They were all much the same kind of men before the war; but now the men who have been at the front are worth twice the others. I don't think they *know* that they are doing more work, and doing it better than they used to do. It is unconscious. Simply, they are twice the men they were.'

And in the towns, in London, where, through the Play Centres, I know something of the London boy, how the discipline, the food, the open air, the straining and stimulating of every power and sense that the war has brought about, seems to be transforming and hardening the race! In the noble and Pauline sense, I mean. These lanky, restless lads have indeed 'endured hardness'.

Ah, let us take what comfort we can from these facts: — for they are facts — in face of these crowded graveyards in the battle zone, and all the hideous wastage of war. They mean, surely, that a new heat of intelligence, a new passion of sympathy and justice has been roused in our midst by this vast and terrible effort, which, when the war is over, will burn out of itself the rotten things in our social structure, and make reforms easy which, but for the war, might have rent us in sunder. Employers and employed, townsman and peasant, rich and poor — in the ears of all, the same still small voice, in the lulls of the war tempest, seems to have been urging the same message. More life — more opportunity — more leisure — more joy — more beauty! — for the masses of plain men and women, who have gone so bare in the past, and are now putting forth their just and ardent claim on the future.

Let me recall a few more personal landmarks in the eighteen years that have passed since 'Eleanor' appeared, before I close.

Midway in the course of them, 1908 was marked out for me, for whom a yearly visit to Italy or France, and occasionally to Germany, made the limits of possible travel, by the great event of a spring spent in the United States and Canada. We saw nothing more in the States than every tourist sees, New York, Boston, Philadelphia, Washington, and a few other towns; but the interest of every hour seemed to renew in me a nervous energy and a capacity for enjoyment that had been flagging before. Our week at Washington at the British Embassy with Mr and Mrs Bryce, as they then were, our first acquaintance with Mr Roosevelt, then at the White House, and with American men of politics and affairs, like Mr Root, Mr Garfield and Mr Bacon — set all of it in spring sunshine, amid a sheen of white magnolias and May leaf — will always stay with me as a time of pleasure, unmixed and unspoilt, such as one's fairy godmother seldom provides without some medicinal drawback! And to find the Jusserands there so entirely in their right place — he so unchanged from the old British Museum days when we knew him first — was one of the chief items in the delightful whole. So too was the discussion of the President, first with one Ambassador and then with another. For who could help discussing him! And what true and admiring friends he had in both these able men who knew him through and through, and were daily in contact with him, both as diplomats and in social life.

Then Philadelphia, where I lectured on behalf of the London Play Centres; Boston, with Mrs Fields and Sarah Orne Jewett — a pair of friends, gentle, eager, distinguished, whom none who loved them will forget; Cambridge, and our last sight of Charles Eliot Norton, standing to bid us farewell on the steps of Shady Hill; Hawthorne's house at Concord; and the lovely shore of Newport. The wonderful new scenes unrolled themselves day by day; kind faces and welcoming voices were always round us, and it was indeed hard to tear ourselves away.

But at the end of April we went north to Canada for yet another chapter of quickened life. A week at Montreal, first, with Sir William van Horne, then Ottawa, and a week with Lord and Lady Grey; and finally the never-to-be-forgotten experience of three weeks in the 'Saskatchewan', Sir William's car on the Canadian Pacific railway, which took us first from Toronto to Vancouver, and then from Vancouver to Quebec. So in a swallow's flight from sea to sea I saw the marvellous land, wherein perhaps, in a far hidden future, lies the destiny of our race.

Of all this — of the historic figures of Sir William van Horne, of beloved Lord Grey, of Sir Wilfrid Laurier, and Sir Robert Borden, as they were ten years ago, there would be much to say. But my present task is done.

Nor is there any room here for those experiences of the war, and of the actual fighting front, to which I have already given utterance in 'England's Effort' and 'Towards the Goal'. Some day, perhaps, if these 'Recollections' find an audience, and when peace has loosened our tongues, and abolished that very necessary person the Censor, there will be something more to be written. But now, at any rate, I lay down my pen. For a while these Recollections, during the hours I have been at work on them, have swept me out of the shadow of the vast and tragic struggle in which we live, into days long past on which there is still sunlight — though it be a ghostly sunlight; and above them, the sky of normal life. But the dream and the illusion are done. The shadow descends again and the evening paper comes in, bringing yet another mad speech of a guilty Emperor to desecrate yet another Christmas Eve.

The heart of the world is set on peace. But for us, the Allies, in whose hands lies the infant hope of the future, it must be a peace worthy of our dead, and of their sacrifice. 'Let us gird up the loins of our minds. In due time we shall reap, if we faint not.'

And meanwhile, across the Western ocean, America through these winter days, sends incessantly the long procession of her men and ships to the help of the old world, and of an undying cause. Silently they come, for there are powers of evil lying in wait for them. But 'still they come'. The air thickens, as it were, with the sense of an ever-gathering host. On this side and on that, it is the Army of Freedom, and of Judgement.

Mary A. Ward

Christmas Eve, 1917.